Sex Crimes Investigation

Catching and Prosecuting the Perpetrators

Robert L. Snow

Westport, Connecticut
London

Library of Congress Cataloging-in-Publication Data

Snow, Robert L.
    Sex crimes investigation: catching and prosecuting the perpetrators/Robert L. Snow.
        p. cm.
    Includes bibliographical references and index.
    ISBN 0–275–98934–8
    1. Sex crimes—Investigation—United States.   2. Sex crimes—United States.
    3. Trials (Sex crimes)—United States.   I. Title.
    HV8079.S48S48   2006
    363.25'953—dc22   2005036342

British Library Cataloguing in Publication Data is available.

Library of Congress Catalog Card Number: 2005036342
ISBN: 0–275–98934–8

First published in 2006

Praeger Publishers, 88 Post Road West, Westport, CT 06881
An imprint of Greenwood Publishing Group, Inc.
www.praeger.com

Printed in the United States of America

The paper used in this book complies with the
Permanent Paper Standard issued by the National
Information Standards Organization (Z39.48–1984).

10 9 8 7 6 5 4 3 2 1

To Jon, Miranda, Taylor Michael, and Alexander Robert, with love

Contents

Preface

No one really knows its extent. No one really knows how many times it happens every year. The only thing experts are sure of is that the problem of sex crimes in our country is far worse than the public could ever imagine.

Over the years a number of national surveys have attempted to uncover the true extent of sex crimes in America, usually through interviews with households and individuals, sometimes involving thousands of subjects. These studies differ in their conclusions about the problem's severity and breadth, but they all say the problem is many times worse than what is reported to the police. It doesn't take much deduction to figure out why these surveys differ in their estimates of the true extent of the sex crimes. Given the very personal nature of a sexual assault, it is not surprising that anonymous, individual interviews, as opposed to interviews with entire families present, show the greatest discrepancy between the officially reported number and the actual number of sex crimes that occur every year. One estimate, based on private, anonymous interviews, found that victims reported fewer than one in six adult rapes to the police. For reasons ranging from embarrassment to self-blame, sex crimes victims often simply don't want to make their victimization public by reporting it to the police. Consequently, the police and the public have no idea of the true extent of the problem.

Sex crimes involving children present an even larger problem. When researchers begin attempting to estimate the scope of the problem of sex crimes involving minors, they soon find that it is impossible to uncover the true total. This is because, although thousands of children are sexually molested by strangers every year, many more are molested every year by someone they know and trust, often a family member. This last fact significantly lessens the chances that a sex crime against a child will be reported to the police, or even reported anonymously to a researcher.

This dearth of reporting, experts find, comes because being sexually molested by someone a child feels he or she should be able to depend on and trust can be such a traumatic and life-shattering event that many victims, throughout their entire lives, never tell anyone, even their closest confidants, what happened. For some young victims, being sexually molested by a loved one is so completely unthinkable that they don't even remember it. To deal with the unspeakable horror, the victims' minds totally blank out any conscious memory of the event. And because sex crimes against children often involve family members, many times other family members, in a misguided attempt to keep the family intact, try to hide the abuse from the police and deal with it themselves.

As with adult rapes, the true number of sex crimes committed every year against children, if it could be determined and published, would no doubt stun and dismay the American public. When my wife Melanie worked as a child abuse detective for the Indianapolis Police Department, it seemed that every night she would come home with stories more horrible than the night before. And she was just one of a half-dozen child abuse detectives in just one city in the United States. Multiplied nationally, the numbers seemed incredible to me, especially since I knew that the reported incidents were only a small fraction of the real total. Listening to my wife's cases, I learned that no family, no matter how blue or white collar, was exempt from having a sexual abuser in its midst. It simply occurred everywhere.

The first thing I discovered during my research and writing of this book was that it takes a special type of person to want to be a sex crimes detective. These detectives often face a daunting, uphill task from the very start. From the moment they are assigned the case, they are likely to encounter roadblocks in every direction.

Sex crimes detectives may even find themselves encountering resistance from within the criminal justice system itself. Prosecutors, they discover, are often reluctant to file charges on cases that involve important people or which don't appear to have an excellent chance of being won. Another roadblock comes from the public's refusal to acknowledge the widespread existence of sex crimes. The idea of sex crimes is so repugnant that many people simply refuse to believe that such crimes, particularly against children, actually occur in large numbers, or occur at all within their own social class. These same individuals will likewise often simply refuse to believe that certain people, again usually within their own social class, could commit such crimes, no matter how apparent their guilt is.

As a result, sex crimes detectives must often work harder and longer than other detectives in order to gain the cooperation of witnesses and collect the evidence they need. They must often work harder and longer than other detectives just to get people to even talk to them about a possible perpetrator. They must deal with victims who often, for reasons of shame and embarrassment, don't tell them the complete story about what happened during the crime, or distort the facts about what really happened. The successful investigation of a sex crime requires a detective whose skills, dedication, and plain hard work and determination can overcome these roadblocks.

I wrote this book because I wanted to show readers the heroic efforts of America's sex crimes detectives. I wanted to showcase the men and women who daily fight these incredibly difficult battles in order to bring those who commit sex crimes to justice. I decided that the best way to do this was by taking readers step-by-step through all the hard work that goes into a successful police investigation. I wanted to give readers a concrete sense of the many intricate and complex tasks that sex crimes detectives must accomplish if they hope to obtain a conviction against a sex offender, including such delicate undertakings as the crime scene search, witness and victim interviews, suspect interrogation, and pretrial preparation.

Along with showing and explaining each of these tasks, this book includes many interviews with sex crimes investigators and other professionals, as well as dozens of true-life anecdotes. These are intended to let readers see that what I'm talking about is not just academic theory, but that it relates to actual cases; that the problem of sex crimes in America is real, and that successfully investigating and prosecuting a sexual predator is a task that only the best of detectives can accomplish consistently.

Perhaps most important, I wrote this book because I wanted readers to understand the true breadth of the problem of sex crimes in America.

I wanted readers to see that the impact of a sexual assault can be devastating, and that its victims can be anyone. I truly believe that only when America understands the severity of the problem, the viciousness of sexual predators, and the crushing impact that a sexual attack can have on a victim will the public demand that more be done to prevent these attacks. Perhaps through this, future victims can be spared.

PART I

Rape

CHAPTER 1

The Crime

I had been a police officer for only a little over a year when I first discovered how dangerous and resistant to rehabilitation sex criminals are. As I look back now over my 37 years as a police officer, I'm surprised it took that long.

On a warm summer afternoon in 1970, I was driving my police car north on Sherman Drive from Raymond Street on the southeast side of Indianapolis. As I topped the hill I noticed two cars off the road just ahead, one pinning the other against a fence and appearing to have run it off the blacktop. But what sent a chill of adrenaline racing out my fingertips was that as I drove up on the scene, I could see that a man was at that moment pulling a woman out of her car with one hand, while in the other he brandished a large semiautomatic pistol.

Having already responded to at least several hundred domestic dispute runs in my year on the force, I immediately surmised that I had stumbled onto some type of argument between a husband and wife or between a boyfriend and girlfriend. Very likely, I continued my quick conjecture, the wife or girlfriend had decided to leave some situation and the husband or boyfriend had decided otherwise. By now I knew that these quarrels, while usually not deadly, could still be exceedingly dangerous. Consequently, I radioed for assistance as I slid to a stop behind the cars, jumped out, and leveled my own firearm at the man.

"Don't move!" I yelled.

The man, momentarily surprised by my sudden appearance, recovered quickly and jerked the gun down out of sight, tossing it into some weeds behind him, apparently hoping I hadn't seen it. He then raised his hands, palms outward.

"Hey look, officer, my girlfriend and I were just having a little argument. It's no big deal. Really. Look, I'll just leave."

I ran up to the two cars, keeping my revolver aimed at him. Since my backup hadn't arrived yet, I handcuffed the man, just in case he suddenly decided he didn't want to be cooperative any longer. Even though he was well dressed and groomed, and even though he now seemed to want to work out a peaceful resolution, I had seen the gun, and I knew that domestic disputes had the tendency to flare up without warning.

"Look, officer, you don't have to handcuff me," he said, moving his now-restrained arms around to the side facing me, as if to emphasize his words. "It was just a little argument is all. I wasn't going to hurt her. Really. Just unhandcuff me and I'll leave. Really. No problem."

The woman, as if in shock, hadn't said anything yet. She just looked at me and then at the man, her mouth moving but no words coming out. The man, on the other hand, wouldn't shut up, and kept telling me that everything was fine and that if I'd just unhandcuff him he'd leave and there'd be no more problems. When my backup finally arrived, I had the other officer put the man in the back seat of his police car. Domestic dispute or not, the use of the firearm in a public place had made this an incident for which an informal solution, used with most domestic disputes at that time, was not possible.

"I don't know that man!" the woman finally blurted out after we'd locked him safely away from her. "I've never seen him in my life! He ran me off the road and then pulled a gun on me!" She took several gulps of air and waved her arms as if trying to repel the memory of what had just happened. "He told me he was going to rape me! He said that if I begged hard enough maybe he wouldn't kill me."

A little checking confirmed that indeed she apparently didn't know him. He had been released from prison a few days earlier, and a receipt in his car showed he had purchased the firearm only hours before. According to our Records Branch, he had received his last prison sentence, and the two before that, for rape (in those days the sentence for rape in Indiana was 2 to 21 years, which meant with good behavior a person usually served only 18 months). I shuddered to think of what he had planned for the woman if I hadn't happened along.

Rape is defined in most states as sexual intercourse by force or threats and against a person's will. In addition, in most states rape also includes sexual intercourse with individuals who cannot consent to it because they are unconscious, drugged, or mentally unable to give consent. Along with rape, there are also several other penetrating sex crimes that involve force or threats, such as forced sodomy, both oral and anal, so when I talk about rape in this book, readers can assume I'm also talking about these crimes.

Along with this, readers should be aware that, although women are the most numerous victims, they aren't the only victims of sex crimes such as rape and forced sodomy. A recent report by the U.S. Department of Justice shows that, from 1992 to 2000, males were the victims of 6 percent of the sexual assaults in America.[1] This is particularly true in the case of sex crimes against children, in which males constitute a large number of the victims. Therefore, when I use the feminine pronoun when discussing the victims of sex crimes, readers can assume I also mean males. In addition to this, while national arrest records show that the majority of sex offenders in our country are men, a large number of women also commit sex offenses, especially sex crimes involving children. And so, when I use the male pronoun when speaking of sex offenders, readers can assume that I also mean females. As documentation of this last fact concerning female sex offenders, a study of 216 college men who had been sexually abused as children found that almost half of these men had been sexually abused by a woman, a number of them by their own mothers. Interestingly, none of the men studied had reported the incidents, even though many of them said that the sexual abuse had had a major negative effect on their lives.[2]

While the definition of rape I gave above may seem clear to anyone reading this book, many people in our country apparently don't understand what constitutes a rape. For example, in a study of college men, 84 percent of those men who had committed an act that met the legal definition of rape didn't think the act constituted rape.[3] Also unclear to many men is the fact that even sexual intercourse between married couples can meet the legal definition of rape if the interaction involves force, threats, and so forth. On July 5, 1993, marital rape became a crime in all 50 states. These laws were necessary because researchers have found that between 10 and

14 percent of all women will experience rape at some time during their marriage,[4] and that marital rape, not surprisingly, is most likely to occur in those marriages marked by other types of violence.[5]

But no matter what the perpetrators believe about the legitimacy of what they're doing, or under what circumstances a rape occurs, women, the police and others find, often fear this crime more than any other. They fear rape not only because of the very real threat of death, physical injury (which occurred in 38% of the rapes from 1992 to 2000),[6] and disease, but also because rape is not just a physical attack on their bodies, but also an attack on their dignity, self-esteem, and sense of security.

Rape is also probably the only crime in which the victim is routinely blamed as much for the incident as the perpetrator. Many people mistakenly believe that rape victims "asked for it" and actually brought on the attack through their actions, dress, and demeanor. As we will see, however, these factors really mean very little to rapists when they are looking for a victim. Still, these factors will often make a prosecutor reluctant to file charges for an alleged rape, even though these same factors are very seldom involved in decisions of whether or not to file charges for crimes such as burglary, robbery, or vehicle theft. And, while the victims of most other crimes, such as burglary, robbery, or vehicle theft, may be temporarily traumatized by the incident, they can usually recover quickly and move on with few lingering aftereffects. Not so with rape. Because rape is not just an assault on a person's body, but also an assault on that person's dignity, self-image, and feelings of personal security, many rape victims never fully recover from the attack. At the very best, rape victims are left with a lingering fear and anxiety that never leaves. But for many rape victims, it's much worse. In the following incident involving serial rapist Duncan Proctor, one of his victims, a 13-year-old girl, became so traumatized, and so feared the return of the rapist, that she eventually killed herself.

On March 4, 1998, Duncan Proctor sat slumped in a wheelchair in a South Carolina courtroom, his body crushed and paralyzed from an automobile accident six years earlier. However, few, if any, of the people present felt sorry for him.

On that day, it took the jury only 45 minutes to convict Proctor of four counts of rape and one count of burglary. "The evidence was overwhelming against him," one juror said. "There was really no defense," said another juror. "I hate he's in the shape he's in," commented a third juror, "but there's no way we were going to vote not guilty given the evidence against him."[7] The judge in the case sentenced Proctor to a term of life imprisonment plus 30 years.

The following month, a different jury convicted Proctor of yet another rape, and the judge in this case sentenced him to an additional life sentence. Under South Carolina law, this means that Proctor can never be considered for parole.

The story of Duncan Proctor's clandestine career as the criminal who would become known as the "Lowcountry Serial Rapist," believed to have raped at least 30 women, began long before his 1998 trials. When Proctor served in the Air Force during the 1980s, military police observed him several times following women late at night. Eventually, because of his odd and disturbing behavior, military officials sent him for counseling; while there, he admitted to being a window peeper. In 1988, after the Air Force discharged Proctor because of his sexual and psychological problems, he and his family moved into a house close to Charleston Air Force Base, where Proctor had been assigned before being discharged. Proctor's wife would later say that he took the involuntary discharge hard and became fixated on pornography, and that consequently they soon began having marital difficulties.

In February 1990, a series of rapes began occurring in the area close to where Proctor and his family lived. Before the police could be certain that the same man had committed all of the attacks, Proctor had already sexually assaulted 16 women in the Charleston area. When Proctor assaulted a 17th woman on June 15, 1991, the police issued a public warning that they had a serial rapist on the loose, and they consequently formed the Serial Rape Task Force. Even though local businesses offered a $20,000 reward for the rapist's capture, the police investigation stalled because of a lack of evidence and leads. Proctor would rape five more women in 1991.

The police task force continued trying to identify the Lowcountry Serial Rapist, but found to their dismay that he was always extremely cautious and took special steps to ensure that he wouldn't be caught or identified. Before breaking into a victim's home, the rapist would first cut the telephone lines. He would also always wear a ski mask and gloves, and would blindfold his victims before raping them. If the women had any small children present in the home, he would threaten to harm the children unless the victims cooperated.

Finally, Proctor slipped up and left a fingerprint at the scene of one of his rapes. Recovering this crucial piece of evidence, the police finally had a substantial lead to work from. At about the same time, Proctor's wife, finding possible evidence from the rapes hidden in their home and becoming alarmed by the strange behavior of Proctor's comings and goings, called the police and told them that she suspected her husband might be the serial rapist they were looking for.

As the police started assembling their case against Proctor, they also began a surveillance of him. However, Proctor apparently spotted the police tailing him while he was in his car and, in an attempt to slip away, ran several traffic lights. The police went after him. A few moments after a police car had pulled him to the side of the road, ostensibly for the traffic violations, Proctor suddenly sped off at high speed. The police gave chase. At one point during the pursuit, Proctor fired a gun at the police, shattering a police cruiser's window. Eventually, after being chased for 15 miles, Proctor lost control of his car on Interstate 26. Colliding with a police vehicle, Proctor's car left the road at high speed and smashed into a tree. It took 45 minutes for rescue workers to cut Proctor from the wreckage of his car. Although none of the emergency workers at the scene expected Proctor to live, he did.

Afterward, when the police searched Proctor's house, they found a gun that had been stolen from the home of a victim during a rape. Proctor's wife also told the police that she had found a ski mask and some personal property belonging to another rape victim hidden in their home.

Although Proctor suffered extensive spinal damage and brain injury in the crash and spent almost six years in a nursing care center, State Solicitor David Schwacke regularly checked on him. When it seemed to Schwacke that Proctor had recovered sufficiently to stand trial, he sent a physician to examine him. The doctor made a determination that Proctor had indeed recovered significantly and was now competent to stand trial. Proctor's attorneys, Patricia Kennedy and Lori Proctor (no relation to Duncan), naturally objected, insisting that their client was mentally and physically unable to assist them in their defense of him. A court, however, ruled that Proctor was competent to stand trial, and two separate juries eventually convicted him. His attorneys soon afterward appealed the convictions.

On April 19, 2004, the South Carolina Supreme Court ruled that Proctor had been properly convicted, and so let his sentences stand. Proctor's attorneys, unsuccessful in their arguments about Proctor's competency to stand trial, had switched tactics in their appeal and unsuccessfully attempted to discredit the DNA evidence that prosecutors had shown linked Proctor to one of the rapes.

"I think this is a good ruling . . . on behalf of the victims in this case," said State Solicitor Ralph Hoisington. "I think it's a relief for the victims by not dragging them through another trial."[8]

Many of the women sexually assaulted by Proctor felt the same. "I'm glad it's over, and I'm glad he got what he deserved," said one of Proctor's victims. "We got justice twice—once when he was put in a wheelchair and again when he was put in prison."[9]

While some people might be shocked that an individual could take comfort in the fact that another person has become paralyzed and wheelchair bound, this is likely because these people don't know the trauma, both physical and emotional, that a rape can bring. They don't understand how a sexual assault can injure a person for life. A rape is not just a physical attack on a person's body, like a punch, slap, or even a gunshot. Many studies, which we will discuss later, show that sexual assault victims often suffer a lifetime of psychological and emotional problems because of their assault. A rape victim can never again feel truly safe.

Although many women very justifiably fear rape, its cause, experts in the field find, is often misunderstood. An interesting misconception many people have about rape is that they believe it is a crime driven by sexual lust or passion. However, this often isn't the case. Actually, the police and others who deal with this crime find, rather than an aggressive act of sexual fulfillment, rape is more often simply an act of violence in which the perpetrator happens to use sex as the weapon.

"It is now generally accepted that, although sexual assaults are characterized by the involvement of forcible sexual behavior, the causes of sexual assault are rooted in inappropriate psychological reactions to violent impulse, not sexuality," said Dr. William Ernoehazy in an article about rape in a medical journal. "A constellation of different psychological classifications has been identified to characterize the sexual assailant, but the psychodynamics involved in all cases are rooted in feelings of inadequacy, unchanneled rage (e.g., impulse control disorders), and other aberrant character disorders."[10]

As one of the possible causes, or perhaps an effect, of the character disorders cited by Dr. Ernoehazy, a study of rapists reported in the *Journal of Sex Research* found that these individuals generally had much less heterosocial competence than non–sex offenders.[11] In other words, rapists many times have a hard time responding appropriately to members of the opposite sex. This can often lead to frustration and anger, which these men then attempt to deal with through rape.

Another investigation, this one an in-depth study of 41 serial rapists who had committed a total of at least 837 rapes, conducted by the FBI's National Center for the Analysis of Violent Crime, confirmed Dr. Ernoehazy's remarks. This study found that the rapists had experienced sexual dysfunction during a third of their rapes, and that the majority of them reported low levels of pleasure from the sexual intercourse itself.[12] Another study, this one of 170 rapists, also found that the rapists had experienced sexual dysfunction in over a third of their rapes.[13] The pleasure for rapists, researchers find, is often not in the sex. It is in the violence, power, and domination.

Throughout the FBI study of the 41 serial rapists, and contrary to the belief of many, researchers found that the accessibility of the victim, rather than her style of dress, her demeanor, her attractiveness, or any other attribute, was by far the largest factor in determining whether or not these men would attempt the crime. Only 15 percent of these rapists said that a victim's clothing had anything at all to do with selecting her as a victim, while a fourth of them said they had no specific physical qualities that they looked for in a victim, only that she was accessible and available to be raped.

However, when the FBI compiled a summary of the attributes of these rapists themselves, they found that, contrary to the stereotype of a rapist, the majority of them were neat and well groomed. More than half of them held steady jobs, were or had been married, were above average in intelligence, and had spent their childhoods in average or above average socioeconomic conditions.

However, the FBI study also discovered that most of these men saw themselves as being macho and attempted to display this through their dress, vehicles, and attitude. Many of these men had also been sexually abused as children, didn't get along well with their parents, and had been confined in an institution at some time during their youth. The study also found that these serial rapists, along with the 837 rapes they admitted to, had additionally committed more than 5,000 minor sex crimes, such as voyeurism, exhibitionism, obscene telephone calls, and so forth.

A final finding was that these serial rapists, along with the sexual assaults and minor sex crimes, had also been involved in a number of other serious crimes, most often burglary.[14] A study in Florida, for example, found that the most common previous criminal conviction for a sex offender was burglary.[15] One of the 41 serial rapists studied by the FBI told researchers that he had entered more than 5,000 homes during his criminal career. A number of rapists also told researchers that they often prepared for a rape by determining a woman's schedule through voyeuristic activities.[16] Additionally, it should be noted that a large number of these rapists, having experience as burglars, would also enter a potential victim's home before the rape so that they would be familiar with the layout of the house. This is why home security, discussed in Chapter 8, is so important. This crucial need to protect one's home from intrusion is dramatically underscored by the fact that in over 50 percent of the 837 rapes admitted to by the subjects of the FBI study, the rapists assaulted the victims in the victims' own homes.[17]

Regardless of where a rape is committed or who the victim is, the police over the years have found that rapists will generally use one of three tactics of approach to initiate a rape.

1. Con

   With this method the rapist feels confident in his ability to interact with his victims. Consequently, he will use some ruse in order to persuade his victims to either accompany him to a secluded area or to allow him to enter their homes, places of business, and so forth. In August 2004, for example, a court in New York convicted Luis Acosta of nine rapes. He reportedly gained entrance to his victims' apartments by claiming to be a plumber there to do some work.

   As another example, serial murderer and rapist Ted Bundy reportedly used a fake arm cast in order to make himself appear nonthreatening to potential victims. Many rape victims later tell the police that the rapist who used the con approach seemed at first to be very pleasant, even charming, and that consequently they saw no problem in giving him a ride, letting him inside their home, and so forth.

   In a bizarre use of this con approach, Canadian police report that in October 2004 a well-dressed and charming man approached women in the Vancouver area and offered them jobs in a security company. Once he had gotten their interest and gained their confidence, he told them that he needed their help in reenacting a sex crime so that he could figure out how to solve it. According to the police, at least four women agreed to undress and place themselves in compromising positions, and were then raped by the man.

Another case, this one in Denver, Colorado, involved a former college drama major who convinced women that he was a doctor. He managed to gain their confidence enough to get them into vulnerable positions before sexually assaulting them. While out on bail for these offenses, he again began approaching women, now convincing them that he was an undercover police officer before sexually assaulting them. In April 2005, he pled guilty to felony sexual assault charges.

2. Blitz

The rapist who employs this method of approach usually doesn't feel confident in his ability to interact pleasantly with his victims. He knows he doesn't have the skill to persuade them to trust him, and so he simply attacks them suddenly and violently, with no forewarning. Victims assaulted by rapists using this tactic often have no chance to negotiate or even to fight back. Once the rapist has violently subdued his victims, he will either sexually assault them right there or transport them to a secluded spot, often after binding and gagging them.

3. Surprise

With this method of approach a rapist will sexually assault a woman after slipping into her home and awakening her in bed, or he will hide in the back seat of her car or in some bushes and grab the woman when she nears him. While not as violent as those who use the blitz approach, these rapists still often threaten their victims, occasionally with a weapon, in order to gain their compliance.

Along with the various victim approaches rapists will use, the police and those who study sex offenders have also found that there are basically five types of rapists. Yet, while I may list certain attributes for each category of rapist this is not to say that any one rapist will fall entirely and exclusively within that category. While a rapist will usually belong predominantly to one category, he may also share some of the traits of the other categories.

1. Power Reassurance Rapist

   This rapist has doubts about his masculinity and ability to attract a woman he finds desirable as a sexual partner. Consequently, during the rape he acts out a fantasy that his victim is actually a willing sex partner and that she is enjoying the sexual interaction.

   A power reassurance rapist will usually surprise his victim in her home or other location and then use just what force he needs to in order to accomplish the rape. Too much force or violence spoils his fantasy of the victim being a willing partner. However, if the victim does resist or refuse to perform a sex act, he will often try to negotiate with her. Since he is fantasizing that his victim is cooperating willingly, he will occasionally make her tell him how much she is enjoying the sex, how great a lover he is, and so forth. He will seldom use profanity or verbally abuse the victim.

   This type of rapist, the police find, will also often take a photograph or some kind of souvenir from the victim or her home, and he may even call the victim later, apologizing for what happened and asking for a date. Since this type of rapist doesn't want violence or a confrontation, he will usually select women who live by themselves or with small children, many times finding out this information ahead of time through voyeuristic activities. These rapists will in addition often have previously scouted several other victims so that they will have a backup in the event an attempt with the first woman selected fails for some reason.

2. Power Assertive Rapist

   A power assertive rapist feels that as a man he has a right to demand and expect sex from a woman. When he sexually assaults a woman he doesn't believe that he is raping her but simply expressing his virility and superiority as a man. This will often happen after a date or soon after meeting a woman in a bar, restaurant, or similar location. Unlike most other rapists, there is little fantasy involved in his assaults; rather, the crime is more situational. He has met a woman and, after what he considers as sufficient courtship or expense on his part, he deserves, demands, and gets sex. If asked, he likely wouldn't consider his actions as rape, even though during the sex act he uses force and is basically concerned only about his own pleasure.

Because this type of rapist believes that he is so masculine and virile, he will usually display this attitude in his style of dress, the car he drives, the job he holds, and so forth. In addition, he will often use a great deal of profanity in his interactions with others because he sees this as being macho. He will also dislike authority, and will possibly have been institutionalized during some period of his life because of an incident involving his aggressive behavior and disdain for authority.

3. Anger Retaliatory Rapist

This type of rapist hates women and wants to punish them. Somewhere in his history he has, or imagined he has, been wronged by a woman. He is seething with anger toward women and uses sex as a weapon against them. As might be expected, these men have explosive tempers, and they will often have extensive police records as a result. This type of rapist is the most likely to use the blitz approach and will often use much more force than is necessary in order to gain compliance from the victim, many times resulting in serious physical injury. There can be no negotiation with this type of rapist, only increased violence if the victim resists. The anger retaliatory rapist, researchers find, may look for a victim who in some way represents the woman he feels has wronged him. Because of his hatred of women, an anger retaliatory rapist will often want to humiliate his victims by leaving them naked in public afterward or through various deviant sexual activities.

4. Anger Excitation Rapist

These individuals, as a group, are the most dangerous of all rapists. Commonly called sadists, these rapists become sexually excited when they make their victims suffer physical and emotional pain. An anger excitation rapist, the police find, is very fantasy driven in that he will usually have a very specific ritual he plays out with his victims. This ritual involves a scenario that he has fantasized about, often for years, and has found sexually excites him tremendously. Whether this ritual involves a type of sex act, the order of the sex acts, physically abusing his victims during the sex acts, or humiliating his victims depends, of course, on the individual's fantasy.

In Houston, Texas, the police recently arrested a sexual sadist who had raped both women and men. In one of the cases he had two of his victims perform sex acts on each other as he watched. In other cases he would sexually assault his victims with objects. According to Houston sex crimes detective Julie Hardin, "[Some of the acts] were so deviant and disgusting . . . that's how we knew [the crimes] were related. He had some fascinations I can't go into now."[18]

Because sexual assaults by anger excitation rapists are so fantasy driven, all conditions must usually be perfect in order for these rapists to obtain sexual satisfaction. Consequently, this type of rapist will often plan and research his attacks in great detail, even going so far as to rehearse parts of them with prostitutes and others.

In order to become sexually stimulated and to achieve real sexual satisfaction, this type of rapist often extensively tortures his victims both physically and emotionally. Anger excitation rapists may not only assault their victims with razors, whips, pliers, teeth, and so forth, but also often describe in great detail the tortures they are going to inflict on their victims and then make them plead for their lives. All of this activity sexually stimulates an anger excitation rapist. Some of these rapists, the police find, are also involved in piquerism, which is the gaining of sexual excitement through seeing blood flow, often from slashing and stabbing the victim.

Sadly, because of the extremely violent and cruel nature of anger excitation rapists, a victim stands a good chance of being murdered during an attack. A victim can also possibly be murdered simply out of frustration. As mentioned above, this type of rapist is tremendously fantasy driven, but since fantasies are always perfect and victims seldom act as the rapist has fantasized for many years they will, he may become angrier and even more violent when his fantasy doesn't go as planned. Also, the police find, an anger excitation rapist will usually keep a record of his attacks, in written, photographic, audio, or video form, and he will often take a souvenir from his victims. Between his attacks, he will use the recording and souvenir to relive and reexperience an incident while masturbating.

5. Opportunist Rapist

An opportunist rapist didn't originally plan to rape anyone. Usually, he is a robber or burglar who suddenly discovers that he has a female whom he finds attractive totally under his power and control. Although generally not overly violent, he will use the force necessary to complete the rape. While the first four types of rapists, once they have successfully completed their first rape, will usually continue with the assaults because they find that the act has temporarily satisfied the need or drive that instigated it, this last type of criminal is often a one-time rapist. However, he can also occasionally become a true rapist, who then begins to rob or burglarize simply for the opportunity to rape his victims. Also falling into this last category would be rapists that sexually assault women who, through their own actions, such as an unwise overindulgence of drugs or alcohol, become unconscious or otherwise unable to resist.

As can be seen in several of the categories of rapists above, for many of these men the pleasure of rape is not in the sex; it often doesn't have as much to do with lust, passion, and sexual gratification as it does with using violence to dominate someone. Rape is often actually an attempt by men with serious psychological problems to compensate for these problems by forcing someone to submit to their will. If all rapes were simply acts of passion and sexual lust, then only young, attractive individuals would need fear them. But this is by no means the case. The reality is that anyone can become the victim of rape, from the smallest infant to the most frail and infirm elderly person.

In February 2005, a judge in Houston, Texas, sentenced 35-year-old Keith Samuel Cook to a term of 50 years in prison for the rape of his girlfriend's 6-week-old baby. In another case, the police in Winton Hills, Ohio, arrested a 31-year-old man who raped a 3-year-old live on the Internet. During my experience as commander of the Indianapolis Police Department Homicide Branch, we had a case in which a woman murdered her boyfriend's baby by throwing the infant against a wall. She told us she did it because the baby wouldn't stop crying. We later found out that the reason the baby was crying was because his father had anally raped him.

At the opposite end of the age scale, in Detroit in November 2004, the police arrested a handyman who had been hired to complete some repairs for a 74-year-old woman. The woman accused him of raping her and stealing her car, which the police later found parked at the suspect's mother's house. In February 2005, in Dallas, the police broke into a house and rescued an 80-year-old woman who was being sexually assaulted by a 30-year-old man. The woman had called the police and said she thought someone was breaking into her home. The victim apparently dropped the telephone, but the police operator could hear glass breaking and then the woman screaming for help, and so she dispatched officers to rescue her.

As mentioned earlier, many women greatly fear the possibility of being raped—and with good reason. A study of men at a major university found that 35 percent of those interviewed said they might commit rape if they were absolutely certain they could get away with it.[19] Studies at other universities have found that as much as 60 percent of the men questioned say they might commit rape.[20] In a further study, researchers found that 1 out of every 12 male college students interviewed had engaged in an act that could be legally defined as rape, though the large majority of these men insisted that the act they committed wasn't rape.[21]

This belief of the men in the study above that forcible sex is not rape is unfortunately a reflection of many of the values that television and movies portray as being commonly held in our country. In dozens of movies men forcibly have sex with women who, the movies suggest, actually enjoy this type of aggression. I once saw a movie starring James Coburn in which the character he played sexually assaulted a young woman, and, when questioned about it, claimed it wasn't rape but simply "assault with a friendly weapon." This, of course, drew a huge round of laughter from the audience, and later in the movie the victim also brushed off the assault as not being a serious matter. In literally hundreds of movies, the plot suggests that women want men who are aggressive and won't take no for an answer. These movies tell viewers that women want men who are as persistent as stalkers. And of course, by the movie's end these men almost always win over the women. Interestingly, in a study conducted about sexual myths, nearly 7 percent of the people questioned said that they believe all women secretly want to be raped.[22]

"These myths prevail because it is often difficult to separate rape from 'normal' heterosexual behavior in American society due to the aggressive-passive, dominant-submissive nature of gender relationships," said the author of a book about rape in America.[23]

Because of the values movies portray as being common, and as the studies cited above show, many men seriously consider committing rape, and unfortunately, every year many men actually do commit rape. According to national statistics compiled by the FBI, in 2003, the police in the United States received 93,433 reports of rape, or one for every 5.6 minutes of the year.[24] Records also show that in 2002, almost 20 percent of the rapes committed in the United States involved two or more attackers, and in almost 4 percent of the reported rapes, four or more rapists attacked the woman.[25] Another set of statistics compiled by the federal government shows that a third of all rape victims in our country are under the age of 17, and 8 percent are under the age of 12, with the most common age of a rape victim in the United States being 14.[26] These figures, it should be warned, however, are only averages, and no woman, no matter how rich or poor, no matter how old or young, no matter how beautiful or average, is immune from the threat of rape.

However, as alarming as the above statistics are, they are not the true picture or scope of the problem. Because rape is such a personal crime in that, besides a physical attack, it is also an attack on a person's feelings of self-worth; because rape victims are so often treated "differently" by the public and even members of their own families; and because, as we shall see later, the perpetrators of sexual attacks are so often well known to their victims, many of the rapes committed every year in our country are never reported to the police. What the actual number of rapes occurring every year in our country is may range anywhere from three to seven times the reported number, depending on which expert's opinion is taken.

A report, for example, by the U.S. Department of Health and Human Services states, "Only 16 percent of rapes are ever reported to the police. In a survey of victims who did not report rape or attempted rape to the police, victims gave the following reasons for not making a report: 43 percent thought nothing could be done; 27 percent thought it was a private matter; 12 percent were afraid of the police response; and 12 percent thought it was not important enough."[27]

This report goes on to state that the National Women's Study found that rapists attack at least 683,000 women every year in the United States, even though fewer than 100,000 of these victims report the rapes. Interestingly, another report from the U.S. government, this one from the Bureau of Justice Statistics, stated that only a little over 300,000 women are raped every year in our country.[28] However, an article by the National Center for Victims of Crime explained this difference, "One significant methodological difference is that the National Women's Study interviewed individuals by telephone, allowing women greater confidence in their anonymity. The Bureau of Justice Statistics conducted face-to-face interviews, in some cases with entire families present, which could have possibly deterred disclosure."[29]

Another study found that female rape victims are one-and-a-half times more likely to report a rape than are male victims. Male victims fear the police and society's reaction even more than females do. Factors that increase the odds that a rape victim, either male or female, will report the crime include whether the rapist was a stranger, whether another crime such as robbery accompanied the assault, and the amount of physical violence that occurred during the rape. This last reason, researchers have found, is the most important in determining whether male victims will report a rape, apparently because it shows that the male victim was over-powered and couldn't prevent the crime.[30] However, even for females, studies show that a physical injury doubles the likelihood of reporting a rape to the police. Studies also show though that the closer the relation-ship between the victim and the rapist, the less likely it is that the rape will be reported.[31]

"I don't really have any stats on it, but I'd say that at least half of the rapes go unreported," Detective Dan Dove of the Provo, Utah, Police Department told me.[32]

In an effort to increase the likelihood of victims reporting rape, a number of jurisdictions have initiated programs that allow rape victims to take part in what is known as "blind reporting." What this entails is allowing victims to report a rape but at the same time not requiring them to give any personal information that would identify them. This affords the police the opportunity to gain information about a sexual predator in the community, and perhaps even make it possible for them to stop him before he can attack again. Since the majority of rapes go unreported, this also gives the police a better idea of the true number of rapes being committed in their community. At the same time, this procedure gives rape victims a chance to interact anonymously with the police, and, if the interaction is positive, time to decide whether or not they want to come forward and make a formal police complaint.

Many rape victims, researchers have found, particularly immediately after the crime, have confused feelings about what happened, and may wonder if they were partly to blame, particularly in rapes committed by intimates or acquaintances. Consequently, they are often reluctant to report them. Many rape victims also fear that taking part in a formal police investigation will steal control away from them just as the rape did.

Blind reporting allows these rape victims the time to think and consider their options before committing to a formal police investigation.

"Blind reporting lets victims take the investigative process one step at a time," said an article in the *FBI Law Enforcement Bulletin*, "allowing time to build trust between the investigator and the victim and making the whole process feel more manageable."[33]

Another reason though that many rapes are not reported to the police is because they occur in institutions where the victims either are not believed, such as in jails and prisons, or where the victims cannot tell what happened because of some physical or mental infirmity. A study done of residents confined to a psychiatric institution, for example, found that 22 out of 58 residents questioned reported a sexual assault by a staff member or other resident.[34] Nursing homes are another institution in which detectives find that sexual assault occurs but is seldom reported. An investigation by a television station in California found that 52 registered sex offenders lived in California nursing homes.[35]

Keep in mind, too, that an unknown number of the rapes that occur every year in our country are not reported to the police because the victims aren't certain of what happened, or even aware that a rape occurred, since they were under the influence of a "rape drug." Drugs such as Rohyphol, Gamma Hydroxy Butyrate, and Ketamine Hydrochloride have been increasingly associated with rapes in the last few years. Given to unsuspecting victims, these drugs can cause drowsiness, loss of inhibitions, unconsciousness, and amnesia. Victims often tell investigators that they recall a sensation of drunkenness that didn't correspond to the level of the alcohol they had consumed and then a large gap in their memories. The fact that the victims of these drugs often cannot remember what happened makes them very popular with rapists. Slipped into an unsuspecting victim's drink, these drugs can make a woman an easy target for a rapist.

In a 1997 case in California, a court convicted two men of over 50 sexual assaults of women drugged by Gamma Hydroxy Butyrate. Many of the women didn't know that they had been sexually assaulted until the police discovered photographs the men had taken of their victims during the assaults.

But whether reported or not, rape is still the crime that many women fear most. And unfortunately, this fear of rape can figure very prominently in women's lives and force them to construct their daily activities in an attempt to deal with it. Many women, it has been found, shy away from various social activities because of their fear of rape. In a book about sexual assault, *The Female Fear*, the authors state that two-thirds of the women they spoke with said they were afraid to venture out into their own neighborhoods after dark because of the fear of rape.[36] Further, this fear is not just some baseless anxiety. According to figures compiled by the National Center for Victims of Crime, one out of every eight women in the United States has been the victim of a forcible rape at some time during her life.[37] An interesting study, *The Sexual Victimization of College Women*, shows an even greater risk for college women. According to this report, college women stand a one-in-four chance of being raped some time during their four years at college.[38]

Interestingly though, while incidents such as the one involving serial rapist Duncan Proctor, in which a rapist unknown to the victim attacks her, occur tens of thousands of times each year in our country, this is not the most common type of rape. Most rapes, about two-thirds of the total each year, as is demonstrated in the following incident, occur between a man and a woman who know each other, and who often know each other very well. And unfortunately, most of these rapes are never reported.

At around 5:00 P.M. on August 13, 2002, a motorist in Oregon City, Oregon, stopped to help a woman he saw running down the road wrapped in a blue tarp. When he asked her what was wrong, she told him between hysterical sobs that Ward Weaver, the father of her boyfriend, had just raped her. The motorist, who said the 19-year-old woman was "extremely upset, crying and shaking," took her to a nearby shoe store, where she called 911.[39]

The young victim told the responding police officer that she had picked up Weaver, who had a suspended driver's license, at his job and was supposed to drive him to a court appearance he had that day. On the way to court, though, she said, Weaver asked her to stop by his house for a moment so he could pick up some things. The victim went into the house to use the bathroom. When she came out, Weaver called to her from his daughter's room, "Come here a second; I want to show you something."[40] Not suspecting anything, since Weaver was her boyfriend's father and had never seemed dangerous, the victim walked into the room.

However, once she was in the room, the woman claimed, Weaver forced her to the floor and began kissing her. The victim told the police that she tried to push him away and that when this didn't work, she began to kick and struggle in earnest. Weaver grabbed her throat and began strangling her until she stopped resisting. When Weaver began taking her clothes off, she began struggling again, and once more he choked her until she stopped fighting him. The strangling began anew when the victim unsuccessfully fought to stop Weaver from having sexual intercourse with her. The victim said that after Ward had finished raping her, she feared he was going to kill her, and so she tried to reason with him, asking him to consider what his grandchildren would think about what he was doing.

Apparently this last comment had an effect on Weaver, and he let the victim up off of the floor. She seized the opportunity and fled from the house, grabbing a blue tarp on the way out to cover herself. The police, who said the victim had injuries consistent with her story, arrested Weaver for the rape later that day.

When Weaver's son, Francis, heard about his father's arrest for raping his girlfriend, he apparently became incensed. He called the police and told them that his father had confessed to him that he had murdered two 13-year-old girls, friends of Ward Weaver's daughter, who had been reported missing from an apartment complex next to where Ward Weaver lived.

The police knew Ward Weaver well. He had been in trouble a number of times in the past and was already under suspicion in the disappearance of the two girls. Weeks earlier, Weaver had appeared on the television program *Good Morning, America*, proclaiming his innocence to host Charlie Gibson. Acting on the information provided by Weaver's son, the police found the remains of one of the girls in a shed behind the Weaver house and the other under a concrete slab Weaver had recently poured at his house. Weaver had stood on this slab when he gave interviews to reporters, during which he proclaimed his innocence in the disappearance of his daughter's two friends.

While Weaver was in jail awaiting trial on the rape charges involving his son's girlfriend, another woman also accused Weaver of sexually assaulting her. Along with this new charge, Weaver had at one time been accused of sexually assaulting one of the 13-year-old girls whose body the police eventually found on his property. Both girls, because they had been friends of his daughter, had often spent time at the Weaver house.

On September 22, 2004, Weaver pled guilty to seven of 17 charges the prosecutor had filed against him, which included murder and sex abuse, and pled no contest to the remaining 10 charges. The judge in the case, however, found Weaver guilty on all 17 charges, which included rape and sexual assault. Weaver received a sentence of life imprisonment with no parole.

"The judge said he was pure evil," commented Tami Weaver, Ward Weaver's sister. "I've known that since I was nine. No one believed me. Now maybe they'll believe me."[41]

While the victim in the incident above reported her rape immediately to the police, unfortunately many victims of this type of rape never tell. Their rapist, as in the Weaver case, is often a relative, close friend, or acquaintance. Because of this, the victims many times don't understand how the incident happened. Often victims wonder if perhaps they are to blame, if perhaps through some action they brought on the attack. In addition, since they know their attacker well, they also many times worry about what will happen to the person if they call the police. Consequently, they often don't.

Unfortunately, researchers often find, another reason many women don't report rape is because they worry that the criminal justice system will be unsympathetic to them. While, as a police officer, I would like to say that this is no longer so, readers have only to look at how the alleged victim in the 2004 Kobe Bryant rape case was maligned to see that unsympathetic treatment of rape victims still occurs.

Yet, while travesties such as the Kobe Bryant case obviously still do occur, they are in the minority. Most rape victims today enjoy much more support and privacy than victims in the past did. Most police departments now train and screen their sex crimes detectives for sensitivity to victims. Successfully investigating a rape, police departments have found, requires a detective who can be the kind of person a victim feels she can trust and confide in. Detectives need to be both supportive and sympathetic to the victim, yet at the same time hard-nosed enough not to flinch from confronting a suspect and making an arrest, no matter who the alleged rapist is.

As I've shown in this chapter, rape can be a devastating event to the victim. It can be a violent and savage intrusion into a person's feelings of privacy and dignity. And it can also easily be an incident victims don't want to talk about. Still, it is crucial that women report rape and coop-erate in its prosecution. Many rapists, the police find, don't commit the act just once, but will continue to rape, often dozens or even hundreds of times, until caught and punished. Not reporting a rape gives the rapist free rein to continue. As we shall see in the next two chapters, reporting a rape begins a complex process that only the best of detectives can complete successfully, but, when completed successfully, can save many other women from having to suffer through the life-shattering consequences of being raped.

CHAPTER 2

The Investigation

July 29, 1996, was the birthday of Piper Streyle's two-year-old son Nathan. Although she had planned to give a birthday party for him later that day, she never attended it.

According to police reports, on the morning of July 29th, 28-year-old Piper was at her home in Sioux Falls, South Dakota, with Nathan and his three-year-old sister Shaina. Piper's husband Vance, a plumber, had left for work at a little after 6:00 A.M. In the mornings, before taking the children to the babysitter and then heading for work at the Southeastern Children's Center in Sioux Falls, Piper liked to spend time with Nathan and Shaina. However, at around 9:30 A.M., the police believe, someone entered the Streyle home and got into a violent struggle with Piper.

When a worker at the Southeastern Children's Center telephoned after Piper didn't show up for her job, and found that, instead of Piper, a frightened, crying Shaina answered the telephone, she notified the Sheriff's Department. Deputies sent to check on the family's welfare discovered the living room of the Streyle home in disarray, Piper's purse and glasses lying on the floor. In a rear bedroom, the deputies found the two young children, terrified but safe.

The three-year-old told the police that a man had come in, argued with their mother, and then fired a gun. Shaina said that her mother had yelled for her and her brother to run and hide as the man grabbed Piper and began dragging her out of the house. The little girl also reportedly told investigators, "Mommy's going to die."[1] On the driveway of the home the police located a shell casing from a 9mm pistol.

Although the police gathered what little evidence they could at the house, the investigators didn't have much to go on until Vance, called home from his job, suddenly remembered something. He told the police about a strange visit he'd had from a man several days before. He told the sheriff's investigators that a man who called himself Rob Anderson had knocked on the door and then seemed startled when Vance answered it. Vance said Anderson looked for several moments as though he didn't know what to say and then stammered that he had come about signing his children up for a Bible camp that Vance and Piper ran. Vance told Anderson that the camp was over for that year. Piper, however, came to the door and told Anderson to be sure to send his children there next year. The man agreed and gave Vance and Piper his name and telephone number.

This gave the police their first solid lead to follow. After the crime scene search, the police canvassed the neighborhood surrounding the Streyle home, and several people they spoke with told them that they had seen a black Bronco circling the area several times on the morning Piper disappeared. Anderson, the police found, owned a blue Bronco.

Sheriff's investigators asked Anderson to come to the station for an interview, which he did. During the interview Anderson admitted going to the house to ask about the church camp. He even told the detectives that he had gone to the house on the day Piper had disappeared, allegedly to ask for permission to use an archery range on the Streyle property. He said no one answered the door, and so he left.

While detectives were talking with Anderson, other officers persuaded a judge to sign a search warrant for Anderson's car and house. In the Bronco they found receipts for a black, water-based paint, paint brushes, and duct tape, all purchased near the time Piper had disappeared. Technicians who examined Anderson's car said it had been painted recently with the black paint, which would easily wash off. Also inside the Bronco the police found a homemade restraining platform. Made of wood and covered with carpeting, the platform had metal hoops attached so that a person's wrists and ankles could be fastened to it. Stuck on the platform the police found human hairs that DNA analysis later confirmed belonged to Piper. In addition, detectives found something else in the car that would also later become extremely significant in the case: pieces of homewort and black snakeroot, weeds that grow along rivers. Inside Anderson's home, the police search turned up a handcuff key, even though Anderson denied owning any handcuffs. In a laundry basket in Anderson's house they also recovered a pair of jeans stained with blood and semen.

Once Vance picked out Anderson's picture as the man who had come to his home asking about the Bible camp, and Shaina had picked out a picture of him as the man who took their mommy, the police arrested him. However, because they had no body or idea where Piper had been taken, the police could only charge Anderson with kidnapping, even though they suspected that he had also likely raped and murdered Piper.

To bring further charges against Anderson, the police knew they had to find Piper's body, and so they began a massive search. They at first concentrated their search near the Vermillion River, since it was close to the Streyle home. When their first efforts yielded nothing, they went to South Dakota State University for help. Professor Gary Larson examined the homewort and black snakeroot the police had recovered from the back of Anderson's Bronco and then advised the detectives that they were looking along the wrong river. These weeds grew along the Big Sioux River. The police switched their search area and soon found evidence that indeed Piper had been taken to the Big Sioux River. There they recovered the blouse she had worn that day, cut in two. Along with this, the police also found blood-spattered duct tape with hair attached to it that later DNA analysis would confirm came from Piper. In addition, crime lab technicians said, the end of the duct tape matched the roll the police had recovered from Anderson's Bronco. The police also recovered even more evidence of Anderson's sexual sadism along the banks of the Big Sioux River: a length of rope and chain, a vibrator, and a used candle.

In May 1997, a court found Anderson guilty of Piper's kidnapping and sentenced him to a term of life imprisonment. The police, however, because of the evidence found near the Big Sioux River, had no doubt that Anderson was a sexual sadist who had raped and tortured Piper before killing her, and they weren't ready to give up their investigation just yet.

As a part of their continuing investigation, the police questioned Jamie Hammer, a friend of Anderson's. He eventually told detectives that both he and Anderson had shared a fascination with the idea of raping, torturing, and killing women. He said that he and Anderson had often discussed how they could carry out such a plan without getting caught. Finally, he admitted, they and another person who also shared the same fantasies, a man by the name of Glen Walker, decided to actually do it. The three men placed "wheel poppers," devices the police use to deflate the tires of fleeing vehicles, into the roadway. When a woman Anderson had previously selected as a victim ran over the device and had a flat tire, she stopped to change it. Anderson grabbed the woman as soon as she got out of the car and dragged her off the road into some woods. However, the woman struggled with Anderson and managed to break free and escape. Two years later, when the police arrested Anderson for Piper's kidnapping, this woman identified Anderson as the man who had also attacked her.

Detectives soon discovered that Anderson and Walker had been involved in at least one other kidnapping. In prison, Anderson talked extensively about his crimes to his cellmate, a man named Terry Brunner. He bragged to Brunner about how he had kidnapped, raped, tortured, and then strangled Piper, afterward throwing her body into the Big Sioux River. He also told Brunner about another abduction, rape, torture, and murder that he and Glen Walker had carried out, later burying the victim's body under a bush. Anderson told Brunner that he had taken trophies from his victims, items of jewelry the women had worn, and that these items were hidden, along with the gun he had used in his crimes, in a wall in his grandmother's basement.

Anderson also revealed to Brunner that he worried about Walker. He feared that Walker would break down if the police ever questioned him. He told Brunner, who was scheduled to be released from prison soon, that he wanted him to murder Walker in order to keep him from talking.

Instead, Brunner went to the police and told them everything Anderson had said. The police found Anderson's gun and the jewelry belonging to his victims just where Anderson had told Brunner he'd hidden them. Just as Anderson feared, under police questioning Walker broke down and told the detectives the location of the body Anderson had buried, which the police later recovered. The police then charged Anderson with the rape and murder of Piper, and the rape, kidnapping, and murder of the woman whose body they recovered.

At the trial, which took place in March 1999, a jury found Anderson guilty of the rape and murder of Piper, and also guilty of the kidnapping and murder of the second woman. The judge sentenced Anderson to death by lethal injection. Glen Walker worked out a deal with the prosecutor and received 30 years in prison.

Although Anderson appealed his convictions, he wouldn't live to see the South Dakota Supreme Court, on May 30, 2003, decide against him and let the convictions stand. On March 30, 2003, in the early morning, prison officials found Anderson hanging from a sheet in his cell, an apparent suicide.

"There are a lot of women who will sleep better knowing that this guy is deceased," said South Dakota State Attorney General Larry Long. "He was a danger as long as he was alive and had any chance of getting out of prison."[2]

What the incident above shows is that, in the investigation of a rape case, information and evidence can come from many different sources. Competent sex crimes investigators know that they must not overlook any source, no matter how unlikely, such as the weeds in the above case, when looking for evidence during their investigation.

"Rape is one of the most difficult crimes to investigate and prove," Johnson County (Indiana) Prosecutor Lance Hamner told me. "Only thoroughly trained, highly motivated investigators consistently achieve success in this very specialized field of criminal investigation."[3]

The investigation of a rape begins as do most criminal investigations, with the report of the crime to the police. This report can be made by the victim of the crime or, as often happens with sex crimes, by someone the victim has told about the crime, called an "outcry witness." If the victim is still at the location where the rape occurred, most police departments will send a uniformed police officer to the scene. This officer's first duty is to ensure the safety of the victim and others in the area. Following this, the officer will briefly interview the victim as to what happened. The officer will not only want to be certain that a crime occurred, but also to learn whether the alleged rapist is still in the area. If not, which way did he flee? What was he wearing? Was he armed?

However the most important aspect of the first contact between the police and a rape victim is for the officer to maintain a professional, nonjudgmental attitude. It is much too early in the investigation to make any assumptions about the veracity of the complaint. Also, often victims will tell officers about actions they took or events they were involved in before the rape that the officers find unbelievably careless or stupid.

However, police departments train their officers to keep their opinions to themselves, and instead to reassure the victim as to her safety, and simply record any information she gives without appearing judgmental or disapproving.

Even more than with other crimes, which can certainly be disturbing to the victim, a rape can be a life-shattering event. A victim's most private feelings of dignity and self-esteem have been violated, she very likely feared she was going to die, and quite often she has suffered some type of physical injury. Therefore, in addition to the officer requesting medical assistance for the victim, most major police departments also make rape counselors available. These counselors can not only comfort and reassure the victim, but can also help guide her through the intricacies of the criminal justice system.

"Some sexual assault victims feel as though they have contributed to their victimization in some way, while others are angry over the violation and demand immediate justice," victim assistance counselor Senobia Pervine told me. "My job as a victim assistance counselor, regardless of the victim's reaction to the attack, is to make her aware of the sexual assault examination procedures, as well as the criminal justice system process. This empowers the victims in regaining control of their lives instead of just letting them be thrust unprepared into the system and feeling retraumatized."[4]

Once the first responding uniformed officer is certain the area and the victim are safe, and he or she has enough preliminary information to put out a description of the suspect, the officer's next duty is to protect the crime scene. No matter how small, every piece of evidence must be collected from a crime scene, because when presented as a whole, all of this evidence, along with witness testimony, can add up to convincing proof of guilt.

Officers usually block off the area with yellow crime scene tape to prevent entry by anyone but authorized personnel. The evidence at a rape scene can be as small and fragile as a single human hair or a drop of body fluid, which could easily be lost or destroyed if the officers didn't protect the crime scene. Also, experience has shown that it is much better to make a crime scene larger than necessary and then reduce it down later than to try to expand a crime scene after sightseers and the news media have already been in the area. The crime scene must therefore include all areas where the suspect may have been. If the victim saw the suspect standing in a doorway a block from the attack, then that doorway becomes a crime scene as it may contain fingerprints, cigarette butts, toothpicks, coffee cups, or other evidence that could help identify the suspect.

Police departments also teach uniformed police officers to never pick up or handle any evidence at a crime scene, or to allow anyone else, including other uniformed police officers, witnesses, and family members, to touch or pick up evidence. Rather, officers are taught to leave the evidence exactly where it was found until a crime lab technician can process it. The only time evidence might be picked up and/or handled is in extreme situations involving officer and bystander safety or when letting evidence stay where it was found will cause more harm than picking it up, such as leaving a semen-stained handkerchief lying in the rain, or leaving an important document lying on the ground when it is windy, for example.

Additionally, police departments teach officers never to do anything that would change the crime scene from the way they found it. The U.S. Department of Justice document *Crime Scene Investigation: A Guide for Law Enforcement* states, "Persons should not smoke, chew tobacco, use the telephone or bathroom, eat or drink, move any items, including weapons (unless necessary for the safety and well-being of persons at the scene), adjust the thermometer or open windows or doors (maintain scene as found), touch anything unnecessarily (note and document any items moved), reposition moved item, litter, or spit within the established boundaries of the scene."[5] While this may sound like common sense, many pieces of evidence have been ruined by the carelessness of police officers at a crime scene.

"A crime scene is in perfect condition until the arrival of the first police officer," says retired Detective Sergeant David W. Rivers of the Miami Police Department. "It goes to hell in direct geometric proportion to the number and rank of the supervisors that show up."[6]

If medical personnel are summoned to the crime scene for a seriously injured rape victim, the initially responding officers must guide them through the crime scene so that they will disrupt as little evidence as possible. The officers will note the names and unit numbers of the medical personnel for the case file. However, sex crimes detectives find that witnesses or victims of a rape will often call for medical personnel before calling for the police; for this reason, it is important that police departments train all local emergency responders in the importance of preserving a crime scene.

Once the officers have secured the crime scene, their next responsibility is to locate and detain any witnesses to the crime. It is important to do this as soon as possible because witnesses, for a number of reasons, often don't want to stay around.

It is also important not just to detain but also separate the witnesses so that each person's story is just that: his or her own version of what happened. The police find that many people who don't feel certain of what they saw will become certain if they hear it from another person, and will become especially certain if they hear it from several people. In addition, individuals can change their minds about what they saw if they hear a different version from several other people. Separating witnesses can also stop collusion between individuals who may want to help the suspect or reduce their own culpability in the crime by telling the police the exact same story.

The first arriving police officers must also be alert to the possibility of destruction of evidence by the victim. Rape victims will naturally want to distance themselves from the rape, and so consequently may want to bathe, brush their teeth, change clothing, and so forth. The first arriving officers must be certain that the victim understands how important her waiting for a medical examination is to the possibility of solving the crime and thereby sparing other women the trauma she has undergone. However, if the officers find that the woman has already bathed or changed her clothing, they will collect as evidence the clothing worn during the assault and any washcloths and towels used to bathe. The officers must also be certain that the victim doesn't destroy any evidence through attempts to clean up the scene, such as by making a bed, flushing a used condom or tissue down the toilet, and so forth.

The initial contact between the victim and the sex crimes detective, who will be summoned by the uniformed officers once it is established that a crime has likely been committed, will set the tone for the entire investigation. The detective can have a victim who is cooperative and helpful in the investigation, or one who is withdrawn and uncooperative, all depending on how he or she handles the initial contact. The victim has already had her privacy violently assaulted, and so the detective will not attempt to start off on a first name basis, but instead use the title Ms., Mrs., or Miss. The detective will introduce him- or herself, express regret for what has occurred, and reassure the victim that what happened was in no way her fault. The detective will also express to the victim that his or her goal is to conduct a professional investigation, during which the victim will receive every courtesy possible.

Experienced sex crimes detectives know that the initial reaction rape victims exhibit to the attack means very little about what may have happened. Depending on their psychological makeup, victims will react differently, even to the exact same circumstances. Some victims may be hysterical and crying, some may be extremely angry, and some may even laugh when they tell what happened. While victims may laugh, the situation was, of course, not funny to them. This is simply their way of coping.

It is during the initial interview with the victim that a sex crimes detective's interpersonal skills must be at their best. A victim, detectives know, will be watching for the reactions to her words, and so to encourage continued cooperation, detectives must be both sympathetic and nonjudgmental. Sex crimes detectives know they must be able to show empathy and understanding for the victim's plight, yet also make her aware of the need to obtain the information necessary to go forward with the investigation. It has been found that rape victims respond best to detectives who are both concerned about them and professional in their job as investigators.

It is also extremely important during the crime scene interview to protect the victim's privacy and dignity. She has just had these violated, and good sex crimes detectives know they must not compound the problem by asking her delicate questions where others can hear the responses. Depending on the victim's condition, it is important to obtain at least a quick version of what happened so that the detective will have an idea of what areas encompass the crime scene and what to look for there.

"If the victim has a serious injury and needs to go to the hospital, I'll just ask for a quick version of what happened so I'll know what to look for at the crime scene," Indianapolis sex crimes detective Larry Cahill told me. "If she's not seriously injured and we're waiting for Victim Assistance to get there, I may ask for a much more thorough story."[7]

Because even many highly educated people don't know what legally constitutes rape, a sex crimes detective can't simply ask a victim "Were you raped?" Instead, the detective must have the victim tell in her own words exactly what happened. While a person may have been the victim of a sex crime, it may not have been rape. For example, I had a case once in which a man forced a woman to watch as he masturbated and then ejaculated on her. Although this was certainly a crime, it doesn't meet the legal definition of rape.

Unlike crimes such as robbery and burglary, in which a physical location is the sole crime scene, with the crime of rape the victim's body also becomes a crime scene that must be protected in order to avoid a loss of evidence. It is almost impossible to rape someone and not leave some evidence behind. A single hair, through DNA analysis, can point to a specific person as the suspect. For this reason, sex crimes detectives, after they are sure they have enough information about what happened in order to process the crime scene, will usually send a rape victim to a hospital or other medical facility for an examination. However, before a rape victim is transported she will usually be visually inspected to be certain that no trace evidence (hairs, fibers, etc.) will be lost in transit.

At medical facilities in most large jurisdictions, the examining physician will use a rape kit. These are kits that have been put together specifically for use with rape victims so that no piece of potential evidence will be overlooked. Although kits may vary in minor detail from jurisdiction to jurisdiction, most contain at minimum the following items:

1. A tube for a blood draw from the victim to use for exclusion during DNA testing (if the victim has had consensual sex within the previous 72 hours, blood will also be needed from that sex partner).
2. A mechanism for brushing the victim's head to collect any of the suspect's hair or other evidence left there, and a mechanism to collect sample head hairs from the victim.
3. A mechanism for brushing the pubic area of the victim to collect any of the suspect's pubic hair or other evidence left there, and a mechanism to collect sample pubic hairs from the victim.
4. Vaginal, oral, and anal swabs.
5. A mechanism for collecting fingernail scrapings.
6. A urine test for rape drugs.

In addition, most rape kits will contain a large sheet of white paper. If the victim is still wearing the clothing she wore during the rape, she will be asked to undress over the paper, which will catch any evidence that may fall off. Each piece of clothing she wore during the attack will then be taken and packaged separately as evidence (the victim will have been instructed to bring along a second set of clothing).

Before the exam, the rape victim will usually be interviewed by a doctor or nurse. Depending on how much information the victim was able to give the detectives at the scene, a detective may or may not be present at this interview. The purpose of this interview is to guide the physician or nurse in knowing what to look for as evidence, and where to look. For example, if the victim says that during the attack she was forcibly restrained, the examiner can document this during the examination and take photographs of her ankles and wrists. Any bite marks a suspect made can be documented and photographed, as it is possible to show that a specific person made the bite mark. If the victim tells about the suspect licking some part of her body, the examiner will look there for saliva samples. In addition, the examiner will ask the victim on what parts of her body the suspect ejaculated, and will again collect any evidence. Since many victims are embarrassed or reluctant to talk about oral and anal sex, often during rape exams medical personnel simply collect swabs from these areas as a matter of routine.

The medical personnel doing the exam will also look for injuries that would substantiate a sexual assault, including bruising, abrasions, and tearing of the tissue around the genital area. In the genital area, the examiner may use a colposcope, which magnifies the view and can find injuries not apparent to simple visual inspection. Depending on the fantasies of the rapist, body parts other than the genitals may also have been targeted for attack, such as the breasts, buttocks, feet, and so forth. Additionally, the examiner will look for defensive wounds on the victim, which would corroborate her story of fighting the suspect, and damage the rapist's story if he claims the sex was consensual.

However, the absence of any injuries does not necessarily mean that an attack didn't take place. This could result from the report being delayed, the attack not being vaginal, or an unaggressive rapist with a victim who feared for her life and didn't resist. Or, a lack of discernible injuries may reflect inexperience on the part of the examiner. Far too often, medical personnel doing the exam don't see enough rape cases to know exactly what to look for.

To correct this problem, in the late 1970s several cities started the Sexual Assault Nurse Examiner (SANE) program. This program provides nurses who have undergone extensive training in dealing with sexual assault victims. In many communities these nurses are on call and will respond to hospitals or clinics where rape victims have been taken. In addition to receiving training on how to examine sexual assault victims and document any evidence they find of an assault, they have also been instructed concerning how to maintain a proper chain of custody with evidence (which we will talk about later) so that anything they find during the exam can be used in court. Additionally, these nurses have received training in how to deal with sexually transmitted diseases and in the intricacies of crisis intervention. And since these are professionals who want to deal with sexual assault victims, the interaction with them will be a much more positive experience for the victim than would be one with a doctor or nurse who only occasionally or seldom sees a sexual assault victim and may not realize the legal and emotional complexities of a sexual assault. Having a SANE program, in addition to helping sex crimes detectives in the collection of evidence, can also greatly reduce the emotional stress of a rape victim, and can make her much more willing to want to continue cooperating with the investigation.

"Where they exist, SANE programs have made a profound difference in the quality of care provided to sexual assault victims," says a U.S. Department of Justice research document. The document then adds, "In addition to helping preserve the victim's dignity and reduce psychological trauma, SANE programs are enhancing evidence collection for more efficient investigations and better prosecutions."[8]

Along with SANE, a number of communities have also formed Sexual Assault Response Teams (SART). These are groups of professionals, including police officers, prosecutors, rape crisis counselors, and medical personnel, who are trained to work together as a team in the investigation of sexual assault.

"Coordinating the efforts of all the parties and agencies involved in sexual assault investigation may be the most important thing a jurisdiction can do to insure that cases are handled, investigated, and prosecuted expeditiously," said an in-depth report on sexual assault investigation.[9]

During the medical examination of the rape victim, back at the crime scene, the search for evidence continues. Special Agent Kimberly A. Crawford of the FBI says, "With recent advances in evidence detection technology and forensic analysis, crime scene searches have become possibly the most important component in many criminal investigations."[10]

However, before anything at all can be done at a crime scene, the detective must first decide whether a search warrant is needed in order to properly process the area. Although search warrants aren't needed for rapes that take place on public streets or in a public area, any time detectives must enter a vehicle or building where people have an expectation of privacy, obtaining a search warrant is a good idea.

While police officers may legally enter vehicles and buildings without a warrant in emergency situations, the U.S. Supreme Court in *Mincey v. Arizona* ruled that a crime scene in and of itself does not constitute an exigent circumstance.[11] The Supreme Court has also held that all searches without a warrant are presumed to be unreasonable; and therefore, when making warrantless searches, the burden falls onto the state to show that exigent circumstances did exist and that the search was reasonable.[12] Consequently, if there is any doubt at all, a sex crimes detective will obtain a search warrant.

Before the actual search for evidence at a crime scene begins, the area must first be meticulously documented as it was found. Experienced sex crimes detectives know that it is simply not possible to take too many photographs or videos of the crime scene, and that taking too few may leave out the ones needed most. If the path and activities of the rapist are known, a photographic or video sequence will be taken. Also, whenever a witness tells the police that he or she stood in a certain spot and saw something important in the investigation, a photograph is taken from this point of view in order to confirm or refute that what the witness said could be true.

Along with photographs and video, a sketch will also be made of the crime scene. While photographs and video can document a scene, distances are often distorted in these and they may be cluttered with items unrelated to the crime. A sketch, on the other hand, includes careful distance measurements and only contains those items relevant to the investigation.

To supplement all of this recording of the crime scene, it is also important for the detective to ascertain whether there are any surveillance cameras near the crime scene. Surveillance cameras are becoming much more common and they may have recorded the suspect entering and leaving the scene. When I was in charge of the Homicide Branch, we had a case in which a suspect murdered a man in his apartment, and we recovered surveillance tapes of him leaving the victim's apartment several times carrying out stolen property.

Once a search warrant has, if necessary, been obtained, and the scene has been documented using photography, video, and sketches, the sex crimes detective is almost ready to begin the in-depth search for physical evidence of the crime. Finding this physical evidence can be crucial to a case because it can help establish the key elements needed to prove the crime in court, link a suspect to the crime, corroborate or refute suspect and witness statements, or may possibly prove that a person believed guilty is actually not the perpetrator after all.

Respected criminologist Leon MacDonell had this to say about the importance of physical evidence: "Physical evidence cannot be intimidated. It does not forget. It doesn't get excited at the moment something is happening—like people do. It sits there and waits to be detected, preserved, evaluated, and explained. This is what physical evidence is all about. In the course of a trial, defense and prosecuting attorneys may lie, witnesses may lie, the defendant certainly may lie. Even the judge may lie. Only the evidence never lies."[13]

Before conducting an in-depth search, the sex crimes detective will conduct a preliminary walk-through of the crime scene to see what additional equipment (alternate light sources for finding evidence, specialized fingerprint recovery equipment, and the like) will be needed. Because of the possibility of pathogens, everyone entering the crime scene usually wears, at a minimum, latex gloves. Other crime scenes, depending on their nature, can demand more stringent health protection. During the initial walk-through, depending on the results of the interview with the victim, the detective will make a mental "shopping list" of the evidence that needs to be looked for in various parts of the crime scene. As more facts surface, items can be added to or deleted from this list.

The initial walk-through also gives the detective the chance to look for very fragile evidence that is easily lost or destroyed. He or she will have this evidence processed first. The sex crimes detective will also at this time start the documentation of the scene. Keeping a flowing narrative of everything that occurs at the crime scene makes completing reports later much easier. Some detectives do this using a tape recorder. Others use a notebook. Any alterations of the crime scene by medical technicians, other police officers, or anyone else who happened into the scene will be noted in the narrative during the initial walk-through. This would include items touched or moved, windows or doors opened or shut, lights turned on or off, and so forth.

After the initial walk-through, the detective will begin to earnestly search the crime scene for physical evidence, which will almost always be there. It simply must be found. Depending on whether the rapist was a stranger to the victim or an acquaintance, the police will look for different evidence. In a stranger rape, just proof that a suspect was at the crime scene when he claims not to have been can be damning. With an acquaintance or domestic rape, the suspect's presence at the crime scene doesn't prove anything. Instead, the detective must concentrate on looking for evidence that shows that force or threats were used.

"The crime scene is critical to any police investigation, and, until processing of the scene is complete, the only person or persons in the crime scene, other than the crime scene technician, should be the primary detective and his or her partner," Bill Pender, a former police officer and now a crime scene technician, told me. "The crime scene is as much the primary detective's as it is the crime lab's, and it should be a joint partnership in working the scene."[14]

How does a detective find evidence at a crime scene? He or she does it by conducting a methodical search of the crime scene, paying particular attention to possible entry and exit points, where perpetrators many times drop or throw away valuable evidence. Witnesses can often guide the search for evidence by telling the detective what to look for and where it might be. Depending on the size of the crime scene, various methods can be used to search it, including breaking the crime scene into grids and strips, spiraling outward from the site of the attack, or using a point-to-point search, in which the detective moves from one piece of evidence to another.

Experienced sex crimes detectives have often found that in searching for physical evidence it is helpful to attempt to think like the criminal. What would I do next? What would I have touched? Most important, however, is that whenever a piece of evidence is located at a crime scene, it is documented as it was found by photographs and inclusion in the crime scene narrative.

When vehicles are evidence, before searching them the detective will note whether there is a key in the vehicle, what position the key is in, the odometer reading, the position of the gear shift, how much fuel is in the gas tank, whether the lights are on or off, the vehicle's license number, and the VIN (vehicle identification number, located on the dash and visible through the driver's side windshield). Also, the detective will usually have someone at the crime scene record the license plate numbers of all cars near the area. Some rapists will panic and run afterward, meaning to come back and get their car later.

In crime scenes that involve wooded or high-weed areas, an entrance and exit to the crime scene must be designated, as well as a pathway through it. Otherwise it becomes much too easy to step on evidence that may be hidden by high weeds, leaves, and so forth. Many times in such a crime scene, metal detectors must be used in order to find metallic evidence that might be hidden in the leaves or high weeds.

Detectives are taught to remember that crime scenes are three-dimensional. Criminals have often been known to throw valuable evidence up onto roofs when leaving crime scenes.

If the rape occurred in a building, the sex crimes detective will look for tool marks on the windows, pried doors, broken glass, and so forth. Rapists will also many times leave fingerprints at the point of entry, and may have left cigarette butts outside the entry point.

However, no matter where the rape occurred, the sex crimes detective will examine the area of the attack looking for any evidence left behind by the rapist, including clothing, bodily fluids, fingerprints, condoms, and so forth. Often the use of alternate lighting sources is needed to find this and other evidence at the scene of a rape. Ultraviolet light, for example, can make fingerprints stand out, and can help in finding semen stains and various fibers. Semen, incidentally, can be found in many places at a crime scene depending on the fantasies of the rapist. In addition to being on the victim, it may be found on the floor, walls, bedding, furniture, and other places.

When looking for blood, crime scene technicians often use the chemical luminol. This chemical can detect blood that has been diluted up to 10,000 times. Therefore, it is possible to find blood even in areas that have been scrupulously cleaned. When sprayed as a fine mist, luminol reacts with blood and causes it to glow a light blue color. This can only be seen in darkness and may last for only a few minutes. Therefore, the crime lab technician using luminol usually has someone standing by with a camera ready to take photographs of the blood traces. Evidence of blood at a crime scene, incidentally, can include not only the victim's blood but also blood from the suspect. Particularly when a rape involves a violent struggle, rapists are often injured and leave some of their own blood behind.

Along with searching the location of the attack, a sex crimes detective will also attempt to find the rapist's exit from the crime scene. Rapists will often drop or throw away such things as used condoms, cigarette butts, and pieces of the victim's clothing when leaving.

There are certain items of evidence that sex crimes detectives especially want to find at a crime scene. These are identification-specific items that can conclusively connect a certain person to the crime scene.

They are particularly important if the victim doesn't know the suspect and he would have had no reason to be at the scene. A few of these are bodily fluids, hairs, fingerprints, footprints, shoe prints, and tire tracks. These can often prove crucial to the case, because once detectives have located shoe prints or tire tracks, for example, they can then compare these patterns to known patterns using one of several computer programs that will match the patterns found to a specific brand of shoe or tire. The detective will then know exactly what shoe or tire to look for, and when found can compare it to the evidence left at the crime scene. Footprints can be compared by taking an inked impression of any suspect's feet.

Any fingerprints recovered at a crime scene, after excluding the victim's and those of any other individuals who would have had legal access to the area, will be run through the police department's Automated Fingerprint Identification System (AFIS) and, if no match is found, sent to the FBI's National Integrated AFIS. Until a few decades ago, the recovery of a fingerprint at a crime scene held little value if the police didn't have a known suspect to compare it against. For many years law enforcement agencies had no realistic way to compare a fingerprint recovered at a crime scene against the millions of individual fingerprints they routinely had on file. However, that was before the advent of the AFIS, a complex computer system that analyzes fingerprints digitally and then stores these digital images in its memory. Then, when a fingerprint recovered at a crime scene is inserted into AFIS, the computer analyzes the fingerprint digitally and compares it against the millions stored in its memory. Usually in just a few minutes, the computer brings up the closest matches to the analyzed fingerprint, a task that would take years if done manually. Following this, a fingerprint technician visually examines the ten or so fingerprints given by the computer against the evidentiary fingerprint to find the correct match.

In 2003, the Indianapolis Police Department became the first police department in the United States to use AFIS for the comparison of not only fingerprints, but also palm prints. Detectives find that nearly as often as recovering fingerprints, they recover palm prints at rape crime scenes. These, like fingerprints, are unique to each individual. It is expected that within the next few years, most other major cities in the United States will follow Indianapolis' example.

"Police departments with an AFIS system were thankful to have the ability to identify latent fingerprints, and at the same frustrated over their inability to identify palm prints from unknown suspects, which constituted 30 to 40 percent of their crime scene lifts," Royce Taylor, a former police officer and now AFIS consultant to the Indianapolis Police Department, told me. "Since June of 2003, our palm print system has allowed us to identify over 260 out of 1,350 submissions. This now gives police officers the ability to positively identify crime scene prints, regardless of what part of the hand they came from."[15]

Despite the impressions given by television or movies, in reality fingerprints can't be recovered from absolutely anything touched. Some surfaces simply don't retain fingerprints. Still, many surfaces do, and at a crime scene one of the most important jobs of a sex crimes detective is to locate objects that may contain fingerprints, and then protect them until they can be processed by a crime scene technician.

Recent scientific advances have now made it possible to find and recover fingerprints from surfaces that, while able to retain fingerprints, do not show the fingerprints when visually inspected. Crime scene technicians now use various alternate lighting systems that emit spectrums of light other than visible, and under which fingerprints undetectable in normal light become visible and can be recovered.

Along with these alternate lighting systems, another way to bring out visually undetectable fingerprints is through the use of one of the key ingredients of Super Glue, a chemical called cyanoacrylate. It has been found that cyanoacrylate, when heated in a closed container, will stick to visually undetectable fingerprint residue and make it visible. The police in Los Angeles solved the case of the infamous Night Stalker rapes and murders using this method. The police had recovered a vehicle used by the Night Stalker, but didn't see any detectable fingerprints. So they constructed a building around the vehicle and filled it with heated cyanoacrylate fumes, which eventually adhered to and made visible a fingerprint that led to the apprehension of the Night Stalker. There is even a device that uses cyanoacrylate fumes to find fingerprints on corpses, and a robot that can spray cyanoacrylate fumes onto suspected bombs.

In addition to cyanoacrylate, scientists have found other chemicals that will enhance fingerprints. For example, on porous surfaces such as paper or wood, the chemical ninhydrin will react with the amino acids in human perspiration and turn any fingerprint a violet color. Occasionally, crime lab technicians will also utilize iodine fuming to bring out undetectable fingerprints.

Along with fingerprints, any body fluids, skin cells, hair, or other bodily residue recovered at the crime scene can be analyzed for DNA, which can identify the bodily substance as belonging to a specific person. As shown in many major cases in the last few years, DNA analysis has become a major force in modern criminal investigation. DNA, or deoxyribonucleic acid, is of course the blueprint for our bodies that all of us carry in most of our cells, and it is as unique as a fingerprint (except in identical twins).

Because of this, sex crimes detectives now minutely inspect all rape scenes. A rapist, they know, is almost certain to have left some bodily residue, and consequently DNA, behind, not only from the rape but also from any struggle beforehand. DNA, it has been found, can be retrieved from such things as sweat, skin cells, blood, hair, semen, dandruff, mucus, and earwax. Almost any bodily part left behind, no matter how small, will contain DNA. In addition to all of the above, detectives also search the crime scene for any object that might contain a suspect's saliva, which can also be analyzed for DNA. This saliva can come from where the suspect bit or licked the victim, from food he may have tasted, or from cigarette butts.

"DNA is a wonderful tool, and I believe in it very much," Bill Pender, a former police officer and now a crime scene technician, told me. "I see it as a tool police officers can use working for a conviction, and at the same time a tool that can set innocent suspects free."[16]

In addition to everything else it can do, DNA analysis can also often tell a sex crimes detective if the same suspect has committed several attacks or if they are by separate rapists. For example, in December 2004, because of the similarity of several sexual assaults, the police in Chicago warned the public that they possibly had a serial rapist on the loose. However, subsequent DNA testing of semen samples showed that two different men had committed the attacks.

To assist in making suspect identifications through DNA, most states have now established DNA banks in which they store samples taken from individuals convicted in their states of violent crimes. And because of the success of DNA identification, in 1998 the FBI set up the Combined DNA Index System, or CODIS, which links nationally the information stored in the various state DNA banks. With CODIS, the DNA recovered from a rape scene in Oregon can be matched to a criminal arrested for a violent crime in Florida. As of July 2005, the FBI had over 2.5 million convicted offender profiles stored in CODIS, and the system had produced over 25,000 "hits," or DNA matches, between crime scene DNA and a suspect.

In addition to recovering all of the physical evidence we have talked about so far, often samples of the soil around crime scenes will be collected. This can become important later if a suspect who claims to have never been in the area of the rape has matching soil on his shoes or clothing. Detectives likewise collect samples of other items that might turn up on a suspect, such as carpet fiber, animal hair, and sometimes even dust that is specific to the area.

If the police should apprehend a suspect very soon after a rape, the sex crimes detective will likely take the suspect's clothing as evidence, as it will almost certainly contain evidence of the assault. Officers will also record and photograph any injuries the suspect may have sustained. Even if the suspect is not caught until some time after the rape, it is still worthwhile to search his residence for clothing. Amazingly, sex crimes detectives have been able to find, even long after an attack and still hanging in a suspect's closet, clothing covered with the suspect's semen and skin cells from the victim.

Once evidence has been recovered during a rape investigation it is crucial, if this evidence is to be used in court, to establish and maintain a chain of custody. What this means is that sex crimes detectives must be able to testify in court that the items presented as evidence are the same items they found during the investigation, and that they have been stored in a secure facility since then. To do this, detectives at a crime scene will secure evidentiary items recovered there, mark the evidence uniquely in some way (e.g., with the detective's initials and the date), record information about the evidence in their report, and then send this evidence to the police department property room or some other secure storage facility. Afterward, if anyone, such as crime lab technicians, wants to examine or test the evidence, they must sign the evidence in and out and state their purpose for obtaining it. A proper chain of custody establishes exactly where the evidence has been at all times and who has had contact with it.

A number of items specific to rape cases require special handling at the secure storage facility. For example, blood and other bodily fluids must be allowed to dry before storing. Also, items meant for DNA analysis must be protected from ultraviolet light, which can degrade the sample.

But just as important as the physical evidence found at a rape scene is what is missing. Are there items the rapist took with him? Many rapists will take souvenirs and trophies in order to help them fantasize as they masturbate later. These can include such things as the victim's underwear, jewelry, and photographs.

In rapes by acquaintances and intimates, sex crimes detectives will search for evidence not that the suspect was at the scene or even that he had sex with the victim, but rather that he used force or threats. This evidence can come from injuries to the victim and suspect, torn clothing, broken furniture, weapons recovered, and so forth. But often in acquaintance and intimate rape cases this evidence comes from the statements of the victim and suspect and from interviews with any witnesses the police can locate.

In order to locate every witness possible, sex crimes detectives will likely canvass the neighborhood near the crime scene to see if anyone heard or knows something that could be important to the investigation. Often, people will have heard or seen something that they didn't realize was significant at the time, but which may well help solve the crime, such as witnesses who saw the rapist lingering in the area beforehand. The canvass is often repeated the next day and a week to a month afterward in order to interview people who weren't at home when the first canvass was conducted.

For many witnesses at a rape scene, particularly minor witnesses, the interview will be conducted right away near the crime scene. It is important to talk to these witnesses not just while the event is fresh in their minds, but also before they have had time to worry about whether or not they should become involved. If interviews are conducted a day or two later, the shock and excitement of the crime will have worn off and the person often isn't as willing to get involved and tell everything he or she saw. Sex crimes detectives conduct these on-the-scene interviews one-on-one, usually in a police car or at some other location where the interviewee and detective won't be disturbed, and most are tape-recorded. Witnesses with more in-depth information, or who sex crimes detectives suspect may be more involved than just as witnesses, are usually taken to the police station for an interview.

Typically, detectives try to establish rapport with witnesses to be interviewed. Establishing rapport can mean the difference between a meaningful statement and just yes or no answers. For rapport to be built, the detective, no matter what the demeanor of the person being questioned, must appear cordial and friendly. Rapport building can start simply by inquiring about the welfare of the witness. The detective must also appear nonjudgmental and fair, and only interested only in arriving at the truth and clearing up the matter under investigation. Establishing good rapport means never talking down to people or appearing to look down on them and their lifestyle. Quite the opposite, building rapport means appearing to the individuals being questioned as a person who holds values very similar to theirs.

Experienced sex crimes detectives have found that during a trial, while the jurors naturally give a considerable amount of weight to physical evidence that connects someone to a crime, they also listen attentively to the testimony of witnesses and defendants. Therefore, collecting recorded statements from witnesses and suspects before a trial can be crucial to the success of the prosecution, because during the trial, individuals often tend to change or distort testimony given right after a rape. Many criminal trials, unfortunately, don't take place until some months after the crime, and many circumstances can change during this time that make individuals want to modify or even deny things they may have said to the police right after the rape.

Since rapes, and particularly serial rapes, are of intense interest to the public, the news media will often show up at rape scenes. Most news media outlets have policies against releasing the names of rape victims, and most won't. However, many news media outlets aren't as scrupulous when it comes to releasing other details, such as the victim's place of employment, the exact location of the rape, and similar details that can sometimes pinpoint who the victim is. Sex crimes detectives must therefore be extremely cautious about what facts they release to the news media. Nothing will make a victim more uncooperative than if she thinks the police gave the news media the information that identified her.

On the other hand, the news media can be of tremendous assistance to a sex crimes detective when it is vital that information be distributed to the public. For example, the sketch of a rapist, his description, or his mode of operation, if distributed by the news media, can often bring in many meaningful tips. Therefore, maintaining a friendly, but professional, relationship between the police and the news media can work to the benefit of both sides.

"News media outlets usually have access to a sexual assault victim's name, address, and so forth, which we treat as gingerly as an egg," Tom Spalding, a reporter for the Gannett newspaper chain, told me. "If we tell the story of rape victim Margaret Jones, 20, of 1113 Main Street, that story would be no more fascinating or helpful to readers than simply saying 'a 20-year-old Eastside rape victim.' There's no point in embarrassing someone who's already been traumatized enough."[17]

Once the investigation has been finished at the crime scene and the victim has finished her examination at the hospital, the investigator must set up an in-depth interview with the victim. Most sex crimes detectives like to have this interview as soon as possible. But no matter when it is, the manner in which this interview is conducted can make the difference between whether the victim will cooperate and assist in the investigation or become withdrawn and reluctant to help. The victim lost control of her life during the rape, her self-esteem was violated, she may have been brutalized, and she very likely feared she was going to die. Therefore, detectives who want rape victims to cooperate in the investigation must be sympathetic to the trauma the victims went through, must be respectful of the victims' need to regain control, and must appear extremely professional.

A popular misconception is that only females can successfully interview female victims about a sexual assault. This is not true. Police departments have found that a successful interview generally depends more on the compassion, concern, sympathy, and professionalism of the interviewer than it does on gender.

At the interview, investigators have learned, the emotional state of a rape victim can be anything from quiet acceptance to feelings of shame and worthlessness to rage and anger. A good sex crimes detective will recognize this and tailor the interview to the victim's emotional state. For example, victims who are expressing rage and anger may allow this to spread to all men, including a male interviewer, which would be an exception to the rule in the previous paragraph. Other victims may need an interviewer, male or female, who is particularly supportive and reassuring.

To start the interview off with the best probability of success, the detective will try to give the victim as much control as possible. The detective will allow her to decide where she wants to sit and how she wants to be addressed. The investigator will then explain to the victim exactly what has happened so far in the investigation, and what will happen next and in the future. This allows the victim to regain some sense of control. The sex crimes detective must also remember that he or she is conducting an interview, not an interrogation, and that it is an interview with a very traumatized victim.

Above all, therefore, the victim's privacy during the interview must be assured. A victim cannot be expected to talk about very intimate things in an open office. A quiet, private office is much more conducive to a successful interview. Also, an experienced interviewer will never touch a rape victim. She could easily misinterpret this.

In addition to the setting, the people present during the interview should also be controlled. Having anyone but the investigating sex crimes detective present during the interview will often prove counterproductive. A rape victim may be reluctant to talk about degrading acts, facts that can be crucial to an investigation, in front of a friend or family member.

During the interview, an experienced sex crimes detective will reassure the victim that no matter what she did or what mistakes she may have made, these don't justify rape. The victim will also be told that her case is very important and that her help is needed in order to take a dangerous criminal off the streets, a criminal who will almost certainly victimize other women if he isn't. And while the detective will usually start off with general questions in order to put the victim at ease, eventually the victim will need to tell exactly what the rapist said and did, and what he made the victim say and do. This is crucial to being able to establish the type of rapist the investigator is dealing with. If the detective can determine the exact ritual of the rapist, this can occasionally pinpoint one specific offender. Therefore, what the detective needs to know are all of the physical, sexual, and verbal behaviors of the suspect. Often the things a rapist did or had the victim do don't seem to make sense, but they do to the rapist. They fit into his fantasy and motivate him.

It is also important to know, besides the major sex acts, about minor acts such as kissing, fondling, disrobing, and so forth. These too can tell about the rapist's fantasies. Once the motivation and fantasies of a rapist are known, it is much easier for a sex crimes detective to profile the offender.

Just as important as his actions, the exact wording a rapist used or had the victim use has often been found to be crucial to an investigation because it can show the rapist's motivation. A rapist who forces his victim to say, "I want you to make love to me," has a far different motivation than does a rapist who uses, or demands that the victim use, much cruder terms.

When asking about the actions of the victim, the detective must be certain to always use professional, nonjudgmental language. The victim has undoubtedly already wondered whether her actions somehow contributed to the attack, and the detective will get much more cooperation from the victim by asking, "Tell me what happened after your car broke down," then by asking, "What were you doing driving around in that kind of neighborhood at night?"

Often, however, no matter how professional the interview, sex crimes detectives will find that victims lie about or distort parts of their story. This doesn't mean that a rape didn't occur. Rather, the victims may be embarrassed by some of the rapist's deviant actions, or by actions the rapist forced them to take, and omit or lie about them. Victims are also often embarrassed to tell about things they did that they know were foolish and made the rape easier, or to admit to acts before the rape that they know are illegal, such as drug use with the suspect. Still, no matter what the detective finally gets the victim to say or tell about, he or she must remain nonjudgmental. We have all done stupid things, but that doesn't mean we deserve to be victimized.

During the interview, the detective will also have to ask about any sexual dysfunction of the rapist. This has been found to happen in about a third of all rapes. This again can tell the investigator volumes about the rapist, particularly if the victim can describe to the detective exactly when and under what circumstances the dysfunction occurred. To obtain this information though, the detective will have to have established a very empathetic and professional relationship with the victim.

Of course, during the interview the detective will also want the victim to give a detailed physical description of the rapist. If the victim saw a birthmark, tattoo, or scar in an area not usually exposed, this can greatly add to her credibility.

The interview will also focus on any action the rapist took to avoid detection, as these actions can show his experience as a rapist. Did he wear a mask or disguise, gloves, a condom? Did he attempt to destroy any evidence of his presence? Did he appear to know his way around the victim's home, indicating he had previously scouted it?

It is also very important to find out during the interview what kind of control the rapist used. This can also tell the detective much about the type of rapist he or she is dealing with. This, however, can be a touchy subject, because while some rapists may use brutal control, other rapists employ what the detective might consider very minimal control. However, the detective must remember the circumstances under which the victim was assaulted. She was likely surprised and frightened, and very possibly worried that resistance would lead to physical violence. Still, victims will often be embarrassed to tell the detective that the rapist's presence alone intimidated them, and so they may exaggerate or even lie about weapons or threats. They may also exaggerate or lie about the resistance they put up. However, it is important to learn whether the victim truly resisted and what the rapist's response was to this resistance. This again can pinpoint the type of rapist and assist in narrowing down the suspects.

Sex crimes detectives also always inquire if the suspect took anything from the victim or her home. Even if the victim says no, the detective will usually still ask her to inventory her personal items such as underwear, jewelry, photographs, and so forth, which some rapists may take as souvenirs or trophies. Finding an object belonging to the victim hidden in the suspect's home can be damning evidence.

Finally, although it will mean touching on an extremely delicate subject, since the victim may have been attacked without provocation, the sex crimes detective will need to know about anything from the victim's past that could have an effect on the case or cast doubt on her story, such as false claims made in the past, previous arrests and convictions, and so forth. Any good defense attorney will almost certainly find out this information, and the prosecution must be ready with a rebuttal.

At the conclusion of the interview, the sex crimes detective confirms that the victim understands what is to follow in the investigation. The victim will be given a telephone number she can call if she suddenly recalls information important to the case or wants to know the status of the investigation. She will again be reassured that her case will receive every effort possible to solve it. The detective will usually then allow the victim to ask any questions she may have, and if a rape or victim assistance counselor hasn't already contacted her, the detective will see that she has this opportunity. Finally, before the victim leaves, good sex crimes detectives will always do something else: they will express how appreciative they are that the victim has been so much help.

Following the victim interview, if the police already have a suspect in a stranger rape case, they may ask the victim and any witnesses to view a photo lineup. To do this, the police insert the suspect's photograph into a display with a half dozen or so photographs of other individuals, and then ask the victim and witnesses to see if the display contains the person they saw. To be valid, the suspect's photograph must not stand out in any significant way from the other photographs, and the individuals in the other photographs must resemble the suspect in significant physical features. For example, the suspect's photograph must be the same size and format as the others, and it wouldn't be valid to have the photograph of a bearded suspect put in with photographs of clean-shaven individuals. The computer mug shot program we use at the Indianapolis Police Department has a feature that allows us to let the computer randomly select photographs of other individuals who match the significant physical features of the suspect.

If for some reason the police decide to use a live lineup of suspects, the same safeguards apply. The other individuals in the lineup must generally fit the suspect's physical features. Many detectives, however, find that they often have much better luck getting an identification from a photo lineup than from a live one. Even though the live lineup subjects usually cannot see the victim or witnesses, this procedure is still much more stressful for them. Also, a photo lineup is naturally much easier and less costly to put together than a live lineup.

In those cases in which the police don't have a suspect, the sex crimes detective must begin developing one. The detective does this by first having the crime lab attempt to link evidence left at the crime scene, such as hair, bodily fluids, clothing, tire tracks, and so forth, to a specific individual. Second, information about possible suspects, besides coming from the victim, can also come from witnesses who may have seen someone at or leaving the scene. Since criminals may often brag about their crimes, the detective will check with his or her own and other detectives' informants to see if any of them have heard of someone bragging about the case.

When attempting to identify a rapist, a detective must also learn to look at the crime not just from the victim's point of view, or even from the law enforcement point of view, but also from the rapist's point of view. Doing this will make sense of things that otherwise don't. When a detective looks at things in terms of a rapist's motivations and fantasies, he or she can then understand what seem like strange and even bizarre actions. Through their experience, sex crimes detectives realize that many rapists have no concern or empathy for their victims. Things that would be ghastly to most of us, such as inflicting pain during sex, are normal to these people. The usual moral constraints have no sway with many of these individuals. If sex crimes detectives can learn to look at a rape from this point of view, it may enable them to understand the actions of a rapist. But for the detective to truly think like the rapist, he or she must know everything that the rapist did, including how he made contact with the victim, what he said or did to her, and the type and sequence of the sex acts (anal sex followed by oral sex, for example, will often denote an anger retaliatory rapist or sexual sadist who wants to degrade and humiliate the victim).

Many rapists are well known to the police from their past acts, their modes of operation, and specific rituals. Sufficient, precise information about the rapist's actions will often enable the police to pinpoint the rapist's identity. Consequently, when looking to profile a rapist, the sex crimes detective will also need to know such things as how the suspect restrained and controlled the victim, what he had her do or say, the response of the rapist to resistance by the victim, and any minor sex acts committed, such as kissing, fondling, or a careful undressing of the victim (these last acts can often denote a power reassurance rapist). One of the most important things a detective needs to know is the amount and type of force or violence the rapist used, along with when it was used. This can speak volumes about his motivation and fantasies. Many times, violence occurs during a rape because the rapist has fantasized for years before actually attempting to act out his fantasy. Fantasies will always be perfect, but human responses aren't, and the rapist can become frustrated when his fantasy is ruined.

While developing suspects, noting specific behaviors is very important because most rapists practice a number of paraphilias. The *Diagnostic and Statistical Manual of Mental Disorders* explains: "The paraphilias are characterized by recurrent, intense sexual urges, fantasies, or situations."[18] A few examples of paraphilias are voyeurism, exhibitionism, fetishism, sadism, masochism, transvestitism, and koproalia (saying obscene things). Very few sex criminals are just rapists, just exhibitionists, or just voyeurs. Most are involved in a number of deviant sexual acts and practice several paraphilias. This is important information to know because, for example, a rapist who forced a victim to slowly disrobe while he watched could well have a police record as a voyeur. A rapist who forced the victim to watch as he undressed could well have a record as an exhibitionist.

If there is no apparent suspect in a rape, sex crimes detectives will check with other detectives in the office and with their counterparts in nearby police departments to see if they've had similar cases. Occasionally, they may all be working on different cases committed by the same suspect, and one side will have the piece of evidence the other needs to make an identification.

Sometimes, when searching for a suspect, a sex crimes detective will also utilize the services of a professional profiler. This is a person who, using the information given by the victim and witnesses, and by analyzing the evidence at the crime scene, attempts to develop a profile of the type of person who would commit such a crime.

Brent E. Turvey, in his book *Criminal Profiling*, describes his occupation this way: "Criminal profiling is the inference of offender traits from physical and/or behavioral evidence." However, he also adds the following caveat, "Any discipline that involves interpreting the multidetermined nature of human behavior cannot be referred to as a hard science with a straight face." He goes on to say this about criminal profiling, "It cannot typically point to a specific person, or individuate one suspect from all others. It can, however, give insight into *general* personality and characteristics of the person responsible."[19]

While behavioral profiles can be useful, they are only guidelines and few rapists will fit the exact profile given. It is also possible, and often more useful, to obtain a geographical profile. By examining the locations of the rapes, the entry and exit routes to the crime scene, and when the rapes occurred, a profiler can often give the detective an indication of where the rapist lives.

In addition, rapists generally have a very high recidivism rate. One study, for example, showed that, within 25 years of an arrest, rapists have a 39 percent chance of being arrested for another sex crime.[20] And this study result, of course, was just for the reported cases of recidivism. Since most sex crimes are never reported, the real rate of recidivism is likely many times higher. Consequently, once sex crimes detectives have gotten a physical description of the suspect, his mode of operation, and his specific behaviors, they will then look at their records and see who fits the profile. Very, very often, a rapist the police are trying to identify already has a record as a sex offender.

Finally, if a rapist has a ritual that is especially idiosyncratic it can be beneficial for a sex crimes detective to contact the vice branch. The sex crimes detective can ask the vice investigators to check with local prostitutes to see if any of them have had a customer with such a fantasy. It is not unusual for a rapist to have first attempted to act out his fantasy with a prostitute.

Once a suspect has finally been identified through the methods above, and enough evidence points toward his guilt, a sex crimes detective will likely obtain a warrant to search his house, car, storage locker, and any other place that may contain further evidence of his guilt. This is another reason why sex crimes detectives need all of the detailed information about a rapist described above. Detailed information about the rapist's behaviors and methods can assist the detective greatly when writing up a search warrant. Certain fantasies will require specific materials. For instance, a sexual sadist will likely have a large collection of bondage magazines, handcuffs, chains, padded restraints, whips, and so forth.

What are the detectives looking for when serving a search warrant? Naturally, they will look for evidence connected to the rape under investigation. In the Piper Streyle case at the beginning of this chapter, for example, detectives searching the suspect's car found the victim's hair attached to his homemade restraining platform, proof that he had kidnapped her. They also found receipts for recent purchases that may have been used in the rape. Detectives will naturally look for any items that may have been taken from the victim or the victim's home during the attack, including not just souvenirs and trophies but also items of value meant for resale. They will look for restraining devices, rape drugs, videotapes, photos, audiotapes, and for pornography specific to the rapist's fantasies. Many rapists, treasuring their pornography collection, will hide this material, along with souvenirs and trophies, beneath loose floorboards, inside walls, above false ceilings, and similar locations. Good intelligence from acquaintances of the suspect can often aid greatly in finding these hiding places.

If the rapist has a computer, the detectives will usually confiscate it and look on it for e-mails that discuss the rape with others who have similar interests, for written documentation of the rape, and for documents and files relating to the rapist's fantasies. Amazingly, sex crimes detectives find that many sex criminals will keep detailed records of their crimes, and that they will often share this information with others.

A search warrant will also often be obtained to take a DNA sample from the suspect, that is, if his DNA isn't already on file in the state or national DNA file. This can usually be done by taking a swab from the mouth.

When serving a search warrant, in addition to looking for direct evidence that can tie a suspect to a rape, the police search for collateral evidence that, while not part of the crime, can show that a suspect is likely to have committed the type of crime the police are investigating. These items, while not pinpointing the suspect to a specific crime, may instead show the suspect's fantasies, sexual interests, and inclinations. Combined with direct evidence, collateral evidence can be a powerful weapon to use in court. A few examples, besides pornography, are fetish items such as restraining devices, latex clothing, leather whips, and vibrators; news stories collected about a rape or series of rapes the police believe the suspect committed; and scholarly books and articles about the suspect's particular sexual deviance. Regarding these last items, often investigators find that sex offenders spend large amounts of time attempting to justify and rationalize their behaviors, and will use this scholarly material in an attempt to do so. Another important item detectives search for is any information relating to future targets. Many rapists plan their attacks in great detail and may have picked targets for the next two or three rapes.

Many rapists, interestingly enough, are involved in consensual sexual relationships at the same time they are committing rapes. Therefore, if a suspected rapist is involved in a relationship with a woman, it can be very advantageous for the detective to talk with the woman. Quite often the rapist has expressed some of his fantasies to the woman and may have attempted to act them out. The fantasies and rituals of a rapist tend to be very stable over time. It can thus also be worthwhile to attempt to locate ex-wives and ex-girlfriends of a suspected rapist to learn whether he has expressed or acted out with them the fantasies he exhibited during the rape.

After a suspect has finally been identified (or the victim already knows and has named him), the alleged rapist will be brought in for interrogation. If the victim knew her attacker, often the suspect will not deny having sexual intercourse with the victim, but he will insist that the sex was consensual. The detective's task then is to show that it wasn't consensual. This can be done through injuries to the victim, evidence left at the scene, witness statements, and through inconsistencies in the story that the alleged rapist tells the detective.

During the investigation, it is also possible that the sex crimes detective may discover evidence that does point to the incident being a consensual act, or that suggests that the act didn't occur at all. This type of false rape reporting does occur, and for various reasons. And because it does occur, there are certain signs that a sex crimes detective looks for which indicate that an individual may be making a false report.

It must be remembered, however, that there is a difference between a false accusation of rape and a rape victim who recants her accusation. A victim may recant for a number of reasons having nothing to do with the veracity of her complaint. She may worry that the criminal justice system will not be sympathetic to her plight. She may fear the stress of undergoing a cross-examination by a defense attorney who will attempt to portray her as a slut. She may also have found that, since the accusation of rape, loved ones now seem distant and afraid to talk to her, and she wants things to go back to the way they were before the rape. Or, if the attacker was someone close to her, she may be under intense pressure from family members to drop the case.

Recantations aside, however, all sex crimes detectives have also occasionally encountered actual false accusations of rape. These, too, may occur for a number of reasons. A woman may be angry with a man and want to hurt him. A prostitute may not have been paid or have been robbed by a customer. Occasionally, a sex act was consensual but then something happened, and the only solution the woman sees is to claim rape. This would involve, for example, a husband finding out about an affair, parents finding out about the sexual activity of their under-aged daughter, or a woman involved in an affair who suddenly becomes frightened that she might be pregnant or have contracted a sexually transmitted disease.

A false report of rape can also be used as a means of bringing about a change in a seemingly intolerable life situation. For example, a young woman who doesn't want to stay any longer at college may claim to have been raped. Another example is the case of Jennifer Wilbanks, who disappeared from her home in Georgia on April 26, 2005, just days before her wedding. Several days later, she showed up in Las Vegas, claiming to have been kidnapped and sexually assaulted. As it turned out, none of this really happened. She simply wasn't sure she wanted to go through with the wedding. On June 2, 2005, she pled no contest to charges of making a false statement. Lastly, a woman may make a false accusation of rape because she craves sympathy and attention and thinks that claiming to be a rape victim is the best way to get it.

A research team studied 45 cases of false rape reports taken over a nine-year period in a midwestern city. They found that the women, who later admitted the claims were fabricated, could not be distinguished in any unique way from those whose reports were true. According to the researcher's report, "The study of these 45 cases of false rape allegations inexorably led to the conclusion that these false charges were able to serve three major functions for the complainants: providing an alibi, a means of gaining revenge, and a platform for seeking attention/sympathy." The study report ends with this concern: "One of the most haunting and serious implications of false rape allegations concerns the possibility of miscarried justice. . . . Merely to be a rape suspect, even for a day or two, translates into psychological and social trauma."[21]

There are a number of warning signs that can tell sex crimes investigators they should be alert to the possibility, but only the possibility, of a false report. These include:

1. Alleged rape victims who tell friends and coworkers about a rape, but who don't want to involve the police.
2. Alleged victims who cannot give a description of the attacker, or who give only a very generic description.
3. Alleged victims who claim they put up a vigorous struggle, but show no injuries consistent with this. Some victims will claim to have fought like an action figure, but have no cuts or bruises.
4. Alleged victims who are uncertain of the details of the alleged assault. Real victims remember odors, sequence of events, words, and so forth.
5. Cases in which officers can find no evidence that a rape occurred, and the alleged victim refuses a medical examination.
6. Cases in which the alleged crime scene shows no sign of the incident.
7. Cases in which even though the alleged rape victim has wounds, they are not consistent with her story. For example, reported defensive wounds that are not on the part of the body they should be.
8. Cases in which "hesitation wounds" surround any serious wounds on the alleged rape victim's body. Hesitation wounds are minor wounds the alleged victim inflicted before finally being able to seriously injure herself. Suicide victims who kill themselves with knives often display these. Also, alleged victims seldom injure themselves in the eyes or on the lips, nipples, or genitalia, where a real attacker would and where it really hurts.

It must be remembered, however, that any of these signs, while pointing to the possibility of a false accusation, can also be present in real rapes. Fortunately, victims with true accusations are usually willing to give supporting evidence to their claims, while those making false accusations will often feign outrage and indignation if asked for more evidence. The best way to handle a possible false accusation is to simply present the victim with the inconsistencies in a positive way and ask her to explain them. Some detectives, if they think the victim is making up a story, will ask about events in reverse of the order given. This will often confuse those who have fabricated a story. Also, detectives suspecting a false report will interview the last person the alleged victim saw before the reported assault. If it is a false report, this witness will often give information contrary to what the victim is saying.

A serious problem arises, however, when the police suspect that a victim is making a false accusation of rape and she has named a specific suspect. Do the police arrest him, even though they suspect he might be innocent, or do they delay arresting him and risk having him rape another person if they are wrong and it isn't a false accusation after all? This is a judgment call, and the police must look at the overall circumstances of the case. The safety of innocent victims is of paramount importance, but an accusation of rape, even if later proven to be false, can be devastating to a person's life and future.

Consequently, in these incidents, the police must look at all aspects of the case. Was there any violence involved that can be supported by visible injuries or other evidence? What is the history of the alleged rapist? Does he have a record of such attacks or of violence? Has the alleged victim made false reports before? Are there signs the victim craves sympathy and attention? What is the relationship between the alleged victim and the alleged perpetrator? Has there been a recent development in the relationship that might encourage a false report? And most important, what is the evidence in the case? Which way does it point?

Sex crimes detectives must consider all of these questions when deciding whether to make an immediate arrest or to wait until more evidence has been collected. The sex crimes detective must weigh an alleged victim's safety, and the public's safety, against an alleged attacker's reputation.

One sign that might lead those unacquainted with rape to suspect a false report is when a report of rape is delayed, often for days or weeks. Experienced sex crimes detectives, however, aren't as worried about this because they understand the conflicting dynamics involved. If the rapist is well known to the victim, she may delay reporting the crime because she's worried about getting him into trouble, or that she won't be believed. The victim may also hesitate to report the incident because she wonders if she could have been partly responsible for the attack or worry that people will think so.

In a case of stranger rape, the victim may delay reporting because the suspect threatened to come back and hurt her or her family if she did. The victim may also delay reporting because she fears the publicity that will come from making a public accusation and the difficulties she will have working her way through the criminal justice system.

Once an apparently truthful report of rape has been made and a suspect identified, the suspect's profile determines the methods that will be used in questioning him. Since each type of rapist has a different psychological makeup that compels him to rape, the approach of the police interrogation, if it is to be successful, must match the rapist's makeup. The goal of any police interrogation is to break down the resistance of a criminal who knows he is guilty, and to find some way for him to confess while still maintaining his feelings of self-worth and dignity. Even the most heinous criminals like to think of themselves in a positive light, and a good interrogator will facilitate this when bringing about a confession.

It has been said that the best sex crimes detective is able to both empathize with the victim and become a buddy to the suspect. Yet, while the detective may certainly feel sympathy for the victim, he or she really doesn't want to be a friend or give support to a rape suspect. Sex crimes detectives generally feel only disgust and repugnance for rapists. But to conduct a successful interrogation, the detective must put personal feelings aside, and the rapist must be made to believe that the detective is someone who understands him and the stresses and pressures he is under. Sex crimes detectives who can do this are much more likely to obtain confessions and admissions. Offenders, it has been found, are much more likely to respond to interrogators who seem sympathetic to them and treat them with respect.

"Convicted felons have explained that they more likely would confess to an investigator who treated them with respect and recognized their value as a person," said David E. Zulawski and Douglas E. Wicklander in an article in *Law and Order* magazine.[22]

Before beginning a suspect interrogation, sex crimes detectives usually attempt to find out all they can about the individual: his or her background, criminal record, and what physical evidence and testimony connects the suspect to the crime. Some detectives even use a checklist to make certain they have investigated the suspect's background and lifestyle thoroughly. It is important in the interrogation of a sex offender to have facts about a suspect that can counter, if necessary, any excuses, alibis, or false information the suspect offers. Relevant facts might include such things as job performance, demeanor at work and home, relationships with others, financial and personal problems, and so forth. It is also important to know about the suspect's temperament and likely attitude before the interrogation begins. With these facts, a detective can decide on the best way to approach and break down a suspect.

"I feel that preparation and research is the very crux of a successful interrogation with a sexual assault suspect," said Captain Tom Tittle of the Marion County (Florida) Sheriff's Department, who also teaches classes on sexual assault investigation for the Public Agency Training Council. "Knowing the allegations, background if it's available, and reviewing the statements helps a detective direct the interview greatly. Going in 'cold' is the last resort."[23]

Before conducting the formal interrogation, some detectives like first to have an informal interview with rape suspects. During this informal interview the detectives can attempt to establish rapport and can also obtain information on the suspects' propensity to commit such acts, along with likely alibis. In addition, all of the information gained in these pre-interrogation interviews can then be used in the planning of the actual interrogation.

"The most productive interviews are planned well in advance," said an article in the *FBI Law Enforcement Bulletin*. "Except in exigent circumstances, competent investigators have learned to invest time in the initial information gathering process."[24]

However, before the police can question a suspect in custody about a rape, there are certain legal barriers that must first be overcome. The U.S. Supreme Court requires that police officers, before a custodial interrogation, advise suspects of their Miranda rights against self-incrimination. These rights warnings come from the famous 1966 *Miranda v. Arizona* case.[25] Although attempts have been made through legislation to override the necessity of giving these warnings, the U.S. Supreme Court in the recent *Dickerson v. United States* case recognized the Miranda rights as having reached "Constitutional proportions."[26] What this means is that the Supreme Court has ruled that Congress cannot legally pass a law that would restrict the necessity of giving these rights warnings, as they are now considered an integral part of the United States Constitution. The Miranda rights warnings are the following:

1. You have the right to remain silent.
2. Any statements made can be used against you.
3. You have the right to have an attorney present during questioning.
4. An attorney will be appointed for you if you cannot afford one.

The Miranda warnings, however, apply specifically to the interrogation of individuals in police custody. Therefore, they do not apply, and do not have to be given, to suspects who are being questioned voluntarily and are free to call off the questioning and leave whenever they want. However, being in police custody is often a matter of a person's perception, and most sex crimes detectives, if they think they might elicit incriminating information from a rape suspect, will usually give the Miranda warnings even if the suspect came in for questioning voluntarily.

In the interrogation of a rape suspect, the actual questioning will usually take place at the police station, normally in an interrogation room. These are rooms the police have specifically designed for interrogation use. The rooms ensure privacy during the questioning, have good lighting, are painted neutral colors, and allow nothing to interfere with or disturb the interrogation. Our interrogation rooms at the Indianapolis Police Department, in addition to meeting these conditions, are also set up so that the suspects sit against a wall where they and the detectives are visible in a videotape being made of the interrogation.

Making a videotape of an interrogation can be extremely helpful in many investigations, particularly if a suspect confesses or makes incriminating statements. Often, later regretting having said anything, since being a sex criminal is almost universally looked down on, even in prison, suspects will deny making a confession or will claim that the police coerced the confession from them. Having a videotape to play at the trial can quickly deflate such claims.

In addition to the audio- and videotaping of both witness interviews and suspect interrogations, many detectives also maintain an interview log. This log lists everyone interviewed or interrogated during a rape investigation, and contains not only specifics about the case but also about each person interviewed or interrogated, such as the date and time of the interview or interrogation, interviewing officer, location of interview or interrogation, and any specifics about the interview or interrogation that might have a bearing on the case.

To be successful, the interrogation of a rape suspect must be set up and staged as well as any performance given in a theater. During the questioning of a rape suspect, the interrogators sit so that nothing behind them distracts the suspect. The only things rape suspects have to look at are the interrogators. The interrogators also sit in positions that allow them to move closer to the suspect when it becomes appropriate. The suspect, by contrast, is seated with limited room to move away from the interrogators.

Exactly how the interrogators and rape suspects are positioned in relation to each other at the start of the questioning depends on the preferences of the interrogators. Some interrogators, rather than face-to-face, like to start off sitting at a 45-degree angle to the suspects so that the interrogation doesn't begin with a confrontational tone. Most also like to start with them and the rape suspects about six feet apart and with nothing blocking the full view of the suspects, since skilled interrogators watch the total body for body language signs. In the midst of an intense interrogation, body language can often give interrogators clues as to how well certain tactics or lines of questioning are working.

Experienced interrogators also make it a point to maintain good eye contact with rape suspects during an interrogation. However, they don't stare at them, as the suspects can view this as threatening. An occasional break of eye contact can relieve the stress of the suspects and actually help facilitate rapport building. Also, good interrogators attend to their own body language as well. They never cross their legs or fold their arms during the questioning, as this can appear confrontational. Instead, they sit with their feet on the floor, palms visible, and arms open.

For the interrogation to succeed, detectives must be cordial and polite to a suspect no matter what the suspect's attitude and demeanor, even in the face of angry and hostile insults. In addition, good interrogators never show shock, disgust, or any type of judgment, no matter what the suspect tells them. Rather than confrontational and angry, they must appear even-tempered and objective, and always seem interested in and sympathetic to the suspects.

During the questioning, skilled interrogators are always searching for a way to allow the suspects to save face while still confessing to the crime or giving relevant information about their involvement in it. Many suspects want to confess, but they want to do it in a way that paints them as victims themselves: victims of a misunderstanding, victims of unbearable stress, victims of a come-on by the victim, and so forth. Good interrogators are thus always searching for and suggesting scenarios and themes surrounding the crime that will paint the suspects in this light.

To facilitate this search, skilled interrogators must have the ability to be flexible and ready to change tactics if it becomes apparent that a given approach isn't working. No one interrogation technique will work with all rape suspects, since different types have different motivations. That is why it is important for an interrogator to research a rape suspect beforehand and to plan the interrogation tactics, and alternate tactics, based on the crime, its specifics, and the background and temperament of the suspect. Otherwise, if one tactic doesn't work, the interrogator won't know which tactic is the best to use next.

Often during the interrogation, a detective will find that trying to make a rapist realize the damage he has done to a victim, or appealing to the rapist's sense of right and wrong, will be a waste of time. Many rapists have a very distorted view of right and wrong, and many also care absolutely nothing about the welfare of the victims, whom they perceive as nothing more than objects to be used to satisfy their needs. An interrogator will thus be much more successful if he or she concentrates instead on the rapist's needs and fears, such as the fear of going to prison for a long time. Most rapists are extremely self-centered, and will only be interested in things that affect them personally. Usually, only when a rapist believes that talking to the police and giving them information will somehow benefit him will he cooperate.

Experienced interrogators know that few rapists feel much guilt about what they've done because most have justified or rationalized to themselves the acts they've committed, usually through projection and minimization. In projection, even though the suspect knows he committed the act, in his mind the blame for it is projected onto someone else, sometimes even onto the victim. For example, suspects may convince themselves that the victims were the ones who initiated the sexual contact, or that the victims acted in a way that would have made any man believe they wanted sex. In minimization, again suspects realize their involvement, but minimize in their minds their own blame, or see the damage done as minor. For example, they may have convinced themselves that the person they raped wasn't really that badly hurt during the act, or that they did all they could to be gentle during the rape, or that they were actually very considerate because they didn't ejaculate inside the victim. Knowing how rapists rationalize their acts, the experienced detective will use these defense mechanisms to get rapists to make the small admissions that will bring them closer and closer to a full confession.

Before deciding how to use these defense mechanisms against a rapist, however, a sex crimes detective must first know exactly what type of rapist he or she is dealing with, because, as mentioned above, different types of rapists will respond to different types of interrogation techniques. The power reassurance rapist, for example, is the exception to the general rule about the futility of appealing to the plight of the victim and to the suspect's sense of right and wrong. These rapists may genuinely feel remorse for what they have done. A power reassurance rapist has low self-esteem, and so the interrogator may be able to get this person to talk by building him up. A threatening environment, on the other hand, may silence him. Detectives have also found that attempting to reduce some of a power reassurance rapist's guilt by the interrogator minimizing the harm done by the rapist, or by the interrogator projecting some of the guilt for the act onto the victim (her wearing of provocative clothing, for example), will often work with this type of rapist and get him to talk. Also, bringing a file or videotape with the suspect's name on it into the interrogation room and simply laying it somewhere without speaking about it can rattle this type of rapist.

The power assertive rapist, on the other hand, will want to be in charge, and so, instead, the interrogator takes charge immediately and lets the suspect know that a complete investigation has been done and that all of the evidence points to him. Bringing the file or videotape with his name on it to the interrogation will rattle him also.

A sex crimes detective I talked to when researching this book told me about using a variation of this last technique in the recent interrogation of a power assertive rapist. The man had been accused of roughing up a date in a parking lot and forcing her into his car, where he allegedly raped her. The suspect told the detectives that no force had been used, but that the sex had been consensual. Before the interrogation, the detective had arranged for a crime lab technician to stick his head in the door of the interrogation room during the questioning and say, "The videotape had been processed," and then leave without saying anything more.

The suspect, naturally nervous, asked, "What videotape?"

"The videotape of the parking lot," the detective answered very matter-of-factly, looking up from notes he was reading.

The suspect's eyes darted to either side. "What are you talking about?"

The detective shrugged. "They have a security surveillance camera for the parking lot. But don't worry, we'll look at the videotape and verify that she's lying, then you'll be on your way."

The detective said the man immediately began sweating, and then moments later started changing his story and admitting that he might have used a little force with her. Eventually, he gave a complete confession. In fact, there was no actual videotape or surveillance camera.

While it may seem unfair for interrogators who are attempting to get rape suspects to tell the truth to use deception themselves, interrogators often do this because they find it so often works. Interrogators may suggest to suspects that they have more evidence connecting them to the crime than they really do, as in the case of the imaginary videotape, or that they have witnesses they really don't who can place the suspects at the crime scene. In the case of multi-suspect rapes, the interrogator may suggest to the person being questioned that one of the other suspects is at this moment spilling his guts and likely implicating him as the instigator in the rape. Also, interrogators might tell suspects that they are getting ready to have an imaginary piece of evidence analyzed by the crime lab, and that they and the suspects both know that the results will implicate them.

Although it might seem to readers that deception and staging are unethical and would void any confession brought about through such means, the courts have supported this type of interrogation, apparently on the premise that it will only make guilty people confess. Of course, bluffing must be used carefully by interrogators and only at a time in the interrogation when they think it has the best chance of success. A bluff that doesn't work will likely weaken the remainder of the interrogation.

With a power assertive rapist, an interrogator might also try putting part of the blame on the victim, such as suggesting that she led the suspect on with obvious sexual cues. The interrogator might tell the suspect that he or she knows it would be easy for a normal, healthy man to let the wrong signals from a woman cause him to do things he probably shouldn't. Lastly, the interrogator might suggest that, even though the victim said no, how could the suspect know she really meant it considering the sexual signals she was putting out? This tactic gives the suspect a face-saving scenario that he can pursue. Yet another tactic with this type of rapist is to flatter his masculinity and attempt to get him to brag about his conquests.

With the anger retaliatory rapist, using a female interrogator will often only make him angrier, as he usually doesn't interact well with women. However, talking about his anger and the reasons for it may lead him to open up, as this is something he has usually dwelled on for most of his life. Another tactic that will often work with this type of rapist is to convince him that all of the evidence of the investigation conclusively points toward him as the rapist, and that he has no choice but to confess.

The anger excitation rapist often believes that he is smarter than the police and will want to play mind games with them. These individuals are hard to bluff because they often know about police technique. To be successful with this type of rapist, the interrogator should preferably be larger in stature than the rapist and have a very calm and businesslike demeanor. This will lessen the suspect's feelings of control. The interrogator should never try to be this person's friend, as the anger excitation rapist will see this as a sign of weakness. These men can occasionally be made to open up and talk during an interrogation if the detective can guide them to the reasons they enjoy seeing women suffer and the best methods for doing it. Quite often, interrogators find, this type of rapist simply can't resist wanting to talk about it.

Often, the police may believe that some of the statements made by a suspect or witness are not true, that the person is lying. Fortunately, there are a number of ways during an interview or interrogation for a detective to tell whether a subject is telling the truth or not, although none is 100 percent accurate. As a matter of fact, an article in the *FBI Law Enforcement Bulletin* stated, "Repeated studies have shown that traditional methods of detecting deception during interviews succeed only 50 percent of the time, even for experienced law enforcement officers."[27] What this means is that detectives can never depend on any one sign to mean that a rape suspect or a witness is lying, but rather they must watch for clusters of signs that denote deception.

What are some of these signs of deception during the interview of a witness or the interrogation of a suspect? There are many. For starters, all good interrogators question any statement a rape suspect makes that begins with, "To tell you the truth" or "To be honest" or "I swear to God that," and so forth. Individuals use these preambles to impress the interrogator, and such expressions often precede deception. Body language is also telling. For example, lying usually makes people very uncomfortable and nervous, and they will often close their eyes for long periods of time, rub their face and head, or blink constantly. According to the same article in the *FBI Law Enforcement Bulletin*, "Research also has shown that when people are nervous or troubled, their blink rate increases, a phenomenon often seen with liars under stress." Other signs of discomfort and nervousness caused by lying include individuals who fidget in their seats, cross and uncross their legs, drum their fingers, preen by picking real or imagined lint off of their clothing, or who constantly look at the clock.

Interrogators naturally also look for signs that subjects are telling the truth. "Truthfulness is signaled by an acute memory, a perceptive recounting of facts, and flowing narration," said former FBI agent Charles L. Yeschke. "Truthful interviewees display a consistent recollection of details and attempt to dig up related specifics, often offering more information than they were asked for." However, Mr. Yeschke also adds, "When interviewees express themselves in a calculated, disassociated, or awkward manner rather than a smooth, flowing way, something, somewhere, is not altogether right."[28]

Also, a number of studies have found that people who are telling the truth use nonverbal gestures to emphasize their words. Individuals who are lying, on the other hand, although they may plan out what they are going to say, seldom also plan out a presentation, and so, if they do use a lot of nonverbal gestures, these gestures will be out of rhythm with, and don't seem to fit, what they are saying.

Eye contact, on the other hand, is not necessarily a good indicator of deception or honesty with rape suspects. Practiced liars know that many people judge the truthfulness of statements through the amount of eye contact, and so they practice maintaining it. Also, in some cultures it is considered disrespectful for individuals to look at someone of superior status in the eye if that person is accusing them of wrongdoing.

It has been additionally found by interrogators that rape suspects who are lying, in order to decide what to say, will often stall for time when being questioned. They do this by asking to have a question repeated or by trying to misdirect the interrogator through asking him or her a question. Along with stalling for time, according to an article in *FBI Law Enforcement Bulletin*, "Research shows that guilty people often avoid using contractions. Instead of saying, 'It wasn't me,' liars will say, 'It was not me,' to ensure the listener clearly hears the denial."[29]

Although there are always exceptions, interrogators find that people who are telling the truth will tell their stories with a smooth, even flow, and with very little break time to think about what they are going to say. They will want to cooperate with the investigation and, although perhaps nervous at being questioned, will not be overly so. Individuals telling the truth will respond immediately to questions and will refute instantly and clearly any accusations of guilt. Innocent people will usually express surprise or shock at being accused of something they didn't do.

On the other hand, suspected rapists lying during an interrogation will often appear extremely nervous and anxious. When accused of being involved in a rape, they will feign either anger or resignation that they are going to be a scapegoat. Also, they will often respond to accusations of guilt with evasive answers rather than denials, such as saying, "What could make you think that I would want to rape her?" rather than simply saying, "I didn't rape her."

Sex crimes detectives, in those cases in which they believe that witnesses or suspects are lying to them, may offer these individuals the opportunity to take some type of mechanical lie detection test. There are two types of mechanical lie detection devices used by the majority of police departments in the United States: the polygraph and the voice stress analyzer.

The polygraph, which has been around since the 1920s and in use by the police for decades, utilizes various measuring devices attached to the person being questioned to record physiological changes that occur when a person lies. A polygraph measures the changes in the heart rate, electrodermal activity of the skin, blood pressure, and breathing of the person being questioned.

During a polygraph examination, the polygraph operator places tubes around the chest and abdomen of the test subject. The examiner will use these to measure the test subject's respiratory rate, which changes when lying. The polygraph operator also fastens a blood pressure cuff around the test subject's upper arm to measure his or her heart rate and blood pressure, which also change when lying. Finally, the examiner attaches devices called galvanometers to two of the test subject's fingers. The human fingers, research has shown, are some of the most porous spots on the body, and these galvanometers check for increased sweatiness caused by deception. They do this by measuring changes in electrical conductivity caused by increased perspiration.

Most polygraph examiners also now use a device called a countermeasures cushion. This is a cushion the test subject sits on that detects any movement made, no matter how slight. It is so sensitive it can detect the test subject's heartbeat. Operators use these because in the past some subjects, when answering the examiner's questions, attempted to thwart a polygraph test by clenching their buttocks or pressing one of their toes against a tack or rock placed in their shoe. These actions were often successful in confusing the results of a polygraph test. A countermeasures cushion will detect this movement.

Although on television or in the movies, polygraphs are often shown as machines with long needles that scribble jagged lines onto graph paper, polygraph operators seldom use these old, analog-type polygraphs any more. Today examiners use digital polygraphs that display the results of the test on a computer screen, which can be printed out if necessary.

Polygraph examiners usually conduct the test in several segments. There will be a pretest time, during which the polygraph examiner will talk with the test subject, who is hooked up as described above, and explain exactly what is going to occur. He or she will also discuss the questions so that the test subject knows exactly what will be asked. The examiner wants the only stress of the test to be answering the questions, not wondering what the questions will be. During this pretest the examiner will also profile how the test subject is responding. The examiner will then give the actual polygraph test, during which he or she will ask a dozen or so questions. However, only three or four of the questions actually relate to the rape being investigated. The rest will be control questions used to gauge how the subject is responding to the test. Following this, the examiner will often review the test with the subject and allow him or her a chance to offer an explanation for any signs of deception.

Various analytical inquiries into the validity of polygraph tests show their success rate at between 70 and 90 percent. From my own experience with the polygraph, I believe the rate is somewhere in the middle of this range. I know this because as part of my research for another book, I took a polygraph test. During my research I stumbled onto the number 1917. This later turned out to be part of a date, but I didn't know at the time whether it was a date, an address, or simply the number 1917. When the polygraph operator asked me during my test, "Did you know the significance of the *date* 1917 when you found it?" I answered no. The polygraph showed a "significant physiological reaction." I suggested changing the question to "Did you know the significance of the *number* 1917 when you found it?" When I answered no to this phrasing of the question, the polygraph showed a truthful response. I was amazed at how dependent an accurate test is on the phrasing of the questions. This is why the examiner must discuss the questions in great detail with the person being examined before the actual test.

In addition though to being certain of the exact phrasing of the questions, several polygraph operators have told me that the questions must also be phrased so that the test subject doesn't have to think about them, but simply answer yes or no. Thinking about a question will also often bring about a "significant physiological reaction." Therefore, much of a polygraph's success rate rests in the ability of the polygraph operator. He or she must be able to properly phrase the questions, to interpret what the polygraph records, and then be able to use this information to either clear the test subject or document deception.

"Question formulation is the key component in the polygraph testing of a suspected sex offender," Homicide Lieutenant David Phillips, who formally headed the Indianapolis Police Department's Polygraph Unit, told me. "Violent sexual predators, child molesters, and sex offenders such as 'peeping Toms' and 'flashers' share a rich and complicated sexual fantasy life. Evoking this fantasy life during testing with an ill-prepared control or relevant question will distort the charts of a polygraph test administered by an unwary examiner. Particular care is necessary in test preparation and the pre-test interview. The general rule of thumb is to stick to detailed relevant questions about the specific acts that have been alleged and to use lie controls without a sexual component."[30]

Unlike the polygraph, the other mechanical lie detection device used by the police, the voice stress analyzer, doesn't have to be attached to the subject being questioned in order for it to work. This device, rather than measuring physiological changes, measures changes in the frequency modulations of a person's voice. According to the inventor of the device, these changes occur because of the stress brought on when a person lies as compared to the ordinary frequency modulation of a person telling the truth. Many detectives find using the voice stress analyzer more convenient than using the polygraph because it can be used with or without the subject's cooperation, and can be used with tape recordings.

The voice stress analyzer records the frequency modulations graphically onto a computer screen. These can also be printed out on a strip of graph paper. A person trained in the use of the voice stress analyzer then examines the graphs for changes in the frequency modulation when a subject makes certain statements or answers specific questions.

"The voice stress analyzer has value in criminal investigations in that it can often give the suspect the extra push needed to extract the truth," Joe Mason, a former homicide lieutenant, told me. "Additionally, it can provide the investigator with confidence that he or she has the correct suspect and therefore should focus the investigative and interviewing efforts on that person."[31]

As with the polygraph test, however, the success rate of the voice stress analyzer falls short of 100 percent. However, both of these devices can be extremely useful tools for an investigator who doesn't base his or her whole case on them, but instead uses them as just one aspect of the case. Often, just the threat of them will make a suspected rapist stop lying and begin making admissions.

Experienced sex crimes detectives realize that even when rape suspects stop lying, few confessions come full-blown by themselves, but usually only follow a series of small admissions. Consequently, interrogators attempt to get suspects to make these small admissions, such as being in the area of the rape or being with the victim. Following this admission, the interrogator will then attempt to get an admission that places the suspect even closer to the crime, and so forth, until eventually the suspect is involved in the crime. Admissions also come when the interrogator catches the suspect in a lie or discrepancy. To explain these, the suspect must often make a small admission. Enough of these small admissions will eventually lead to a confession.

However, even if a rapist has finally made enough admissions that he eventually admits to a rape, the interrogator must continue the questioning because usually there are more victims, and sometimes many more. Even when making a confession, a rapist will seldom tell about all of his crimes. Once a suspect begins a confession, however, an experienced interrogator never interrupts, but allows the suspect to completely finish before asking about other rapes. Interrupting will break the suspect's train of thought and narrative flow, and can cause important details to be left out. If a suspect does need prodding during a confession, good interrogators always use open-ended questions such as, "Then what happened?" or "What did you do next?" These types of questions encourage the suspects to talk and expound on what happened during the rape. And once suspects have told the interrogator everything they can recall about a rape, they will be more likely, with a little prodding, to tell about other rapes.

Sometimes, however, a rapist who the detective feels certain is guilty simply won't confess or stands on his Miranda rights not to be questioned. In these cases, once the suspect has been identified, and evidence and information from the crime scene, search warrants, interviews, and interrogations have been gathered and collated, a sex crimes detective will then present the case file to a prosecutor. The prosecutor will review the file and, if the evidence appears sufficient, the next step in the criminal justice system handling of a rape case begins: the trial.

CHAPTER 3

The Trial

In 1987, just days before his trial for rape was to begin, Alex Kelly, a former high school wrestling star, fled the country. For the next eight years, using money sent to him by his parents, Kelly reportedly lived and moved around Europe. Then in 1995, having become engaged to a woman named Amy Molitar, Kelly surrendered in Switzerland and eventually returned to the United States for trial.

The woman Kelly had been accused of raping, Adrienne Ortolano, had never given up hope of bringing Kelly to justice, even going so far as to hire an attorney in an attempt to locate him. When Kelly finally went to trial in 1996, Ortolano thought that at last justice might come, but it didn't. The trial ended in a hung jury, meaning that the members of the jury could not come to a unanimous decision. During the trial the victim told the court how she had met Kelly, who was a neighbor, at a party and had accepted a ride home from him. Instead of taking her home, she told the court, he stopped his Jeep Wagoneer, forced her into the rear cargo area, choked her, and then raped her, afterward telling her that he would kill her if she ever told anyone.

Two of the jurors in the case, however, said they couldn't believe that Kelly could keep one hand on the victim's throat and still lower the rear seat of the Jeep, as Ortolano had testified, and consequently they couldn't vote to convict him. In a second trial, in June of 1997, Ortolano told the court that Kelly had taken his hands off of her throat for a few moments to lower the seat, which was the same story she had told the police when she reported the rape. The testimony about Kelly's actions during the first trial, she said, had been simply a misstatement.

Kelly, on the other hand, even though fleeing to Europe, claimed before the trials that the sexual intercourse with Ortolano had been consensual. However, while he proclaimed his innocence outside of court, he decided not to take the stand to testify in either trial.

The jury in the second trial convicted Kelly, and the judge sentenced him to 16 years in prison. Soon afterward, Kelly faced another trial on charges that, just days after the Ortolano rape, he had raped another woman.

On March 3, 2005, after eight years in prison, Kelly appeared for a parole hearing. The Connecticut Parole Board voted unanimously to reject Kelly's application for parole, citing his violent nature and the detrimental impact he had had on his victims' lives. Adrienne Ortolano and Kelly's second victim, Hillary Buchanan, attended the parole hearing and testified about the pain and anguish he had caused them.

"Who knows how many there were before us; I wonder how many there will be if you release him," Buchanan told the parole board.[1]

Kelly appeared calm and repentant when speaking before the parole board, telling them that he had raped the two women because he thought the world owed him something, but that now he knew better. However, when the board rejected his application for parole and told him he could not reapply until May 2008, Kelly became visibly angry and demanded of the board, "Why did we come here?"[2]

The above anecdote illustrates a very important point about rape trials: that members of the jury often scrutinize every word the victim speaks. The smallest discrepancy, such as whether Kelly had taken his hands off of the victim's throat, or kept one hand on, while letting the seat down, can make some jurors want to toss out the victim's entire story. In addition, jurors often scrutinize the victim's actions, and will many times vote to acquit if they think the victim did anything at all to encourage the rapist or didn't do enough to discourage him.

Rape is probably the only crime in our country in which the victim's actions and words are so carefully scrutinized. In a rape trial both the rapist and the victim are on trial, he for the rape, and she to prove that she was a totally innocent victim who did nothing to provoke and everything she could to resist the attack. No other crimes demand this from the victim. In robbery cases no one cares whether the victim had unwisely ventured into a bad area of town; it's still a robbery. In a burglary case no one cares if a victim had flimsy locks on a window; it's still a burglary. But not so with a rape. Because of this extra scrutiny, many victims never report their rape to the authorities, making it a crime the police will never know the true extent of.

"Not only is rape the only crime for which 'consent' can be used as a defense," Johnson County (Indiana) Prosecutor Lance Hamner told me, "but the degradation and humiliation its victims suffer make it the most under-reported and late-reported serious crime law enforcement must combat."[3]

"The demeanor of a rape victim on the stand is very important for the jury," Detective Kevin Hammel of the Trumbull, Connecticut, Police Department told me. "Experienced investigators and prosecutors are well aware of the wide range of emotions a victim can present, but without the experience of working with sexual assault victims, a jury can misread the demeanor of the victim. A victim who expresses little or no emotion or a light or happy demeanor during testimony may mistakenly appear to jurors as less traumatized than she should be."[4]

Along with this extra scrutiny of the victim, because juries are made up of people, no one can ever predict with 100 percent accuracy, no matter what type of case the prosecution presents them with, how the jurors will view the evidence, what testimony they will give the most weight to, what exactly they will do when deliberating, or what decisions they will come to. Our jury system, I've found over the years, can often be far from perfect. Sometimes jurors can reach their decisions in much more puzzling ways than just trying to decide whether or not the defendant could get the seat down with one hand, as in the first Kelly trial. For example, when I worked in the Homicide Branch we once had a murder case in which we thought we had more than enough evidence to support a guilty verdict. However, the jury came back with a not-guilty finding. When we spoke with the jury members afterward one of them stated very matter-of-factly, "Well, we knew the officer was wrong because that's not the way they do it on *NYPD Blue*."

While this was so ludicrous as to be almost humorous, much the background information that juries use to make their decisions, and not just in murder cases but also in rape cases, actually does come from television and movies. Many members of the public watch their favorite television cop shows religiously every week, and unfortunately, some believe that everything they see on the program is true and comes from actual police cases. Just as unfortunate, since most cop shows are totally unrealistic and seldom have the facts rights, police officers usually don't watch them. Consequently, we often don't know the frames of reference juries will use when making their decisions.

A recent magazine article on evidence recovery reflects on the effect that television programs such as *CSI* and others have on the public's perception, "As we keep going forward, the public scrutiny is going to be even five times harder because they believe the shows, what they see and how quick they think that you can turn around crime scene evidence and get the bad guy."[5]

Along with all of their other television-conceived ideas about police work, jurors do often wonder why it sometimes takes the police months to finally arrest the guilty party in a rape case, when every week they watch detectives routinely arrest the bad guy before the end of their favorite television police show. Consequently, juries often give credence to a defense attorney's claim that his or her client is just a fall guy because the police investigation had stalled with no real suspect. After all, nobody on television or in the movies ever takes that long to catch the bad guy.

The truth is that if television or the movies really showed how involved and tedious much of real police work is, if they showed detectives questioning dozens of witnesses, running down hundreds of facts, and trying to collate mountains of evidence, no one would watch the show. It would be much too slow. Writers and producers have to make it look fast and easy.

But besides television and the movies, are there other factors that can cause juries to come to these sometimes odd decisions? Are there other factors that can cause them to side with a defendant when all of the evidence points toward his guilt? Unfortunately, yes there are.

Many members of a jury, no matter what the law says or what instructions the judge gives them, still have their own preconceived notions about rape. Many people, for example, believe that a woman who makes a mistake, such as accepting a ride from someone she doesn't know well or going to a man's apartment or hotel room late at night, is just asking to be raped and shouldn't be surprised when it happens. They believe she is just as much at fault, if not more, than the rapist. Other jurors may believe that if a woman didn't put up a life-and-death struggle then she really wasn't raped. Real victims, they believe, would rather die than be violated. It's also possible that a member of the jury could be one of the 7 percent of people cited in Chapter 1 who believe that all women secretly want to be raped. Since it only takes one juror to create a hung jury, when selecting juries for rape trials prosecutors must make a concerted effort to weed out individuals with these preconceived and erroneous ideas about rape and rape charges. Prosecutors do this through *voir dire*.

The legal process of *voir dire*, which literally means "to speak the truth," is meant to be a mechanism by which the court can find a pool of jurors from the community who will impartially judge the case at hand. This process involves allowing both the prosecution and the defense to question prospective jurors about issues that they believe may affect the person's objectivity. As a part of *voir dire*, both sides have a limited number of peremptory challenges, through which they can remove a certain number of prospective jurors without having to give any reason. After these peremptory challenges are exhausted, however, attorneys must then show cause for eliminating a prospective juror.

And yet, while *voir dire* may be intended to bring about an impartial jury, actually both sides use it for just the opposite reason. Both sides hope to be able to pack the jury with individuals who will be sympathetic to their proposed presentation.

"Attorneys select jurors whom they will be able to persuade, not jurors who will be 'fair and impartial' to both sides," said attorney Marni Becker-Avin in a recent article about jury selection.[6]

Prosecutors and defense attorneys try to select the best jury for their presentation by questioning the jurors in court about issues relating to the case, and in complex cases prospective jurors may also be asked to fill out a lengthy questionnaire concerning their beliefs on certain issues. The questionnaire used in the recent Scott Peterson case in California, in which the state accused Peterson of killing his wife and unborn child because of his involvement in an extramarital affair, reportedly ran 23 pages long. In addition to many other inquiries, the questionnaire asked prospective jurors their feelings concerning extramarital affairs.

It's not just the defense attorneys, however, who read and study these questionnaires, but also jury consultants. These are individuals or firms that, using various psychological principles, can supposedly tell defense attorneys generally what kind of jurors, and even specifically which of the prospective jurors, will most likely be sympathetic to their clients.

Despite all these measures, there have been many rape trials in which carefully picked juries have not come back with the verdict defense attorneys had hoped for. This is usually a direct result of the type of case the sex crimes detectives have put together. To be successful, the detectives and prosecutor must be able to anticipate what the accused rapist's attorney will use as a defense and be ready to counter it. This can often lead to much more investigative work for the detectives. It is not uncommon for prosecutors to give sex crimes detectives long shopping lists of additional items they want investigated or witnesses they want interviewed before they will be ready to charge a defendant with rape or to try the case in court. While detectives will often grumble that some of the items are nit-picking, a good prosecutor doesn't want to be caught unprepared during a trial.

An important issue that often makes rape prosecutions difficult is that victims, both in court and out, and particularly if they accuse someone of stature of the rape, may be vilified by some members of the public, or are at best looked upon with suspicion. For example, in February 2005, the FBI arrested Cedric Augustine of Long Beach, California, for making a threatening communication across state lines. Mr. Augustine had made death threats over the telephone against the woman who had accused basketball star Kobe Bryant of rape.

"We had a ton of people threatening us, but (Augustine) gave us 80 calls and the FBI tracked him," reported Eagle County (Colorado) District Attorney Mike Hurlbert.[7]

Along with possibly being vilified, rape victims, regardless of who is accused and even under the best of circumstances, are going to be forced to undergo an extremely emotional and trying experience during the trial. At very least, the victim will have to face the man who raped her, will be forced to tell the intimate and often humiliating details of the assault in front of the jurors and spectators, and she will have to withstand a vigorous cross-examination by a defense attorney who will try to make the jury believe that she is mistaken or confused about the events she has testified to.

It can be worse for the victim, however, in that defense attorneys, during their cross-examination, may use a different tactic. They may not deny that the sexual intercourse occurred, but instead attempt to show that the defendant had simply had what he, and any normal man, would rightfully believe was consensual sex, given the victim's actions and reputation, Possibly though it will be even worse than this, and the defense attorney will suggest to the jury that the victim is simply a promiscuous liar who not only regularly propositions men, but now also wants to send an innocent man to jail. And while many people might believe that rape shield laws would prevent defense attorneys from doing much of this, unfortunately that isn't always so.

"[The rape shield laws are] not complete protection," said Paul Campos, a law professor at the University of Colorado. "They give rape victims some protection against being blindsided by the introduction of information about their sexual past, but it's far from complete protection by any means."[8]

In 1974, Michigan became the first state to pass a rape shield law. Eventually the federal government and all states (except Arizona) passed rape shield laws. When pressing for the passage of these laws, advocates claimed that they would prevent defense attorneys from steering the attention of the jury away from the guilt of their clients and onto issues such as the woman's dress, demeanor, and past sexual history. They claimed that rape shield laws would stop the type of in-court character assaults that often kept women from filing rape charges.

"Rape shield laws prevent defendants charged with sexual assault from unfairly attacking the victim's morality in an attempt to cast her as unchaste, not worthy of belief, or otherwise 'having asked for it,'" said an article in *Forensic Nurse* magazine. The article also states that rape shield laws are needed because if they were not on the books, "In trial, the jury's attention is diverted away from the issue of the defendant's guilt (assaultive conduct) by putting the victim on trial for her 'promiscuity.'"[9]

According to an article in the *George Washington Law Review* about the history behind rape shield laws, "A chaste woman was considered more likely to have resisted the defendant's sexual advances and to have lodged a legitimate claim of rape. An unchaste woman was considered more likely to have consented to the defendant's advances and to have lied about it later."

The same article stated, "Psychological and sociological research over the past two decades indicates that a complainant's promiscuity or perceived promiscuity with third parties subverts the truth-seeking process by biasing jurors against the woman who has failed to live up to a model of feminine modesty."[10]

Consequently, rape shield laws were needed to prevent this character and reputation inquiry from even becoming an issue. Advocates felt these laws were needed so that a victim's reputation or past is no more of an issue in rape cases than it is in robberies, burglaries, or any other type of criminal case.

Unfortunately though, while meant to protect rape victims from unfair attacks on their character, almost all rape shield laws have exceptions that limit the protection a rape victim has against these verbal assaults. For example, the rape shield law in Colorado, the state in which the Kobe Bryant case would have been held, has two exceptions to the introduction of evidence about a victim's sexual history. One of these exceptions, which almost all rape shield laws on the books include, is the introduction of testimony about the victim's past sexual history with the defendant, apparently based on the lawmakers' belief that a woman is seldom raped by someone she has had sex with in the past. Of course, this isn't true, but lawmakers aren't the only ones who hold to this myth. A study by the University of Illinois at Chicago of rape cases tried in court found that 80 percent of the prosecuted cases involved stranger rapes,[11] even though national statistics show the opposite, that previous intimate partners commit many more of the adult rapes than do strangers.[12]

The other exception in the Colorado rape shield law, also included in many other rape shield laws across the country, is the introduction of any evidence or testimony that could demonstrate that the proof the prosecution has of rape (injuries, semen, etc.) could have come from someone other than the defendant, such as a sexual encounter with another party or parties. This is the claim that Kobe Bryant's attorneys made.

As anyone who follows the news knows, the woman who accused basketball star Kobe Bryant of raping her eventually dropped the charges when the judge in the case decided to allow evidence and testimony about her previous sexual history, which would have essentially turned the trial away from the actions of Kobe Bryant and into an examination of her and her past. While we will likely never know what actually happened in the incident since there was no sworn testimony in open court, Bob Pietrack, the bellman at the hotel where the alleged rape occurred, told reporters that immediately after the alleged incident the victim looked disheveled and upset, as if something terrible had just happened to her.

When some people suggested that she was faking, Pietrack said, "No one can act that well. It took several minutes after we were outside for her to tell me what had happened, in between crying episodes."[13]

Some observers thought that the truth about what had happened that night in Colorado would come out in the civil lawsuit the victim filed against Bryant. However, this also didn't happen. On March 2, 2005, Bryant settled this lawsuit out of court.

"The parties and their attorneys have agreed that no further comments about the matter can or will be made," said a statement from Bryant's attorney.[14]

In general, the 30-year existence of the rape shield laws has demonstrated that they work best when a woman is violently raped by a complete stranger who has a long criminal history. These laws provide much less protection when a woman is raped by a person of stature or by someone with whom she has had a previous intimate history.

Of course, worrying about their reputations in open court is only half the concern many rape victims have. They must also worry about their personal information being passed around outside of court. Even though most major news media outlets have policies about not releasing personal information concerning the victim of sex crimes, personal information, particularly in high-profile cases, still leaks out. For example, the victim in the Kobe Bryant case, along with dozens of vicious rumors about her unchaste character, also had her name, home and e-mail address, and telephone number posted many places on the Internet. The Internet company Terra Lycos said that when the accusations against Kobe Bryant became public, the search for information about his accuser was the most-searched-for Internet item.[15]

"There is such an obvious thirst for information on who this woman is, and there's no lack of people willing to share intimate details of her life," said Bob Cook, a columnist for Flak Magazine.[16]

Of course, the victim's reputation, actions, and past sexual history aside, in any rape trial a conviction will be more likely if, along with the victim's statement, there is also some corroborating evidence. In rapes by individuals known to the victim this evidence can include injuries consistent with the victim's account, injuries to the suspect, witnesses who overheard events leading up to the attack, and statements the suspect made to the police and to others afterward. In stranger rapes this evidence can include the suspect's statement to the police, injuries to the victim, injuries to the suspect, and the victim's description of the suspect, his car, any peculiarities of his anatomy, and so forth. Also vital to the prosecution, particularly in stranger rape cases, is physical evidence such as DNA.

In cases of sexual assault by strangers, the introduction of DNA evidence from semen and other bodily traces has led to the conviction of many rapists in the last decade. For example, in August 2004, a jury convicted Mark Wayne Rathbun of being the Belmont Shore Rapist, who had attacked 14 women over a five-year period. The police stopped Rathbun just minutes after a 911 call about an attempted rape, and samples taken of his DNA connected him to almost all of the rapes attributed to the Belmont Shore Rapist. In another case, this one in January 2004, DNA taken from a dropped cigarette butt led to the arrest of Timothy Ferguson in a rape case. Further DNA comparison linked Ferguson to the rapes of at least five other women ranging in age from 63 to 86.

DNA evidence is so persuasive in stranger rape cases that some states have begun extending the time period for the statute of limitations for sexual offenses. Texas, for example, doubled the time period from 5 to 10 years. Other states are following suit. Some prosecutors, in order to get around the statute of limitations for rape when they have DNA evidence, indict a John Doe on the DNA profile, which can then be replaced on the indictment with a specific name when the lab identifies the DNA.

Speaking about this extension of the statute of limitations for sexual offenses, Edward Mallett, president of the National Association of Criminal Defense Lawyers, said, "We're amazed at the number of innocent people getting exonerated these days because of DNA testing. And I can't think of some philosophic reason that somebody should be able to avoid criminal responsibility just by the passage of time, when science makes it possible to prove their guilt."[17]

Of course, many other types of physical evidence besides DNA can help win a rape case, such as fingerprints, recovered weapons, footprints and tire tracks, and so forth. And along with this direct evidence, the collateral evidence discussed in the last chapter can also be useful in the prosecution of a rape case. While the defense attorney may try to portray the accused as an upstanding, God-fearing father and family man, the introduction of pornography found in the defendant's possession that is similar to facts of the attack, or showing the jury pieces of bondage equipment from the defendant's collection, can paint him in a much different light.

However, regardless of the type of evidence the police have gathered that supports the charge of rape, a victim can't be simply told to show up for court without some preparation. If the case is to be won, the victim must be made aware of what to expect. She also needs to know what each member of the prosecution team's job is and how he or she will help in getting a conviction. It has been found that rape charges are more likely to result in a conviction if the victim is made to feel that she is part of a team effort, and that everyone on the team is committed to obtaining a conviction. A large part of the reason for many rape convictions is the victim's attitude and commitment to see the trial through.

As a patrolman, I once had a case in which the dispatcher sent me to a house where the residents reported that a naked woman had come to their door. When I got there I indeed found a woman, now wrapped in a blanket, who had a severe cut on her throat. Still able to talk as I bandaged her up and we waited for the ambulance, she told me she worked at a local television station and that a man had abducted her as she got into her car in the station parking lot. She said he forced her to drive her car up to a garage behind the house she was now in, where he raped her, and then cut her throat. She said she played dead and he left.

After the woman went to the hospital and the sex crimes detective arrived and took over the investigation, I began a block-by-block search for the woman's car. I found it about a mile away from the crime scene and, as we soon found out, only a block away from the home of a man who had just been released from prison for a very similar rape.

In this case, the victim became totally committed to the investigation and prosecution of her attacker. She assisted the police whenever asked, identified the recently released man as her attacker, religiously appeared in court, and remained very poised throughout the long judicial proceedings, never wavering in her commitment to remove this man from the street. A court eventually convicted the man she identified and sentenced him to a prison term he will never live to see the end of.

For a rape victim to achieve this degree of commitment, she must not only be well acquainted and comfortable with the police officers investigating her case and any rape crisis counselors who are assisting her, but she must also be well acquainted and comfortable with the prosecutor who will be handling her case. The victim must feel that she and the prosecutor will work as a team to gain a conviction.

To accomplish this, good prosecutors will take the time to explain to the victim each phase of the trial so that she will be prepared for what's going to happen. A good prosecutor will also explain to the victim exactly what she should expect during a trial, such as objections by either side, preliminary motions, sudden adjournments for reasons having nothing to do with the case, the right to have questions repeated or explained, and so forth. It has been found that the more aware the victim is of what can and will happen, the more prepared and poised she will be during the trial.

However, probably the most important preparation of the victim is making her aware of what to expect during her cross-examination by the defense attorney. An experienced prosecutor will make sure the victim is aware of all the various tactics the defense attorney may use, such as trying to make her angry, trying to get her to contradict herself, or challenging her credibility and chastity. Some prosecutors, in order to prepare victims for a trial, will have them visit an unrelated trial so they can see a cross-examination. The victim must also be prepared, when the prosecutor asks, to tell in open court about all of the sensitive, embarrassing, and unpleasant things that occurred during the crime. And she must be prepared to talk about all of these things again when cross-examined by the defense attorney.

Most defense attorneys during their cross-examination really don't expect the victim to suddenly break down on the witness stand and admit that she led the accused on and that he is actually innocent, or that she is really a promiscuous liar who is trying to wrongly send a fine, upstanding citizen to prison. Rather, in many rape cases, defense attorneys know or highly suspect that their client is guilty. Their hope is not to be able to prove beyond a reasonable doubt that their client didn't commit the rape, but only to raise even small questions in the jurors' minds, as in the Alex Kelly case, about how many hands it takes to lower a car seat. The prosecution, not the defense, must prove the case beyond a reasonable doubt. The defense doesn't need nearly that level of proof. Even the slightest question in some jurors' minds during a rape trial can make them want to acquit rather than convict.

Defense attorneys attempt to raise these small questions by bringing in their own "experts" to counter what the prosecution witnesses have stated and to give their own interpretation or analysis of evidence. They also try to raise doubt in jurors' minds by getting the victim of the rape and any witnesses for the prosecution to change their testimony on the stand, even in very minor ways, from the statements they gave to the police. Defense attorneys hope that this will then raise questions in the jurors' minds about the credibility of the victim or witnesses.

Attorneys for accused rapists also attempt to raise small doubts in the jurors' minds by employing a tactic called "You can't unring the bell."

In this tactic, defense attorneys suggest scenarios to the jury, such as the victim's accusation of rape actually being part of a plot to get revenge against the defendant, or that their client is the victim of a conspiracy by the police to railroad an innocent man. The prosecutor will, of course, immediately object to these suggestions. But while the judge may sustain the objection and instruct the jury to disregard the statement, defense attorneys know that they have planted the idea in the jurors' minds.

The investigating sex crimes detectives, too, must be prepared, not just to testify but also to be cross-examined by the defense attorney. What can sex crimes detectives expect from defense attorneys during a rape trial?

There are many tactics taught in law schools about how to defend against criminal charges. One of these is a three-pronged tactic that states, first, attack the evidence. If this doesn't work or isn't possible, attack the witnesses. If this doesn't work or isn't possible, attack the police.

How does this three-pronged line of attack come into play during a rape trial? First, defense attorneys attack the evidence by attempting to have any incriminating items collected by sex crimes detectives excluded from the trial, usually by claims that they were obtained illegally or improperly. Defense attorneys may also attack the veracity of laboratory findings, such as a DNA analysis that points to their client. Additionally, they may attack the chain of custody, implying that the evidence has been tampered with, or defense attorneys may simply attack the relevance of the evidence.

If this attack on the evidence fails, defense attorneys will then move on to attacking the state's witnesses. Defense attorneys will question the victim's and any witnesses' credibility, the reliability of what they saw or heard, or may accuse them of wanting revenge against the defendant or of lying against the defendant for various other reasons.

Lastly, when other efforts have failed, defense attorneys attack the police in a variety of ways. They may accuse sex crimes detectives of having a vendetta against their client, particularly if their client has a long arrest record, something often common with rapists. Defense attorneys may also accuse the detectives of doing a sloppy job of investigation and attempting to cover it up by railroading their client. Lastly, defense attorneys may claim that mistakes were made in the police investigation that led to the erroneous arrest and prosecution of their client.

A sex crimes detective testifying on the stand must therefore understand the subtleties of what the defense attorney is trying to do. Usually, the defense attorney doesn't really expect the detective to admit a vendetta or to making a mistake, but only wants to plant the idea in the jurors' minds.

Defense attorneys during their cross-examination also want to raise doubts in the jurors' minds about a sex crimes detective's credibility. They do this by attempting to get detectives to contradict themselves. In many rape trials, defense attorneys take depositions before the actual trial. Depositions are sworn statements taken from the state's witnesses by the defense attorney. These not only allow defense attorneys to get a pretrial look at what testimony will be given at the trial, but defense attorneys often study these statements intensely in the hope that a sex crimes detective will say something on the stand that contradicts, even in some small way, what he or she said in the deposition. If this occurs, the defense attorney will usually instantly attack the detective's credibility, again in the hope of planting a small seed of doubt in the minds of the jurors.

Because of all these tactics used by defense attorneys, there are a number of rules sex crimes detectives have developed over the years that guide them in preparing for a rape trial and for their courtroom testimony and cross-examination. They are:

1. While the investigating sex crimes detective will be the person most intimately acquainted with the facts of the rape case being tried, all of the detectives who have assisted on the case in any capacity may be called to testify, and therefore should also be intimately acquainted with all the facts of their part of the case. However, a few minutes before being called to testify is not the time to review the case. Because rape trials are often complex and time-consuming, they may not take place until many months after the actual crime. Between the time the detective investigated the rape and the actual trial, he or she may have worked a couple dozen other rape cases. Relevant facts can become confused or forgotten. Detectives should therefore give themselves ample time to completely review the case, or at least their part in it, and they should particularly review any depositions they have given in the case, because the defense attorney has most certainly studied them and will jump on any changes in testimony. When jurors see a police officer on the witness stand who seems unsure of the facts of the case, they will often tend to lean toward the defense attorney's argument of reasonable doubt. Testimony from an officer that flows

smoothly and naturally will be given more credence than will the testimony of an officer who fumbles through his or her notes or who simply reads the information to the jury.

2. A strict rule for sex crimes detectives is: "If it's not in the report, it didn't happen." Detectives can be certain that defense attorneys have obtained and read copies of all of the police reports in any rape case. Talking about something on the witness stand that is not included in the official police reports will almost certainly be immediately attacked by defense attorneys as proof of a cover-up and plot to wrongly convict their clients. This information will likely be stricken from the trial anyway because it wasn't given to the defense during what is known as the discovery process, a legal procedure by which defense attorneys receive access to all of the evidence the prosecution has.

3. Sex crimes detectives on the witness stand should answer only the question asked, and never elaborate. Defense attorneys are always looking for information not given to them during the discovery process, and will attempt to get police officers and witnesses alike to provide them with this information by having them elaborate on the questions asked. They often do this by pausing for lengthy periods after the officer or witness has finished answering a question. Many people find long periods of silence like this uncomfortable and will attempt to fill them. Experienced detectives know better and simply patiently wait for the next question.

4. If a sex crimes detective doesn't know the answer to a question, he or she should simply say so and not try to wing it. "No matter how much you know, there is always information that you will not be familiar with," said Dr. Jaine Fraser, a trial and jury psychologist for Dallas's Trial Psychology Institute. "As long as it is truthful, 'I don't know' is always an acceptable answer."[18]

5. Sex crimes detectives on the witness stand should *never* lose their temper, no matter what a defense attorney says or implies. Detectives who lose their temper play very badly in front of juries. It says that perhaps, as the defense attorney has suggested, they are hotheads who are trying to railroad an innocent person after all. Besides, experienced detectives know that the defense attorney usually doesn't really mean it when he or she accuses them of wrongdoing or sloppy police work, but is simply doing it in the hope of influencing the jury.

"It's sometimes the strategy of the defense to make an officer appear angry and upset," says Earl Musick, an attorney and former police officer. "If the defense is successful, the officer has lost the battle."[19]

Just as important as not losing their tempers, sex crimes detectives should never attempt to engage in a battle of wits with a defense attorney. This will also often play badly to the jury, making the officers appear smug and patronizing.

6. The dress and demeanor of a detective can greatly affect the amount of credibility a jury gives his or her testimony. Experienced detectives know to dress conservatively and neatly, and to always be polite and attentive on the stand. How a witness looks and acts affects the jury's perception of the value of that person's testimony. Sex crimes detectives always strive to appear as professionals simply doing a job, and doing it well. But one of the hardest things for many police officers to do when testifying in court is to speak without using police jargon, which the jury may not understand. Detectives must tell about the rape investigation in simple, ordinary language that jurors cannot misinterpret.

7. Sex crimes detectives are usually the ones responsible for bringing the physical evidence of a rape case to court. Experienced detectives know that they must check on this evidence several days before the trial. Property rooms of large police departments can be huge, with thousands of items stored there, and things do get lost or misplaced. The morning of the trial is not the time to begin a search for missing evidence.

8. Since a lengthy period of time often passes between the arrest of a rape suspect and the trial, important witnesses may have moved to a new address or simply disappeared during this time. It is the responsibility of the sex crimes detective to locate these witnesses and to be certain they appear to testify. Again, this is not something to begin doing the day of the trial.

While all of the physical and psychological pain of a sexual assault, accompanied by the emotional turmoil of the ensuing police investigation and trial, can be traumatic and even overwhelming for adult victims, it can be doubly so for children. Children who are sexually assaulted by an adult, especially an adult they should be able to trust, can suffer untold emotional, physical, and psychological damage. This is why individuals who commit these types of crimes against children must be stopped. As we will see in the next three chapters, this is a complex task that only the best of detectives can pursue successfully.

PART II

Sex Offenses against Children

CHAPTER 4

The Crimes

On April 15, 2004, California Superior Court Judge Julie Conger sentenced 72-year-old Kenneth Parnell to a term of 25 years to life in prison. His crime? He had attempted to buy a young boy for $500, allegedly for the purpose of sexually molesting him.

Parnell, who, because of his age and health requires assistance with daily functions, had reportedly asked his caretaker if she could get him a young African-American boy and offered her $500 if she could. At first thinking that Parnell was joking, the caretaker soon realized that he was serious and went to the police.

Working with the authorities, the caretaker returned to Parnell and told him she had a young boy waiting out in her car. Parnell gave her $100 and told her to bring the boy inside. When the police instead arrived and arrested Parnell, they found that he had the additional $400 in his pockets. In his home they also found an assortment of sex toys and pornography. The police charged Parnell with soliciting a kidnapping. However, this wasn't Parnell's first brush with the law involving child molestation.

"He's been a danger to children his entire life," said prosecutor Tim Wellman.[1]

Parnell began his brushes with the law in the 1950s when he served a sentence in jail after being convicted of impersonating a police officer with the intent to abduct and assault a young boy. On December 4, 1972, in Merced, California, Parnell and an accomplice persuaded seven-year-old Steven Stayner to get into a car with them. Parnell then took Stayner to a cabin he lived in near Yosemite Park. To quiet the frightened seven-year-old, Parnell told him that he had called his mother and she said it was okay for him to spend the night. Stayner, believing everything was all right, began playing with the toys Parnell had earlier set out for him.

In the following seven years Parnell would tell Stayner many more lies. He eventually convinced Stayner that his parents didn't want him any longer and that they had given up custody of him. He also told Stayner that he had adopted him and that his new name would be Dennis Parnell.

Because Parnell apparently feared staying in any area long enough to cause people to ask questions, he and Stayner moved 12 times in the following seven years. As another precaution, Parnell would rehearse over and over with Stayner the story he was supposed to tell school authorities about who he was. Amazingly, school personnel never became suspicious, even though most of them had received copies of the missing child posters that Stayner's distraught parents had distributed all around central California.

Finally, after seven years of captivity and near constant physical and sexual abuse from Parnell, something happened that made Stayner at last decide to escape. Parnell apparently decided he wanted to expand his "family," and enlisted the help of an accomplice in kidnapping a five-year-old boy named Timmy White off the street in Ukiah, California. Parnell immediately dyed the five-year-old's hair brown so that people wouldn't associate him with the little blond boy whose picture he knew would soon appear on the inevitable missing child posters.

Stayner, having suffered through years of abuse at the hands of Parnell, and knowing what was in store for the five-year-old, decided he had to do something. Taking the little boy with him, Stayner escaped from Parnell and hitched a ride to the area where he thought White lived. Unable to find the little boy's home, Stayner stopped in at a police station. After hearing Stayner's and White's stories, the police quickly arrested Parnell, who would eventually be sentenced to prison for his acts. However, he would be paroled in the mid-1980s, unrepentant and unchanged.

While the above incident involves the abduction and sexual molestation of a child by a stranger, an incident that is every parent's nightmare and occurs far too many times every year in our country, a much more common occurrence is the molestation of a child by a family member or close friend of the family. I found this out very early in my career.

One afternoon in the early 1970s, still a relatively new police officer, I was patrolling my assigned district. A large railroad yard sat on the northeast edge of my district where lately a number of stolen cars had been dumped. In addition to this, homeless people often camped there and would occasionally vandalize the property. Consequently, I tried to visit the area a couple of times during each shift.

As I pulled in between several of the sets of railroad tracks I came onto a car parked there. Two bare-skinned people inside the car began grabbing clothing and quickly getting dressed as I pulled in behind them. Figuring I had happened onto two lovers, I gave them a few minutes and then walked up to the car, meaning to tell them that they had parked in a dangerous spot. The male in the car, I discovered, was 52 years old. The female turned out to be his 13-year-old niece.

After placing the man under arrest and sending him off in the prisoner wagon, I drove the girl to the hospital for an examination. During the drive she told me her story. The sexual molestation, she said, had been going on for two years. Her mother, the arrested man's sister, was an invalid who depended totally on her brother for support. The uncle began molesting the niece by threatening to throw her and her mother out of the house if she didn't do what he told her to.

I registered the girl at the hospital as a rape victim and, since she was under 16 years old, the hospital required that a relative come and approve the examination. A half-hour or so later, the arrested man's wife showed up at the hospital. Her first words to me were, "It's impossible. She couldn't have been raped. She was with my husband."

I took the woman to a quiet corner and told her what I had found. She shook her head. She didn't believe a word of it. Not a single word. Her husband, she insisted, was a deacon of the church, the loving and affectionate father of four children, and the vice president of a local heating oil company. It simply wasn't true. I was wrong.

However, a moment later the attendants wheeled the young victim past us on her way to the examination. The look the girl gave her aunt was all it took. The woman eventually divorced her husband and the company he worked for fired him. However, he never did stand trial for the molestation, because the victim's mother sent her out of state and refused to allow her to cooperate in the investigation, a fairly common occurrence in child sexual molestation cases.

Unfortunately, little about the problem of child sexual molestation has changed in America since this event. As then, few people today have any idea how widespread child sexual molestation is in our country. Few realize it is an epidemic that claims hundreds of thousands of young victims every year. Yet, child sexual molestation, police officers and child protective service workers know, occurs in every community and in every social class in our country.

"While the reports of child sexual abuse seem to be increasing," Detective Richard Nanan of the Manchester, New Hampshire, Police Department told me, "I believe they are only a third or less of the assaults that actually occur."[2]

"I think the public would be shocked if they knew how much child sexual molestation there is," Detective Dan Dove of the Provo, Utah, Police Department told me. "There's a real lack of awareness about it."[3]

While practically everyone knows that sexual intercourse between an adult and an underaged child is molestation, many don't know that this crime can also encompass many other acts. Child sexual molestation can run on a continuum from talking about sex with children to showing them pornography, from fondling them to actual sex acts, from forcing children to appear in pornography to sexual sadism.

The laws against these various types of sexual contact vary from state to state, with the age limit of consent being around 16 in most states. Statistics show, however, that the peak age for the sexual assault of females in America is 14, while for males it is 4.[4] And, unlike in adult rape cases, consent is not an issue with children, since the law does not recognize children as being able to give consent to have sexual relations. A special problem, however, develops when two individuals, both under the age of consent, have sexual relations. Again, the laws against this act differ from state to state, but most states that forbid it require a specific age difference between the two minors before the act becomes a crime.

However, sexual relations between underaged individuals are greatly in the minority. Most child sexual molestations take place between an adult and a child. How many child sexual molestations occur every year? No one really knows. The problem is so often hidden and unreported that no one can give specific numbers. Yet, studies show that one out of every seven boys and one out of every four girls in our country will be sexually assaulted before reaching the age of 18. According to U.S. Department of Justice statistics, over two-thirds of the victims of sexual assault reported to the police each year in our country are under the age of 18, 14 percent under the age of 6. These statistics also show that the threat of being sexually assaulted at age 20 is half of what it is at age 14, and those age 40 have only a tenth the chance of being sexually assaulted as does a girl of 14. Further statistics show that, like many adult cases, the majority (77%) of the sexual assaults of children take place within a residence.[5]

Moreover, no one knows if even the alarming numbers above are true totals, because the victims of child sexual assault are often too young to report the crime, don't realize that what's happening to them is wrong, or are frightened to report what is happening because the molester is in a position of power and authority over them, such as a parent or guardian. And while some people want to deny that the problem of child sexual molestation is widespread by pointing out that the number of reported cases of child sexual abuse is much smaller than those of other types of child abuse, such as physical abuse and neglect, the actual number of cases is likely many times higher than reported because sexual abuse is so much easier to hide than physical abuse or neglect. Many experts believe that the number of child sexual molestation victims in our country easily runs into the millions. However, we will likely never know the true number because so many victims, throughout their lives, never tell anyone, ever, about the abuse.

Sadly, many of the institutions where child sexual abuse occurs also regularly try to cover it up. Everyone who has watched the news in the last few years knows about the scandal of child sexual abuse in the Catholic Church, abuse that had been covered up and hushed up for decades. While this made front-page news for months, the Catholic Church is by no means the only organization that has concealed the problem.

An article about rampant child sexual molestation within deaf schools had this to say about the covering up of the crime: "First, every effort was made to keep the problem as secret as possible, especially from the media, but also from coworkers, parents, teachers, and boards of directors or other superiors. This was done in part to protect the school or organization, because this kind of publicity can be devastating. It has contributed to the closing of several schools serving deaf youth, for example, the

Nebraska School for the Deaf and the Central North Carolina School for the Deaf."[6] Making this problem even worse, children with disabilities, such as deaf children, are 4 to 10 times as vulnerable to sexual abuse as are other children, according to researchers at the National Resource Center on Child Sexual Abuse.[7]

Another article, this one about the sexual molestation of underaged students by teachers and administrators in public schools, said, "In case after case, teachers or administrators caught molesting students were allowed to resign quietly and move to another school district, sometimes even with a letter of recommendation. In fact, the practice was so common among schools that it was called 'passing the trash.'"[8]

As a part of my research for another book, I attended a molestation prevention program given at a public grade school by Indianapolis police sergeant Terry Hall. This presentation was being given to the parents so that they would know what Sergeant Hall would be presenting to their children. Sergeant Hall, it turned out, had been sexually molested as a child by his uncle, and he spoke freely about this event during his presentation. At the conclusion of his talk two adults, a man and a woman, bolstered by Sergeant Hall's courage to speak about his childhood sexual abuse, wanted to talk about their own. Both said they had never told anyone about it.

It is not uncommon for adults to come forward like this at his talks, and Sergeant Hall told me that he also almost always finds several cases of unreported sexual molestation whenever he gives his talk to children. Unfortunately, because of this record of finding unreported sexual abuse among students, some principals, wanting to protect their institutions, decline to have him speak.

Since most cases of child sexual abuse are never made public, many people like to believe that child molesters are just seedy strangers who hang around playgrounds, and not their neighbors, their relatives, their children's teachers, their religious leaders, or their public servants. However, this simply isn't so. Child molesters are everywhere and can be anyone. Actually, research shows that only 20 to 30 percent of child molesters turn out to be total strangers. According to U.S. Department of Justice statistics, between 75 and 85 percent of sexually abused children are molested by an assailant known to them.[9] An article in USA Today states that 70 to 90 percent of the sexual abuse of children is committed by people known to the children, and that 30 to 40 percent of it is committed by relatives.[10] And while many people may also want to believe that child sexual molestation occurs only in lower-income families, that is only because the problem is much better hidden in higher-income families, where it exists in great numbers.

So, if child molesters aren't strangers who hang around playgrounds, then who exactly are they? Professor David Burton of the University of Michigan said this about child molesters in our society: "I've known MBAs, CEOs, janitors, grocery clerks. The pure numbers indicate that they're everywhere."[11]

Unfortunately, Professor Burton is absolutely correct. With regard to the sexual molestation of students by teachers, a misconception many people hold is that this involves only male teachers. Not so. While most people have heard about sixth-grade teacher Mary Kay Letourneau's affair with an underaged student, by whom she had two children, and for which she consequently spent seven years behind bars, she is by no means the only female teacher who has been sexually involved with an underaged student. In St. Augustine, Florida, a 28-year-old female teacher pled guilty to having sex with a 13-year-old boy. A Long Island, New York, female teacher's aide pled guilty to having sex with a blind, 11-year-old boy. In Tampa, Florida, a 24-year-old female teacher and part-time model has offered a defense of insanity to charges of having sex with a 14-year-old male student. In Tennessee, Florida, Texas, and California, the police have arrested female teachers who now await trial on charges of having had sex with underaged male students. Yet, while their numbers are much larger than most of the public could ever imagine, female teachers who sexually molest students are nevertheless far outnumbered by male teachers who molest students.

Police departments are no more immune from having child molesters within their ranks than schools are. In Glenwood, Minnesota, for example, a court convicted a police officer for having sex with an underaged girl. Other courts have convicted police officers for similar offenses in Orlando, Florida, and Butler County, Ohio. In West Palm Beach, Florida, a court sentenced a police officer to a term of life imprisonment for having had sex with several boys under age 12 whom he had met through a sheriff's youth training program.

Churches have also seen their share of child molestation scandals. The Catholic Church acknowledges that, between 1950 and 2002, victims accused 4,392 priests of child sexual molestation, which was about

4 percent of the active priests during that time. Eighty-one percent of the reported 10,667 victims, the church said, were male.[12]

A report on child sexual molestation within the Catholic Church, issued by a board impaneled by the church, stated, "According to some witnesses, certain sexually immature or conflicted individuals and certain homosexual men appear to have been attracted to the priesthood because they mistakenly viewed the requirement of celibacy as a means of avoiding struggles with their sexual identities."[13]

The same report explained how the problem within the Catholic Church mushroomed into the catastrophe it became, "Faced with serious and potentially inflammatory abuses, Church leaders placed too great an emphasis on the avoidance of scandal in order to protect the reputation of the Church, which ultimately bred far greater scandal and reputational injury."[14] At last report, the scandal will cost the Catholic Church, besides a huge loss in stature, over $3 billion in settlements to victims.[15]

The Catholic Church, however, is by no means the only religious organization to have child molesters in its midst. An elder in the Jehovah's Witnesses contends that the Jehovah's Witnesses Church encourages child molestation by keeping the commission of the crime by its members quiet. He claims that the leadership of the Jehovah's Witnesses has a list of over 23,000 child molesters within their faith.[16]

Other religious organizations face similar problems. A man of the Amish faith in Ohio, for example, recently pled guilty to sexual battery on a three- and a five-year-old girl, while a court convicted an Amish man in Wisconsin of sexual assault on a minor. The Hare Krishna movement, whose members with their shaved heads and saffron robes were fixtures in airports during the 1960s and 1970s, admitted recently to widespread sexual abuse of children within their boarding schools.

Along with religious organizations, groups that cater to children's needs unfortunately also bring with them the threat that the individuals running these groups could be child molesters. In August 2002, a court sentenced a scoutmaster in the Boy Scouts to 8 years in prison for sexually molesting a member of his troop. An Orange County, California, judge in July 2001, sentenced a counselor from the Big Brothers organization, who also happened to be a Boy Scout leader, to 60 years in prison for sexually molesting three boys. An executive director of Big Brothers/Big Sisters in New Jersey pled guilty in December 2004 to having had sex with an underaged boy he met through a mentoring program. In Nevada, a man who worked for a daycare center recently received a prison term of 14 life sentences for molesting nine boys and girls, ages 2 and 3, at the center. A court sentenced a family therapist in California to a term of 90 years in prison for having had sex with a 13-year-old girl he was supposed to counsel.

Being famous or powerful is also no guarantee that the person is not a child molester. Actor Jeffrey Jones, who played the principal in *Ferris Bueller's Day Off*, pled no contest to charges of employing a 14-year-old boy to pose for sexually explicit photos. In 1995, a court convicted former Congressman Mel Reynolds of sexual misconduct with a minor. Former Governor of Oregon Neil Goldschmidt admitted to reporters that he'd had sex with a 14-year-old girl when he was the mayor of Portland, Oregon. The police recently arrested, but then had to release because of diplomatic immunity, a diplomat from the United Arab Emirates who authorities say had solicited sex over the Internet from what he thought was a 13-year-old girl.

Verifying the widespread nature of child sexual abuse throughout our society, researchers Gene G. Abel and Nora Harlow concluded from their study of over 4,000 child molesters, "These results suggest that the act of molesting a child is prompted by a factor outside of the molester's social status or his ethnic group."[17]

These same researchers uncovered some other interesting findings. For example, they found that child molesters are practically indistinguishable from most others in the U.S. population, that only 10 percent of them molested children they didn't know, that 68 percent of their victims were family members, and that the majority of the subjects in the study began to molest before their 20th birthday. These researchers estimate that there are presently at least 40,000,000 adult Americans who were sexually molested as children.[18]

Confirming one of the findings of the study above, Detective Richard Nanan, who investigates child sexual abuse for the Manchester, New Hampshire, Police Department, told me, "I would say that in the majority of cases I investigate, the offenders more often than not are familiar with their victims."[19]

Unfortunately, families, more than any other group, harbor child molesters within their ranks. And while the majority of the family members who sexually molest other family members are male, the police also run into a large number of female child molesters. One study showed that women make up about 20 percent of these offenders.[20] Mothers in

Florida, Texas, Colorado, Tennessee, and Massachusetts, for example, have made the news recently for sexually molesting their own children.

A much more common experience, incest between fathers and daughters, often occurs in families in which the father is the dominant power figure, who many times maintains his authority through threats, intimidation, and violence. Studies of incestuous families show that, to further their control, incestuous fathers will often forbid their daughters from dating or interacting with boys their own age, and often from interacting with anyone outside of the family. Consequently, outsiders usually see these families as reclusive. How much control do fathers in incestuous families wield?

In Fresno, California, on March 12, 2004, the police responded to the report of a disturbance at the home of 57-year-old Marcus Wesson. Two of his nieces, who had previously lived with the Wesson family but told the police they had escaped, had returned to claim the children they left behind. Inside the house, officers could hear what appeared to be an argument going on. In a soft, polite voice, Wesson told the officers that he needed to talk with his family before he could let the children go. The two nieces pleaded with the officers to let them get their children, but, before they could, Wesson walked to a back bedroom and locked himself in with nine of his family members, beginning a police standoff that would last for 80 minutes.

An hour and twenty minutes later, Wesson, now covered with blood, stepped back out the bedroom. Inside, horrified officers found a pile of nine bodies, eight of them children, all shot through the eye. The police arrested Wesson for the murders, but his story would soon take on much more bizarre dimensions.

When investigators began looking into the background of the Wesson family they uncovered a web of incest and absolute, total control by Wesson. Several of the girls in the family told investigators that Wesson had home-schooled them and aggressively discouraged them from having any contact with people who were not part of the family. If they were ever asked by anyone who the fathers of their children were, they were told by Wesson to say that they had been artificially inseminated. DNA testing, however, would later show that Wesson had fathered many of his daughter's and niece's children.

Through talking with family members and others who knew them, the police learned that Wesson had apparently run his family like a religious cult, with himself as the divine leader. His authority was never to be questioned, and his will was law. The police also found that he had rigorously and regularly drilled into the members of his family the belief that they had to be ready to kill each other and then themselves, starting from youngest to oldest, if the authorities ever tried to break up the family.

"In this family, he was Christ himself, the ultimate authority figure who determined life and death," said prosecutor Lisa Gamoian. "But for his suicide pact, for his teachings, none of this would have happened."[21]

Wesson, though seldom having any gainful employment, living most of his life on welfare and often scrounging food for his family out of dumpsters, had, like a cult leader, invented a prestigious past for himself. He told outsiders the fiction that he had once been a top bank executive.

"He told me that he gave up his life in corporate America to raise his family and home-school them and bring them up in a Christian life," said a worker at a harbor where Wesson and his family had once lived on a dilapidated boat.[22]

Even though Wesson's wife, who was 15 when she married the 27-year-old Wesson, was aware that he regularly committed incest with his daughters and nieces, she didn't seemed overly disturbed by this. After his arrest, she affectionately described him to reporters, saying, "He was a very imaginative, loving husband and father. To him, the most valuable, precious things in the world were children."[23]

At Wesson's trial, which took place almost a year after the murders, his defense attorney argued that Wesson didn't kill the nine people in the back bedroom, but that instead one of his nieces had done it and then killed herself. The prosecutor said this didn't matter. Wesson had over the years relentlessly drilled into his family the necessity of taking this action, and so, she told the jury, he was still just as responsible as if he had pulled the trigger himself.

"If you have any sympathy for the defendant, think about the sympathy he showed to the children March 12," the prosecutor told the jury. "Think about the compassion he showed each of his children while he was systematically directing their death."[24]

The jury agreed, and, on June 17, 2005, they found Wesson guilty on 9 counts of murder and on 14 counts of raping and molesting seven of his daughters and nieces. (Although Wesson pled not guilty, his attorneys, after DNA testing had confirmed that he was the father of his daughter's and niece's children, no longer fought the sexual assault charges.) On June 29, 2005, the jury recommended that Wesson receive the death penalty.

Fathers who commit incest, researchers find, do so because they so firmly control every action of their families that they often feel "entitled" to use their children as they see fit. Many of the mothers in these incestuous families, on the other hand, while knowing that what is happening is wrong, don't protest because they too are under the stern control of their husbands. Researchers have found that the mothers in incestuous families may actually come to resent their daughters more than the husbands because they see their role being taken over. Therefore, owing to the sexual abuse by the father and the resentment and rejection by the mother, incest can have devastating effects on the psychological and emotional development of its victims.

While Marcus Wesson and others guilty of incest victimize their own families, readers may wonder where other child molesters, who may have had dozens or even hundreds of victims, could have found them all. At one time nonfamily child molesters had to go out looking for their victims, but today they can do it without leaving their homes. The victims come to them—over the Internet.

Molesters today, in their search for young victims, will visit Internet chatrooms set up to cater to the age group of children they are interested in. In order to be able to interact well with the participants of the chatroom, molesters stay up-to-date on the latest music and music videos, movie and television stars, hobbies, and interests of the age group of children they target. They will also be well aware of the problems these children face in their world. Then, after meeting prospective victims in a chatroom, molesters will spend a considerable amount of time grooming them. They will listen to the problems the children are experiencing and empathize with them. They often spend much more time discussing the issues of the day with children than the children's parents do. Of course, since the end target of this interaction is to have sex with the child, molesters will very gradually interject sex into the conversation. They typically do this in small steps until they have finally broken down the child's inhibitions, and then they set up a meeting.

A report by the National Center for Missing and Exploited Children said that, in a sample of 1,501 children between the ages of 10 and 17 who use the Internet regularly, 1 in 4 had received unsolicited pictures of people having sex, 1 in 5 had received a sexual solicitation, and 1 in 33 had received an aggressive sexual solicitation in which a potential molester had asked to meet them somewhere or had contacted them by telephone or regular mail. Yet, in only 10 percent of these solicitations and in only 3 percent of the incidents of unwanted pornography did anyone report the act to the authorities.[25]

The authorities have found that molesters, in their search for victims, on the Internet or otherwise, often look for a specific type of child, the easiest type to molest, the child who is withdrawn and troubled, the child who is having disputes with his parents or at school. The molester is looking for the child who believes no one understands or cares about him or her.

Kenneth Lanning, a former special agent for the FBI who specialized in child molestation, said this about the selection of children as victims by molesters: "Almost any child can be seduced, but the most vulnerable children tend to be those who come from dysfunctional homes or are victims of emotional neglect."[26]

Once the molester has found this child he will then often spend large amounts of time grooming the victim by listening to him or her, empathizing with the problems the child faces, and making the child think that he really does care and understand. All children naturally crave attention, respect, and affection. Child molesters know this and use it.

During the grooming process, the molester will lead the child subtly and usually unaware into the sexual molestation. The first physical contact between them may be a simple, nonsexual touch, and, following this, each touch will become just a little more intimate. The molester will eventually accomplish his objective of having sex with his victims through both this patient step-by-step process and by simply giving prospective victims the attention and affection they crave.

A child molester will also often spend as much time seducing the adult caretaker of the victim as he does the child. Molesters tend to select as victims children whose parents are overburdened and stressed by the demands of a job. Child molesters will then offer to take over some of the child-care responsibility, which the parents mistakenly see as a godsend.

Why do child molesters go to such great lengths? Why are they willing to expend so much time and energy and take such huge risks? They do it because for many of them, adults hold no sexual allure; children are what sexually arouse them. Many of the most committed child molesters in our society are what are classified as pedophiles. The *Diagnostic and Statistical Manual of Mental Disorders* defines pedophilia as "recurrent, intense, and sexually arousing fantasies, urges, or behaviors involving prepubescent children, generally 13 or younger."[27] Another classification some child molesters fall under is hebephilia, which is a sexual attraction to children

13 to 16, while ephebophilia is a sexual attraction to teenagers. These last two classifications, although not included in the *Diagnostic and Statistical Manual of Mental Disorders*, can still be crimes.

Expanding on the definitions given above, experts who study child molesters usually place them into one of two groups. The first group is called the situational or regressed molester. This person may or may not be a pedophile. His reason for sexually molesting children can often be something other than having a strong sexual attraction to them. For example, he may find himself sexually aroused and the most convenient person available is a child, he may simply be curious about this type of sex, or he may want to get even with someone. With this type of molester, the sexual abuse comes more from the situation he finds himself in than an actual preference for children as sex partners. This type of child molester, as might be expected, will usually have fewer victims than the preferential molester below.

The second type of child molester is the preferential or fixated child molester. This person is usually a true pedophile. He is attracted to children because he finds that they sexually arouse him. The behavior of these individuals is long term, need driven, and very fantasy dependent. Preferential child molesters are often willing to invest large amounts of time and money in the pursuit of child victims, and they may take tremendous risks in the pursuit of their goals. Some of the worst preferential child molesters will spend every dollar they have and use every free moment of their life in the pursuit of child victims.

Preferential child molesters typically have a sexual interest in children of only a certain age group, and will often discard victims once they leave the age group of choice. They will spend as much time and effort seducing a child victim of the age group they prefer as an adult would another adult, using affection, attention, gifts, and other kindnesses. They also know what's important and what's troubling to children. Most important, they listen to them.

Unfortunately, preferential child molesters will often seek jobs that put them in contact with children of the age group they prefer. And since child molesters make it their task to be up-to-date on all of the latest fads, movies and television shows, computer games, Internet sites, and other items of interest to children, they are often seen as "cool" by the kids and may be the most popular teacher, coach, scout leader, and so forth. As these individuals seem to relate so well to children, they are often seen by adults as "amazing with kids," and may even win awards for their work with children. This is why when someone like this is exposed as a child molester, everyone is stunned and asks, "Why would he suddenly become a child molester?" But this isn't what has happened. Instead, what has happened is that this individual was always a child molester who had simply worked hard at getting himself into a position where he could freely molest children.

As an example of this, 63-year-old Dean Arthur Schwartzmiller, who the police found had kept a detailed written log of the over 36,000 sex acts he had engaged in with children over his life, had at one time been a football coach that everyone thought was exceptional with kids. "The parents all thought he was great," said attorney James Kevan. "No one suspected a thing."[28] Only later did it come out that he had apparently been looking for and grooming victims all along. For example, only later did the parents find out that one time the coach had stopped the school bus on the way to a football game to do a "jock strap check."[29]

Whether situational or preferential, the most dangerous child molesters are those who have low levels of social competence, those who have a hard time interacting with others. Unlike child molesters who can woo, groom, and seduce their victims through social interaction, these individuals, in order to satisfy their sexual urges, may violently assault or abduct their victims. This carries a huge danger to the victims because, besides the danger of the assault itself, this type of child molester cannot bribe, sweet talk, or coerce children into being quiet about what happened, and so consequently they often kill them. An FBI study of a small sample of incarcerated child molesters who had abducted their victims found that all of the individuals studied had a high sexual preoccupation with children, two-thirds had low social competence, and three-fourths had sexual deviant desires besides pedophilia, such as voyeurism, fetishism, exhibitionism, and sadism.[30] A national study of nonfamily abductions of children estimates that there are between 3,200 and 4,600 such abductions each year, and that the most common reason for these is sexual assault.[31]

Interestingly, researchers find that even though most preferential child molesters are not as violent as those described above, many will still often spend a large part of their life trying to justify their actions. Most preferential child molesters realize that society sees them and their actions as repugnant, but they nevertheless continually search for validation of what they do. As a part of this validation, many will claim, for example, that they only do what they do because they truly love children and that sex is only a small part of it, although few of these individuals have anything to do with children they are not having sex with.

To rationalize what they are doing, preferential child molesters may also often seek out others who have similar interests. While much of the public might be surprised to know this, there are many national and international organizations that support and encourage sexual relations between adults and children. A few of these are the North American Man Boy Love Association, the Diaper Pail Fraternity, the Rene Guyon Society, the Pedophile Information Exchange, the Child Sensuality Circle, the Pedo-Alert Network, and the Lewis Carroll Collectors Guild.

As might be imagined from the discussion in this chapter, since much of the sexual molestation of children takes place between a child and a family member or a child and a trusted family acquaintance or a child and an upstanding community member, investigation of this crime can often be extremely difficult. And, as we will see in the next chapter, often the hardest part of a child molestation investigation is just getting people to talk about it.

CHAPTER 5

The Investigation

On May 6, 2005, a judge sentenced Molly Daniels of Georgetown, Texas, a small town about 25 miles north of Austin, to a term of 20 years in prison for insurance fraud and hindering apprehension. Her crimes reportedly sprang from a plot to keep her husband out of jail and allow him to have contact with their children after his conviction for sexually assaulting a young girl.

According to investigators, Molly spent weeks surfing the Internet, searching for information on how to make a fire hot enough to destroy a human body, how to stage a car crash so that it looks like an accident, how to make investigators believe that a fire was the result of the car crash and not arson, and how to create a new identity for her husband. After she had collected all of this information, Molly's husband allegedly went to a local graveyard and dug up the body of 81-year-old Charlotte Davis, who had died six month earlier and had been buried in a pauper's grave.

"We felt because she was older, there would not be much family impact, if any," Molly told the jury during her trial.[1]

The couple then reportedly dressed the woman's body in jeans, tennis shoes, and a Harley-Davidson baseball cap with a fishhook attached. Following this, they placed the body in a green Chevrolet, and then, on June 18, 2004, just days before Clayton was scheduled to report for incarceration, allegedly pushed the car off a cliff and set it on fire. The fire burned so intensely that emergency workers responding to the scene found the head and limbs of the body behind the steering wheel totally consumed.

Afterward, Molly told family members and friends that Clayton had died in the car crash. At a memorial service for Clayton, coworkers at the gutter company where Molly worked as a receptionist (which closed down for the day so that the employees could attend the service) gave her $1,000 they had collected. Molly also had a $110,000 life insurance policy on her husband.

Several weeks following the accident, Molly introduced her two children, ages four and one, to her new boyfriend Jake Gregg, who was actually Clayton with his hair dyed black. Molly had earlier forged a Texas driver's license and birth certificate under that new name. To complete the new identity, Molly had made a list on her computer of plastic surgeons in Mexico. Neighbors soon began to notice that the new boyfriend never ventured outside where anyone could see him.

"Before the whole incident, we'd wave and say hello," commented neighbor Scott Regier. "Afterward, when they pulled in the driveway, she would get out of the minivan, open the garage, and he would pull in. The guy never got out."[2]

Upon inspecting the scene of the car crash, investigators immediately became suspicious. They could find no skid marks where the car had left the road, the fire had started in the driver's seat, and they discovered the presence of charcoal-lighter fluid. In addition, DNA taken from Clayton's mother didn't match the DNA taken from the charred corpse.

Although eventually convicted of insurance fraud along with hindering apprehension, Molly tearfully told the jury during her trial that collecting the insurance money wasn't the reason for their actions. "It was about keeping the family together," Molly said. Under the terms of Clayton's conviction for the sexual assault of a young girl, Molly feared that he would not be allowed to have contact with their two small children after his release from jail.

"This wasn't about money," said Molly's attorney Thomas Vasquez. "They could have taken the money and gone to Mexico. She felt everything was falling apart and she had to take action somehow. It was misguided, but (her family) was the motivation."[3]

As bizarre as the above incident was, encountering this type of mindset when it comes to the sexual abuse of children is not that uncommon. Sex crimes investigators often find that the loved ones of individuals accused of the sexual molestation of children, even when the victims are family members, will rally around the accused and attempt to thwart the investigation.

We had just such a case when I headed the Homicide Branch. We had received a call that a 12-year-old girl had overdosed and died after taking a half-dozen of her grandmother's prescribed painkiller OxyContin. At the autopsy, the pathologist found the young girl's rectum to be greatly distended, a condition the pathologist believed had likely been caused by repeated sexual molestation. Although we had a likely suspect, a family member, unfortunately, the only one who could tell us for sure what had happened was dead. The rest of the family not only didn't want to talk to us, but rallied around the suspect and were ready to offer him an alibi for any time period we could ask about.

But sometimes the problem is not just that of family members protecting a molester, it is getting people to believe that the sexual abuse occurred at all. "Society's attitude about child sexual abuse and exploitation can be summed up in one word: denial," said former FBI agent Kenneth V. Lanning, who spent 18 years specializing in the investigation of the sexual victimization of children. "Most people do not want to hear about it and would prefer to pretend that child sexual victimization just does not occur."[4]

Because this tendency toward denial of child sexual abuse runs throughout our country's population, it unfortunately applies to those who serve on juries. Often, no matter how much or what type of evidence or how many witnesses the police produce, some jurors simply refuse to believe that certain people could be child molesters, and consequently they will acquit them.

In addition, while for the young victims having to talk about sexual abuse to their parents and the police can be stressful enough, being forced to testify and then undergo a cross-examination in court can increase this stress tenfold, often making young victims very bad witnesses on the stand. The child molester, on the other hand, is often glib and seemingly sincere on the stand when he falsely proclaims his innocence. This, too, can lead to the acquittal of guilty child molesters. Therefore, rather than having a trial, the aim of every child sexual abuse investigation is to gather enough physical evidence and witness testimony to make a molester not want this information exposed in open court. Law enforcement officials try to spare the young victim the stress of having to testify in court by making the molester want instead to work out a plea bargain with the prosecutor.

"Having a child relive the experience of an abusive situation through a trial could cause unnecessary and avoidable trauma," Detective Richard Nanan of the Manchester, New Hampshire, Police Department told me. "Thus, having a suspect plead guilty would be the ideal outcome to all of these types of cases."[5]

However, before this can be accomplished, before sex crimes detectives can hope to begin gathering the necessary evidence, they need to be aware of where the rest of the family stands. Do they believe the accusation or do they stand behind the accused molester? Do they believe that the incident did happen but that the victim likely instigated the acts? While this may be hard for many readers to accept, that individuals could actually believe that very young children could be the instigators in sex acts between them and adults, and that adults could be powerless against the seductive powers of a young child, it occurs frequently. For example, in March 2005, a jury in Santa Cruz, California, convicted a 36-year-old man of five counts of child molestation involving an 11-year-old girl. When the victim's mother heard of the abuse, believing her daughter to be the instigator, she abandoned her daughter and even testified for the abuser at his trial.

"I hope that now that she has gotten [this] pronouncement from the community," said prosecutor Steve Moore about the conviction, "which she couldn't get from her mom, or obviously from him, she will be closer to recovering from what happened to her."[6]

Sadly, incidents like this are a very common experience. Still, knowing on which side the family stands in relation to a child sexual abuse accusation can be crucial to the investigation because it will affect the gathering of information and evidence. Family members who side with the abuser may try to hide or destroy evidence or try to silence the child. Family members who side with the abuser will often either not want to talk to the police or will get together and work out a story that they all tell. Families that stand behind the victim, on the other hand, can be great sources of information and evidence for the detective. They can confirm that the suspect and the victim were alone at certain times, and they will often know where evidence the sex crimes detective needs is located.

On being assigned a child sexual abuse investigation, and in their search for enough evidence to avoid a trial, sex crimes detectives will treat the area where the molestation took place as they would any other crime scene, and will initiate the activities and measures described in Chapter 2. Further, because the victim is a child and because the perpetrator is often a family member or close friend of the family, there are a number of additional investigative tasks that must be accomplished.

Since most child molesters are family members or acquaintances of the family, merely finding evidence of their presence at the scene has little value. Apart from this, detectives will look for much of the same evidence as they would in an adult sex crime, such as semen stains, pubic hairs, implements used in the crime, and so forth. Like those who sexually assault adults, child molesters, especially those that are not close family members, will often take a souvenir or trophy to use for fantasizing and masturbating later. Detectives will thus ask about these during the interview with the victim and look for them when they search any area controlled by the molester. However, a serious investigative problem with child molestation is that sometimes the crime has been going on for months or even years and in many different locations, which makes a routine crime scene search, if not impossible, at least much more difficult. Still, the detective must attempt to locate the scenes and work them anyway, in the hope of obtaining enough evidence to back up the child's story and increase the likelihood of obtaining a plea bargain. Fortunately, child molesters often leave such evidence behind.

"Need-driven behavior leads to bewildering mistakes," said former FBI agent Kenneth V. Lanning.[7] What agent Lanning means is that preferential child molesters are often so need-driven in their sexual preoccupation with children that they will often make mistakes that stun law enforcement in their stupidity. For example, child molesters may want photographs of themselves and children involved in sex acts so badly they will send their film out for professional processing. Or they may want professional child pornography so badly they will download it onto their company's computer, even knowing that the computer may be routinely audited. Another need-driven mistake often occurs when child molesters have accumulated a large amount of child pornography. Even under investigation by the police, child molesters will often hang onto this evidence, especially homemade pornography that can tie them to a specific crime. Common sense says they should destroy it, but many won't. Child molesters often prize their collection of child pornography more than any other possession, and rather than destroy it, they will try to hide it. Therefore, sex crimes detectives will vigorously search for this evidence, particularly if it involves homemade child pornography, because, if found, it will quickly lead to a guilty plea rather than a trial.

Even when sexually suggestive photographs of children, child pornography, or similar items do not directly connect the suspect to the specific crime, these materials constitute valuable collateral evidence that can help a case tremendously by showing that he is inclined toward such activities. This type of evidence can quickly deflate the cries of outrage from a suspect who claims to have no sexual interest in children. Other forms of collateral evidence might include fantasy writings about child molesting, items from one of the organizations mentioned in the last chapter that support child molesting, and so forth.

Investigators may also find collateral evidence in the guise of extensive collections of what purports to be scholarly or educational material about child molesting. In their attempt to justify and validate what they do to children, many child molesters collect and read scholarly material about their particular sexual interests.

Another item of collateral evidence that investigators look for is intelligence material about possible future victims. Child molesters, detectives find, are often planning one or two victims ahead and may have researched a number of vulnerable targets. As an example of this, in September 2004, a convicted child molester in New York City pled guilty to using fraudulent identification from the Department of Education to gain access to the confidential files of students at two schools. Police believe the man was attempting to gain intelligence on future victims.

In addition, the police find that pedophiles often stay in contact with other pedophiles. They will many times share information and advice about how to successfully recruit and retain victims. They will also occasionally brag about their recent crimes, and this can be damning evidence if they mention in this correspondence the victim in the case the police are investigating.

"Pedophiles' social networks are other pedophiles," said Professor Ann Wolbert Burgess of Boston College, who has written extensively about child sexual abuse. "They socialize, telephone, write letters, E-mail, network, and share strategies for continuing their deviant relationships with children, even when in prison."[8]

Because of this tendency to network, if a child molester has a close circle of friends, the police will almost certainly look into the possibility that they are all child molesters. They do this because child molesters have often been known to share not just information, but also victims and pornography involving their victims. Also, since most preferential child molesters have a certain age range that they are attracted to, they will often pass their victims onto another molester when the children grow out of the desired age range. These victims can consequently often be good sources of information on the molester who once claimed to love them, but has now abandoned them.

Along with the possibility that a group of molesters might be sharing victims, investigators are also always looking for any evidence that a given case is just one small part of a much larger series of molestations by this same abuser. Many child molesters have more than just one victim, and in some cases, such as those involving members of organizations that cater to children, a molester can have dozens of victims.

Sex crimes detectives have found, to their surprise, that many child molesters are avid record keepers who detail each and every molestation. And so, when searching for physical evidence, detectives always look for records of a molester's crimes, in the form of photographs, videos, sound recordings, journals, and so on. For example, in June 2005, the police in San Jose, California, charged Dean Arthur Schwartzmiller with molesting two 12-year-old boys. When the police searched his home they found piles of spiral notebooks filled with the details of more than 36,000 purported sex acts Schwartzmiller had committed with young boys during the previous 35 years.

"I've never seen anything like this," said Sergeant Tom Sims of the San Jose Police Department, talking about Schwartzmiller's extensive record keeping.[9]

However, some types of physical evidence are often simply not available. Since the sexual assault of children is usually discovered after the fact, and often after it has been going on for some time, occasionally for years, unless the child molester was caught in the act, evidence of the abuse can seldom be found during the medical examination of the child. With the exception of extreme cases, such as the one cited earlier involving the young girl who took the overdose of OxyContin, there are often no definitive physical signs of child molesting.

A study on the signs of child molesting concluded, "data collection regarding the physical signs of sexual abuse has preceded careful documentation of characteristics of genitalia and anal anatomy of children who have not been sexually abused and of variations among normal children."[10] What this study is saying is that there has not been enough data collection comparing unmolested children with molested children to be able to say in many cases that a sexual molestation has definitely occurred. Readers should also keep in mind that much child molesting doesn't involve vaginal or anal penetration, but rather oral sex, fondling, making children pose for pornography, and so forth, and consequently will leave no physical signs. One study discovered that medical exams found definite indications of sexual abuse in only 45 percent of cases in which the suspect later confessed.[11]

Even so, in most child molestation cases investigators will send the victims for a medical examination. If the police were fortunate enough to find out about the molestation soon after it occurred, the examiner may find semen, pubic hairs from the molester, saliva on the victim, and so forth. But even in those cases in which the child sexual abuse wasn't reported until some time after it occurred, the medical exam is still necessary to check for pregnancy, sexually transmitted diseases, and obvious injuries as a result of molestation. Unlike the examination of a child's genitalia, which can be inconclusive, pregnancy or a sexually transmitted disease provides clear proof of sexual abuse.

While the search for physical evidence can occasionally turn up definitive proof of child molesting, often much of the important evidence in child sexual abuse cases comes from talking to the victim, the suspect, and any witnesses. This is when an investigator's skill in interviewing and interrogation becomes paramount.

Sex crimes detectives know that they are dealing with an extremely sensitive area when they begin talking to people about a possible child sexual molestation, and they know that they must therefore be prepared to hear stories from people closely involved in the case that are seldom 100 percent true, or even close. According to an article in the FBI Law Enforcement Bulletin, "In virtually every case of child sexual abuse, someone will attempt to deceive investigators. Therefore, investigators must avoid the temptation of accepting initial statements at face value, regardless of how sincere the source appears."[12]

Along with realizing that many people will lie to them, experienced investigators are also aware that since most members of the public find child molestation particularly repugnant, many individuals are likely to have a difficult time accepting that a person they know or that a person of stature in the community could be a child molester. Because of this, detectives may have a difficult time getting cooperation during interviews. Some individuals, for example, may have facts that could help the investigation tremendously, but they don't want to divulge these facts because doing so would force them to face the fact that indeed the person in question might be a child molester.

"People seem more willing to accept a sinister stranger from a different location or father/stepfather from a different socioeconomic background as a child molester than a clergy member, next door neighbor, law enforcement officer, pediatrician, teacher, or volunteer with direct access to children," said Kenneth V. Lanning.[13] However, as we have seen throughout this book, these very individuals are quite often child molesters.

Since the starting point of many child molestation cases is often the child's story about what happened, a meaningful interview with the victim can often be the most important step in the success of the investigation. Therefore, being a good child abuse investigator requires a person who can relate well to children and make them feel secure in talking about the alleged incident. For some people this is simply a natural talent. They relate well to children and children relate well to them. These individuals, of course, make the best child abuse detectives. For others, this skill requires extensive training and experience, but it is a skill that can be acquired. And it must be acquired if a person wants to be a successful child abuse investigator, because if a child feels frightened or intimidated by an investigator, often little meaningful communication will result.

"Whether it's in the office or the young victim's home, I start slowly and try to demystify the police officer aspect (but still letting them know that I am one) and show them I am there to help and can be their friend," Captain Tom Tittle of the Marion County (Florida) Sheriff's Department told me. "I have started conversations about sports, schools they attend, favorite hobbies, and it usually takes off from there."[14]

However, no matter how well a sex crimes detective can relate to children, the initial interview will still often be the most difficult one. That is because this is the meeting at which the detective and the victim will establish their relationship, but more so because during the initial interview by the police, a child sexual abuse victim will usually be under severe emotional stress. This stress has come about because exactly what the molester had said would happen if the victim ever told about the sexual abuse has happened. The suspect, who is often a family member or close family friend, may now be under arrest, the mother and others may be distraught and even hysterical, everyone may be treating the child as if he or she is some kind of freak, and it may look to the child as if he or she is in trouble.

Therefore, an important job of the investigator at the initial interview, after confirming that a sexual molestation likely occurred, is to reassure the young victims that they have done the right thing by reporting the sexual abuse, and that what happened was in no way their fault. The victims must also be assured that they are not in any trouble.

Once the victim has been reassured, the detective can begin to think about the interview. Detectives who want to have a productive interview with young victims never question them in an interrogation room or even at the police department if possible. These surroundings are more likely to frighten children into silence. Investigators find they have much more success if they use a more child-friendly environment. Consequently, a number of cities have founded child advocacy centers, which are offices away from the police department, where detectives, child protective services workers, prosecutors, and others involved in the investigation of child abuse work together. But the most important part about these centers is that they don't look like police stations. Instead, they are very child friendly, with bright colors and lots of toys.

Similar to interviews with adults, detectives will usually first attempt to find out the personality of the child before the actual interview. The detective needs to know whether the child is outgoing and talkative, shy and easily frightened, and so forth. This can have a bearing on how the detective approaches the child. However, even after finding out this, before a meaningful interview with a child molestation victim can begin, the investigator must first have established rapport with the child and made him or her feel safe talking about what has happened. Some investigators have a natural affinity with children and can do this by simply talking with them. Other investigators will do things such as simple magic tricks, or anything else that will put the child at ease and make him or her like the detective. For older children, detectives find, much of this isn't needed. For them, rapport before an interview can often be established simply by treating them as adults and with respect.

Also before getting into the actual interview, sex crimes detectives must be certain that young children know the difference between right and wrong and that telling a lie is wrong. Additionally, detectives will usually try to find out a young child's name for various body parts, so there will be no misunderstanding when the child tells about what happened. Some detectives do this just by talking with the child, some by having children draw pictures, and some by using anatomically correct dolls.

Once the correct setting has been found, rapport established, and the detective is certain the child knows the importance of telling the truth, next the detective must usually deal with the victim's parents. While often the parents may very much want to be in the room while the interview is being conducted, having a parent or other adult present during the interview of a child molestation victim can often prove counterproductive. The young victim will usually not want to discuss intimate and embarrassing details of what has happened in front of them. Consequently, the parents must be persuaded to wait outside.

"I allow young victims to see mom or dad there during the initial conversation, which shows the victims that their parents approve of me speaking to them," Captain Tom Tittle told me. "However, when the conversation starts to be an interview, privacy is a greater conductor of information that will reveal the details of any heinous act."[15]

After this issue is out of the way, the actual interview can begin. Experienced detectives are not surprised if victims at first deny that any molestation took place, no matter what the evidence. They know this occurs because the victims are ashamed or embarrassed, the molester has threatened them or their families, or because the molester is a loved one. Occasionally, the child may not even realize that what has happened is wrong.

During the interview with the victim, the detective wants to learn exactly what happened, what parts of the body it involved, when it happened, at what locations it happened, and how long it has been going on. Since very young victims may have difficulty with dates and times, detectives will often have to have these children relate incidents to events important to the them, such as before or after lunch, before bedtime, before or after Christmas, when it was cold outside, and so forth. Some detectives will ask about a child's favorite television shows so that they can use these as a reference during the interview for what time of day things happened.

Over the years, sex crimes detectives have found a number of important facts they must keep in mind when interviewing children. The first is that their attention span is short, and so detectives must not linger in their questioning about certain events. Another is that during the interview the detective must get down to the child's level and not tower over him or her. Otherwise, rather than building rapport, the detective will appear intimidating. The detective also must be certain during the interview that the child understands the concept of numbers. When a child says that something happened a certain number of times, careful detectives will often have the child count to that number.

In addition, to ensure a productive interview with small children, detectives must remember to use simple sentences and only one- or two-syllable words. Veteran detectives also know that if they ask young children the same question several times, these children will often assume that the answer they gave was wrong, and they may change it. Most important, experienced detectives know they should never interrupt a child when he or she begins a narrative, except with phrases such as "What happened next?"

When interviewing a sexual abuse victim, sex crimes detectives know from experience that very few reported child molestation incidents are the first time the abuse has happened. Often, the sexual abuse can have been ongoing for months or even years. The detective, therefore, needs to find out during the interview how long the abuse has been going on, and if there have been more victims.

During the interview of child victims, no matter how depraved the acts described, detectives know they must never express shock, disgust, or disapproval. Children who know the acts are wrong are often looking to see if the detective disapproves, and may stop talking if they believe so. It is important that the child see the detective as friendly, nonthreatening, and nonjudgmental. Experienced interviewers of children also know that they must be cautious not to ask leading questions because many children will follow the lead. Instead, questions must be open-ended, such as, "Tell me what happened that made your bottom hurt."

For children who have a hard time opening up and talking about what happened, detectives find that asking them to draw a picture of what occurred can often be helpful. These drawings then become evidence in the case just as oral interview answers would be.

During the interview, the detective will also ask about such things as any rewards offered or threats made; any other adults who may have been involved; any devices such as oils, vibrators, lubricants, or pornography used during the molestation; whether the perpetrator took pictures or video; whether the perpetrator kept anything of the child's; whether the perpetrator has a secret hiding place for his materials; whether the victim was given any drugs or alcohol; whether the child and the person being investigated have a secret and what will happen if the child tells the secret; whether the child and the person being investigated ever played games; and whether anyone was touched or undressed during these games. In addition, as in the investigation of adult rape, it is important to know exactly what the perpetrator did and in what order. This can tell the detective what kind of sex offender he or she is dealing with.

An important lesson many veteran sex crimes detectives have learned over the years is that they can never discount any child's story of what happened during the abuse, no matter how bizarre or outlandish it sounds. Child molesters, they have discovered, will often engage in acts with children that they are embarrassed to ask of adults.

A truly difficult victim interview for sex crimes detectives can come when the molestation victim is a child with a mental handicap. Some abusers, it has been found, will specifically select these children as their victims because they know about the added difficulty of proving sexual abuse. They know that these children may be unable tell or describe to the detective what has happened. In these incidents, finding corroborating evidence or witnesses often becomes paramount if the case is to be prosecuted.

Sex crimes detectives must also be prepared to interview victims who, even though undoubtedly sexually molested, will refuse to admit it or talk about it, no matter what the evidence. Sexual molestation, particularly within families, is often intertwined with strong feelings of love and attachment. According to a booklet about child sexual abuse, "Insidiously, most abuse of children happens within this intimate sphere, by trusted and loved family or community members. Because of the sacredness of family and its relationship to community, child sexual abuse is tightly wrapped around issues of love, loyalty, responsibility, and betrayal."[16] These are the cases in which the ability of a sex crimes detective to establish rapport with children and make them want to talk about their abuse becomes crucial. To be successful the sex crimes detective must be able to convince the young victims that what happened was wrong and that they were in no way to blame for it. The children must believe that, regardless of who the abuser was, the right thing to do is to tell the detective about everything that happened.

Once the investigator has obtained all of the information he or she thinks possible from the victim, experienced detectives will ask the victims if there is anything else they want to talk about. Some victims, particularly young ones, will have important information that they were simply waiting for the investigator to ask about. Interviews with child molestation victims, especially if the detective expects continued cooperation, should always conclude with the officer thanking the children for their help, expressing how important their assistance was, and assuring them that they are not in any trouble and are not to blame for what has happened.

Occasionally, when interviewing what they initially believed was a victim of child sexual abuse, the detective will hear a story that doesn't appear to match the facts. They will encounter a story that appears to be a fabrication. Do children ever make false accusations of being sexually molested? Yes, they do, and for various reasons.

Older children have been found to make false reports of sexual abuse for reasons of revenge; to get attention and sympathy; to direct attention away from some wrongdoing of theirs; because of the fear of pregnancy or a sexually transmitted disease through consensual sex with another minor; or to make changes in their environment, such as having a stepfather or boyfriend removed from the house or perhaps moving themselves to a relative's house. Small children, on the other hand, may tell their parents about something that has happened which is misinterpreted by the parents as sexual abuse. When the police investigate it, however, they find that the report was false, although not intentionally so. Finally, in some cases an adult may coach a young child into making a false accusation of sexual abuse against an adult. Fortunately, for most of these coached accusations, in-depth questioning by an investigator will expose the fabrication. Small children who have been coached to make an accusation of sexual abuse are seldom coached about the intimate details they would have if a molestation actually occurred.

Many of the parents of children who are coached into making a false accusation of sexual abuse are going through divorce proceedings.

An accusation of sexual abuse against a parent, it has been found, can add considerable clout to the other parent's standing in areas such as child custody, visitation rights, and so forth. One study of child sexual abuse allegations made during divorce proceedings found that 14 percent of these accusations were deliberate, false allegations.[17] Other studies have found rates between 2 and 8 percent.[18]

Investigators must therefore tread carefully when looking into accusations of child sexual abuse made during divorce proceedings. According to an article in the FBI Law Enforcement Bulletin, "The effects of being wrongly accused of child abuse and taken into custody for such a crime prove almost as heinous as the crime itself." The article goes on to say, "If the police arrest or falsely accuse an innocent person, no number of apologies or retractions can undo the irreparable damaged suffered to that person's reputation."[19]

On the other hand, the detective knows that the accusations made during divorce proceedings could also be true. The child sexual abuse could be the reason for the divorce, or perhaps the child, with the abusing parent now out of the house, is no longer afraid to tell about what has happened. Therefore, in these types of cases all of the facts of the alleged incident must be closely examined and investigated before formal charges are filed.

Sometimes, children who sex crimes detectives believed were telling the truth when they initially told about being sexually abused will recant their stories and claim that they lied when reporting the abuse. This claim of lying, however, often isn't true. The child may be recanting, but he or she wasn't lying when making the original accusation. In one study of 630 cases of child sexual abuse, researchers found that the victims recanted in 22 percent of them.[20] However, in another study, this one of 576 cases of child sexual abuse, researchers found that only 1.4 percent of the recantations were because the original accusations were fabricated.[21]

Why then, as the one study above found, do a fifth of child sexual abuse victims recant their accusations, even though almost all of them were originally telling the truth? Police give a number of reasons for such recantations. After making an accusation of sexual abuse, a child is often put under tremendous pressure by family members to recant, particularly if the abuser is a family member. Many times families will do this because they suddenly realize what's going to happen to them if the criminal investigation is allowed to continue. Often in these cases, the wage earner of the family is now in jail, the family structure is in turmoil, and family members have suddenly come under tremendous public scrutiny. Children also often recant because after telling about the abuse their world comes crashing down around them. Their mother is reduced to hysterics, their father has been taken away, the police have questioned them and other family members several times, and everyone is treating them like a freak. It's just like the molester told them it would be if they ever told about the abuse.

While detectives know that the interview with the child sexual abuse victim can be sensitive, the interview with a nonabusing spouse or intimate partner in a child molesting case can be just as sensitive. Experience has shown that, to be productive, this interview must be conducted privately and always away from the offender. The detective must be able to assess how much this person already knows and where he or she stands on it. If this is the first time the nonabusing spouse or intimate partner has heard about the abuse, the detective may be able to obtain some important corroborating information and evidence. Or he or she may be able to obtain information and evidence that refutes the victim's story.

However, if this isn't news to the nonabusing spouse or intimate partner, and this person appears to be not supportive of the child, but instead solidly on the side of the accused abuser, steps may be necessary to protect the child from what will almost certainly become a hostile and even dangerous home environment. For example, in Atlanta, Georgia, a 12-year-old girl gave birth to a baby that DNA tests showed her mother's boyfriend, Trianthony Cannon, had fathered. After the police arrested Cannon, the mother attempted to get the court to release him and repeatedly threatened her daughter about talking to the police. "Trianthony and Mommy said don't tell anyone because they would take me away," the girl told the court, which eventually sentenced Cannon to a term of life imprisonment plus 80 years and the mother to a term of life imprisonment plus 21 years.[22]

In another incident of a nonabusing parent siding with the abuser, in February 2005, a jury in Houston, Texas, recommended a 50-year prison sentence for Keith Samuel Cook after convicting him of raping his girlfriend's 6-week-old baby. His girlfriend now faces charges of failure to report child abuse. Initially, after finding her baby seriously injured, and after her boyfriend had pleaded with her not to take the baby to the hospital, the mother claimed that she had injured the child while changing its diaper. An aunt, however, saw the injuries to the baby and insisted that it be taken to the hospital.

When interviewing a nonabusing spouse or intimate partner in a child sexual abuse case, the detective must be certain to always appear nonjudgmental of this person's actions or inactions, and present only the appearance of a professional doing a job that must be done. This person may feel very guilty about not knowing what was happening, and to keep good rapport the detective must not show disgust or disapproval, no matter how obvious the signs of abuse appear to have been.

Since the detective wants to find out what, if anything, this person knows about the alleged abuse, and this may be the first time he or she has heard about it, the detective will usually only tell the person the facts from the child's accusation that are absolutely necessary to tell. And investigators will be certain not to tell this individual anything they don't want the suspect to know, as this individual may very possibly go over to the suspect's side. In addition, the detective must be prepared for a number of possible responses from these individuals, ranging from intense rage to very little concern about the child and more concern about what is going to happen to them (loss of income, negative publicity, etc.).

During the interview with nonabusing spouses or intimate partners, in order to obtain important corroborating information and evidence about the abuse, the detective must naturally inquire about the status of the relationship between them and the suspects. The detective will need to know about such things as any violence in their relationship, the status of their sexual relationship, pornography read or possessed by the suspect, the relationship between the suspect and the victim, alcohol or substance abuse, and any history of the suspect being abused as a child. A supportive, nonabusing spouse or intimate partner who believes and wants to help the victim can be a great ally and assist tremendously in the collection of evidence. Depending on the situation, the detective may also need to advise a nonabusing spouse or intimate partner who is afraid of the suspect, or fears the financial repercussions if the investigation goes forward, about the various agencies within the community that can help, such as shelters and similar services.

Occasionally in child sexual abuse cases, both parents, along with other family members, can be nonabusing. However, an interview with the parents of a child molested by someone outside of the family can be just as sensitive as it would be if one of them were the abuser.

Parents often know the abuser very well, may be close friends, trust him implicitly, and have difficulty believing that he could be a child molester. The first step, therefore, is to convince the parents of the truth of the accusation, which can usually be done with information provided by the victim. The detective must then ask about such things as the relationship of the family with the abuser, the abuser's access to the child, and what the child has told them, if anything, about what happened. In such cases, sex crimes detectives can often obtain valuable corroborating evidence from parents, such as times the child was alone with the alleged abuser, sudden and unusual gifts to the child from the alleged abuser, actions of the alleged abuser around the child, and so forth.

Following the interviews with the victim, the victim's family, and any witnesses, the next step in a child sexual abuse investigation is the interrogation of the suspect. Successful questioning requires excellent communications skills on the part of the detective. A document from the U.S. Department of Health and Human Services said this about child abuse investigators: "The investigators chosen for this type of work should be able to communicate and empathize not only with the victim but also with the family and the perpetrator."[23] In other words, the detective must appear as professional, compassionate, and sympathetic to the suspect as he or she does to the victim and witnesses.

Most of the interrogation techniques used with child molesters are the same as those used with suspects in adult rapes, discussed in Chapter 2, although because this crime involves children there are several modifications to the techniques that we will talk about below. However, as with suspects in adult rape cases, before conducting an interrogation of a suspected child molester, detectives will gather as much personal information as possible about the individual and conduct an informal interview in order to find out about his temperament, relationship with witnesses, any criminal history, ability to have committed the crime, likely alibis, and so forth.

During the interrogation of suspected child molesters, privacy is crucial if the detectives want them to open up. Child molesting is repugnant to the general public, and molesters know this, so they will seldom be willing to talk about any acts they have committed if anyone nearby can overhear them. Interrogations, therefore, should, if at all possible, be conducted in the type of interrogation room discussed in Chapter 2.

Usually, at the beginning of a child sexual abuse investigation all a detective has is the word of the victim against the word of the suspect. This is why gathering corroborating evidence and testimony is so very important. Having these to point to during an interrogation will often make the suspect see the futility of continuing to lie, and eventually lead him to confess.

Even the most obviously guilty child molester wants to think that he is not a total monster, and so the interrogator can help him rationalize his behavior with statements such as, "I know you were under a lot of stress," or "Believe me, I've seen a lot worse cases than yours," or "I know that you love her and didn't mean to hurt her." Detectives have found over the years, though, that because the crime is perceived with such disgust by the public, few confessions of child molestation come full-blown. They often come one step at a time. Usually, the detective has to start getting small admissions (the suspect was with the child), then move forward with more admissions (he touched the child over her clothing), and then after enough of these admissions finally move on to the confession.

Even if child molesters admit something to the interrogator, detectives have found that they will seldom admit to everything they have done. Suspects will seldom tell about all of their molestation incidents or all of their victims. This is why when one child in a family has been sexually abused, all of the children must be questioned about abuse. Also, this is why every victim found must be asked if he or she knows of any other victims. Often there will be others, and occasionally many others.

The police have found that child molesters, because again of the public's disgust with the act, very seldom accept full blame for what has happened, no matter what proof the police have. Instead, molesters often try to blame others, including the victim. Molesters will talk about how the victim made the first sexual overture or how provocative she was. Molesters will try to blame even grade-school and younger children of being the sexual aggressor. Some child molesters try to minimize their criminal behavior by saying such things as they truly love children and that they only have sex with those who "consent." This, of course, is a meaningless rationalization because children cannot give consent to have sexual relations with an adult.

According to an article in the *FBI Law Enforcement Bulletin*, "Experienced investigators know that by nature everyone uses an often-unconscious mental process to justify their behavior or cope with personal problems.

Criminals frequently employ these defense mechanisms to rationalize their actions, to project blame onto someone or something else, and to minimize their crimes."[24]

Child molesters, like most people, no matter how heinous their acts, still like to see themselves in a positive light. In Las Vegas, for example, the police discovered during a drug investigation several videotapes of George William Gibbs engaging in sex with two six-year-old girls. Convicted and sentenced to a term of 40 years to life in prison, Gibbs told the judge that the incidents on the tapes were simply an aberration. "I'm not some deviate pedophile running around the streets," he said.[25]

As another example of this, Joseph Edward Duncan III is presently under arrest in Idaho for the murder of an entire family, who authorities believe he killed so that he could have their two young children to molest. He has also spent many years in prison for past child molesting. Duncan had this to say in an Internet blog he kept prior to his arrest for the murders: "I have decided to give up trying to convince people that I am a real person, with honest and good intentions, not some evil monster they should be afraid of."[26]

Because child molesters such as Gibbs and Duncan like to see themselves in a positive light, interrogators who want them eventually to confess must treat them with respect and dignity. The abuser wants to be seen in a good light, and the interrogator is simply carrying on this myth. The abuser who believes that the interrogator understands and respects him will often open up and make admissions.

In addition to treating a suspect with respect and dignity, a good interrogator will never use harsh, accusatory words such as "hurt," "molest," or "rape," but rather use words such as "incident" or "mistake." Experienced interrogators also always search for scenarios that will allow the suspect to confess, but do it in a manner that allows him to still look like a good person who has just made a mistake. Themes or scenarios an interrogator might use can include: that the suspect wasn't to blame, it was a spouse with a low interest in sex that made him do it; that the suspect didn't mean to hurt the child but was just trying to teach him or her about sex; that the suspect was under pressure or stress and had a moment of weakness; that the suspect was himself the victim of sexual abuse as a child; or that it wasn't really the suspect, it was the alcohol or drugs. But to make this work, interrogators must come across as sympathetic to the plight of the suspect and understanding of the pressures that caused him to commit the abuse. They must never show the true disgust they feel.

In cases in which a suspect appears to be just on the verge of confessing, but simply can't seem to do it, and the interrogator finds that he has an emotional attachment to the victim, the interrogator might appeal to the suspect that, since he won't come clean about what happened, now the victim is going to have to go through the tremendous stress of testifying in court. Sometimes this works.

However, in some cases, no matter how much proof the police have, no matter how many witnesses, the suspect simply won't confess and therefore will not want to take part in a plea bargain. In these cases, the detective, as in the rape cases talked about in Chapter 2, will present the physical evidence and statements collected to a prosecutor. If enough evidence is available, then the next step in the criminal justice system begins: the trial.

CHAPTER 6

The Trial

On October 5, 2004, a jury in Farmington, Missouri, deliberated 90 minutes before returning a guilty verdict on 12 felony sex charges against 31-year-old Wilburn L. Nash. His victim: a five-year-old girl. The 12 guilty findings involved six counts of first-degree statutory sodomy, for which the jury recommended Nash receive a life sentence on each, and six counts of first-degree child molestation, for which the jury recommended he receive a sentence of 15 years on each.

During the trial the victim, then six years old, testified on the witness stand about the sexual molestation she had suffered. However, as would be expected with a six-year-old, her testimony wasn't smooth and assured. It was halting and frightened. She couldn't tell the jury how many times Nash had molested her and whether the acts all occurred on one day or were spread out over a long period of time. In the hope of buttressing her testimony, the prosecutor presented evidence from child abuse experts who told the jury that children this victim's age often cannot give exact times of remembered events or the number of times an event occurred.

Fortunately for the prosecution, what really swayed the jury wasn't the child's testimony, but a videotaped confession in which Nash admitted to the events described by the victim, evidence which his attorney tried to discredit by saying that Nash had been "scared to death" by the tactics of the police. Nash's defense attorney claimed that her client had been beaten, threatened, and coerced by the police into making the confession.[1] However, while there was a three-hour interrogation before the confession, on the videotape Nash is shown looking relaxed, with a soft drink and pack of cigarettes on the table in front of him as he is talking. The jury asked the judge for permission to see the taped confession again during deliberations, which the judge allowed.

Despite his confession, during his testimony Nash claimed that the victim had lied on the stand because she was angry with him over some punishment she had received. The prosecutor, however, suggested to the jury that a five-year-old wouldn't have the knowledge to fabricate the story she told, and also reminded the jury that in his confession Nash admitted to doing everything the young victim had accused him of.

"I'm extremely pleased with the outcome," said prosecutor Wendy Wexler Horn about the jury's findings. "It was one of those cases in which the evidence is difficult to listen to—a 5-year-old girl experiencing unspeakable sexual molestation."[2]

After the jury returned with the guilty findings, Nash's attorney asked the jury to consider recommending the minimum sentence for Nash because he had no criminal record and had been sexually abused himself as a child. The jury, however, recommended the maximum sentence. Consequently, Nash will likely never be freed from prison. State law in Missouri requires that those convicted of first-degree statutory sodomy serve 85 percent of their sentence before release.

While the above trial eventually had the outcome the police and prosecutor had hoped for, the case didn't turn out as most sex crimes detectives would have liked it to. In their view, the best outcome for any case involving the sexual molestation of children is a guilty plea by the accused, and not a trial. As was demonstrated in Nash's trial, young sex abuse victims are seldom good witnesses in court. Without Nash's videotaped confession to back up the victim's testimony, the jury very likely would not have given the child's account as much weight. But not only are young victims often poor witnesses for the prosecution, a sexual abuse trial in which a child has to testify against a loved one can also subject the victim to a paralyzing cascade of emotion.

"Children seduced by acquaintance molesters are particularly ashamed, embarrassed, or guilt-ridden about their victimization," said former FBI agent Kenneth V. Lanning. "They often have conflicted feelings about the offender and may find it particularly difficult to confront him in court."[3]

As an example of the emotional impact of such confrontations, in August 2003 in Moffat County, Colorado, the state charged a man with sexually assaulting his daughter. The abuse had come to the attention of the authorities when the victim confided to a family friend about what had been going on. During the trial, the daughter, extremely distraught about having to testify against her father, nevertheless told the court about the sexual abuse that began at age eight and often happened several times a week. Another daughter, confirming her sister's testimony, also appeared on the witness stand and testified against the father.

After the jury returned a finding of guilty to the charges of sexual assault and aggravated incest, the judge ordered the defendant's bond revoked and for the bailiff to take him into custody. As the bailiff led the handcuffed man past his daughter on the way to jail, he leaned toward her and said, "My blood is on your hands now."[4] The daughter broke down into sobs.

The prosecutor, upon viewing the confrontation, said, "He spent six years using shame to control her. He's not going to stop now."[5]

Unfortunately, such emotional confrontations are common in child sexual abuse cases. However, the perpetrator isn't the only factor in bringing about this emotional stress. When brought to court, most young sex abuse victims are frightened of the surroundings, frightened that the person who abused them is sitting only feet away, and confused about what they should be doing. Consequently, these young victims are often attacked and easily confused by defense attorneys, who demand that they recall and relate events just as an adult witness would. When they can't, these defense attorneys will then many times accuse them of lying or being mistaken about the abuse. As might be imagined, having this type of confrontation with a defense attorney only adds to the emotional stress of a child witness.

An article in the *Encyclopedia of Crime and Punishment* had this to say about children testifying in court: "Approximately 95 percent report being frightened to testify and many children report that the day they testified was the worst day of their lives."[6]

But other issues besides stress on the victim also make child sexual abuse trials difficult. Suzanne O'Malley, a prosecutor who specializes in child abuse cases, had this to say when I asked her about the difficulties she faces when prosecuting child molestation cases: "Actually, there are three major problems that keep coming up when I try child sexual abuse cases. First, no one really wants to hear the gritty details about what happened. The very first case I tried involved two kids who were forced not only to have sex with their parents, but also with each other. I got a conviction and, due to the nature of the case, naturally got a lot of media attention. This being my first case I proudly took a copy of a newspaper article about it to my grandfather to show off my accomplishment. He read a couple lines of the article, and then, with a look of disgust, handed it back to me. 'I can't read this stuff,' he told me. 'Just show me where your name is.' Unfortunately, this is a very common reaction, and because of it we lose a lot of potentially good jurors, people whose minds would be in tune to the cruelty and injustice of child sexual abuse, but who don't serve as jurors because they can't stand to hear about it.

"Second, I often run into jurors who believed that the sexual abuse happened, but just couldn't convict. Over and over I've heard jurors say, 'I believed the child, but there wasn't enough evidence,' or 'I know something happened, but I just couldn't convict based on the word of a child.' I often wonder who these jurors think should testify. This is a crime committed against a child in secret. Very, very seldom are there any adult witnesses. It's always amazing to me that so many people feel they can't depend on the word of a child because, in my experience, I've found that children are much more honest than adults, who often have ulterior motives and hidden agendas.

"Finally, for a number of reasons children often don't want to testify. Getting a child to tell about sexual abuse is many times the hardest part of the case. With adults I can usually reason with them and show them the long-term benefits of testifying. Children have a much harder time seeing this. They're naturally worried about what effect testifying against a parent or sibling will have on their family. Or they're worried about getting into trouble because they believe the abuse was their fault. Kids also wonder what the other kids will think about them testifying against a popular coach or teacher. And of course, many times the children love the people who are molesting them, and they don't want to hurt them. Child molesters, I've found over the years, thrive on this kindness of children and will manipulate it to their advantage."[7]

Mrs. O'Malley's comments about why children often don't want to testify in court are borne out by the following example. In July 2001, the local prosecutor charged former Waterbury, Connecticut, Mayor Philip A. Giordano with sexually assaulting two girls, aged eight and ten. A prostitute with whom Giordano had previously fathered a child had reportedly supplied these victims to the mayor. The prostitute eventually turned state's evidence and testified against Giordano at his trial.

Even though the police had accumulated considerable evidence against him, including a taped telephone conversation in which he told the prostitute to bring the youngest girl to his office, Giordano refused to plead guilty and forced the two girls to testify in court about the sexual abuse they had suffered at his hands. How badly did the prospect of having to testify in court about their sexual abuse stress these two young girls?

According to a newspaper article about the trial, "The youngest one . . . became ill from anxiety and lay curled in a fetal position one floor above the courtroom, waiting to testify." About the older girl, the article said, "The older girl spent the evening before her testimony throwing up, all the while reassuring her counselor that she could do it, she could testify."[8]

The court eventually convicted Giordano of sexually assaulting the young girls. The judge sentenced him to a term of 37 years in prison.

There are, fortunately, legal ways around having to have a child testify in open court about sexual abuse. In the case *Maryland v. Craig*, the U.S. Supreme Court, in a five to four decision, said that the guarantee in the Sixth Amendment that a criminal defendant must be able to face all witnesses against him at his trial is not absolute. The Court found that "in certain narrow circumstances, competing interests, if closely examined, may dispense with confrontation at trial." The Court found that a state's interest in protecting the physical and psychological well being of children could outweigh this right of defendants to face their accusers.[9] In the *Maryland v. Craig* case, the judge had allowed a young victim of sexual abuse to testify through closed circuit television rather than in open court. In other states the videotape of an interview with the child can be used in lieu of testimony in open court.

However, such solutions are fraught with difficulty in that different states have different requirements for victims testifying, and in the states that do allow these types of remote testimony for child witnesses, the prosecutor must usually first show that the child will likely be psychologically or physically damaged if forced to testify in open court. Even in these states, problems still develop. In June 2004, for example, the Colorado Supreme Court overturned the conviction of a man found guilty of sexually molesting a seven-year-old boy. They ruled that the prosecution shouldn't have been allowed to use the videotaped interview of the young victim without having the seven-year-old made available for cross-examination by the defense.

In Wisconsin, on the other hand, a state appeals court ruled that "protecting children from emotional trauma is a legitimate legislative purpose" and that a judge erred when he didn't allow the videotaped interviews of two preteen sex abuse victims to be shown to the jury.[10] The judge in this case had not allowed the videotape to be entered into evidence even though the prosecution had made the victims available for cross-examination by the defense.

A much better solution, of course, is the suspect pleading guilty. The detectives, therefore, must focus their investigation on gathering sufficient evidence, both direct and collateral, to erase all doubts about a suspect's guilt, leading him to accept a plea bargain. This, however, can present a challenge.

"Child sexual abuse presents far greater problems in validation than physical abuse, due to the nature of the abuse," said a manual on child abuse published by the U.S. Department of Health and Human Services. The manual goes on to say this about proving child sexual abuse: "First, clear physical evidence is generally lacking, the abuse usually occurs secretly so no credible witnesses exist, often the child has been coerced into silence, and the victims' young age makes their statements problematic on the surface. Second, perpetrators are admitting to very serious felonies if they acknowledge their role in the abuse. Understandably they are reluctant to do so."[11] Even so, if the police can amass enough evidence and witnesses, suspects will often see that a trial is not a good idea, and try to work out the best plea bargain they can get, as the following examples show.

In March 2002, in California, a therapist specializing in the treatment of children pled guilty to 29 counts involving his participation with his wife in sex acts with a 14-year-old-girl. His wife also eventually pled guilty. The police, during their search for evidence, found videos and a written journal documenting the acts, which, of course, the husband and wife didn't want shown in open court.

In North Carolina, a businessman and former chairman of the local Chamber of Commerce pled guilty in January 2005 to seven counts of indecent liberties with children. He had met his victims, the police found through their extensive investigation and questioning of witnesses, through his daughter. This case didn't have to go to trial because the police felt they had amassed enough evidence to sway a jury, which the defendant also apparently believed.

A teacher, athletic coach, and priest who taught at Boston College High School pled guilty in January 2005 to raping and sexually assaulting two of his students. He would reportedly molest his victims after persuading them to take part in naked wrestling drills that he had told them were part of their conditioning regimen. The police, in their investigation, had amassed enough evidence and witness testimony to almost certainly have obtained a conviction if a trial became necessary. The defendant obviously didn't want to risk it.

While it's true that evidence can occasionally be lacking in some child molestation cases, fortunately for the police, gathering evidence on individuals who sexually abuse children is often made easier by the abusers themselves. A number of writers in the area of child sexual abuse investigation call some preferential child molesters "evidence machines." What these writers mean is that, while a person would think that child molesters who had taken pictures of themselves and their victims engaging in sex acts would destroy these once they found out that the police were investigating them, they often don't. While one wouldn't think that child molesters would send e-mails to people they hardly know bragging about child sexual abuse, they often do. And while one would think that child molesters who had taken souvenirs and trophies from their victims would get rid of these once they found out that the police were investigating them, they often don't. The police have only to find these items.

The police, however, search for this evidence not only to avoid a trial, but also because sometimes no matter how much or what type of evidence the police amass, some child molesters, not wanting to admit to their acts and be labeled a sex offender, will insist on going to trial anyway, apparently hoping that the child's testimony will fall apart on the stand and the jury will acquit them. This evidence then, as Nash's videotaped confession did in the case at the beginning of this chapter, can buttress poor testimony by the victim.

Dedicated sex crimes detectives who dig hard enough can sometimes find evidence that depicts the actual sex acts described by the victim on the witness stand. For example, in Chicago in March 2005, a jury watched a video an accused man had made, and the police had worked intensely to find, of the gang rape of an underaged girl. The man, as his defense, had claimed that the sex was consensual, but the video showed otherwise.

As another example of the value of intense evidence collection, a prosecutor in Wisconsin charged a local businessman with sexually assaulting a nine-year-old boy he had met through a mentoring program. When the boy was on the witness stand he told the court how the defendant had shown him large amounts of child pornography, apparently in an attempt to make sex between adults and children look normal, and how the defendant had sexually assaulted him in his office in Monona, Wisconsin.

The defense attorney vigorously attacked the boy's credibility on the stand, pointing out that he was unable to recall exact dates or times of the alleged abuse. The defense attorney also attacked the boy's testimony concerning the types of sexual activity he and the defendant had supposedly engaged in, pointing out that the boy had alternately told the police about episodes of oral and anal sex, and then later denied taking part in either act.

While it is normal for a young boy, fearing that he might be labeled a homosexual, to deny taking part in oral or anal sex, this type of wavering in testimony can still possibly nudge a jury toward a not-guilty finding. This is when strong investigative skills can swing the balance back the other way. In this case, the police recovered from the defendant's home and office computer large amounts of the exact same type of child pornography the victim had described on the witness stand, corroborating the boy's statement. Even more important, the police recovered a semen stain that contained the defendant's DNA from a mouse pad in his office, just where the young victim had said the sex acts occurred.

The jury convicted the man of two counts of repeated sexual assault. They also found him guilty of 16 counts of possession of child pornography.

Unfortunately, the more outrageous and depraved a child molester is in his sexual abuse of children, the harder it often is to prove in court, particularly when corroborating evidence is scant and the case hinges heavily on the victim's testimony. Many child molesters come across as loving parents or relatives, solid community leaders, or devoted volunteers in youth programs. Consequently, jurors often find it difficult to believe that these individuals would commit such depraved acts. It has to be the children's imagination, the defense attorney will certainly suggest. This is when the value of collateral evidence becomes paramount. Showing that the accused person collects child pornography depicting the very acts he is accused of, or has fantasy writing about such acts, can sway a jury.

"Child pornography, especially that produced by the offender, is one of the most valuable pieces of evidence of child sexual victimization that any investigator can have," said former FBI agent Kenneth V. Lanning. "The effects on a jury of viewing seized child pornography are devastating to the defendant's case."[12]

As another way to bolster a young victim's story, sex crimes detectives will also always search for additional victims of the abuser. Detectives have found that the more molestation victims they can locate, the less likely it is that a molester will want to face the possibility of a trial. A jury, both the police and child molesters know, will give the testimony of several victims telling a similar story much more credibility than they will a single victim.

However, while the goal of sex crimes detectives is to uncover enough evidence to persuade child molestation suspects to plead guilty, this does have a down side to it. Occasionally, suspects who have committed what the detectives feel are heinous acts will, after seeing the large amount of evidence the police have recovered, admit the acts, but then work out plea bargains with the prosecutor that amount to only minimal punishment.

Professor Ross Cheit of the University of California at Berkeley studied the results of convictions for child molesting in a New England state. He discovered that from 1985 to 1993, 70 percent of those pleading guilty or found guilty of child molesting didn't receive any jail time at all, only probation.[13] This is frightening when one considers how sexually fixated some preferential child molesters are. What this means is that more children will have to be molested before the person not sent to jail by the court finally will be. And with many preferential child molesters, this is a near certainty.

As an example of this lenient treatment, in February 2005, a minister and former county councilman in South Carolina received only three years of probation for having sex with a 12-year-old girl. In another case, in May 2005 a former police officer in Massachusetts admitted to sexually molesting a 7-year-old girl for over a year. However, the court sentenced him only to four years of probation. Unfortunately, these are only two of far too many lenient sentences for child sexual abuse that have come with a plea bargain.

An article in a New York newspaper said this about lenient sentences for child sexual abusers: "Often the roadblocks to tougher penalties are plea bargains, which district attorneys are tempted to accept because of the prospect of trying to get a conviction with the testimony of children. Though there are laws now that allow the use of videotaped testimony from children, the experience still just adds to the trauma they already have."[14]

In most jurisdictions, although the sex crimes detective may be consulted about a plea bargain, the final decision about these rests with the prosecutor and the court. Therefore, most sex crimes detectives do the best job they can and try not to worry about such things as occasional lenient plea bargains, since they have little or no control over them anyway.

An interesting side note is that many of these molesters who, in the face of a mountain of evidence against them, do plead guilty, nevertheless after this plea still insist that they are actually innocent. "If the case has been put together properly, however, when the dust settles, most of these [child sexual] offenders plead guilty," said former FBI agent Kenneth V. Lanning. He goes on to say, "The last thing they want is all of the details of their behavior to come out in open court. They work the best plea bargain they can, say they are guilty when the judge asks, and then tell everyone else why they are really not guilty."[15]

As agent Lanning points out, detectives who have piles of evidence and reams of witness testimony will often hear offenders, after pleading guilty and admitting to the judge that they committed all the acts alleged, later tell the press or loved ones that they are only pleading guilty because they want to spare the child or their loved ones the stress of a trial. This, of course, is simply flimsy fabrication to hide the fact that if the police presented the evidence they had recovered in open court, then everyone would see how degenerate the accused child molester really is.

Another way in which child molesters try to escape personal responsibility for their actions is to plead "no contest" to the charges, or, in the states where they are allowed, to make an "Alford plea." What this last plea means is that the individuals are pleading guilty to the charges because they believe the police have enough evidence to convict them, but that they still deny committing the crime.

However, if, no matter how hard the detectives work, a suspected child molester won't plead guilty and a trial is necessary, a child witness, in those situations in which closed circuit testimony or a videotaped statement aren't possible, must be prepared for the extreme stress of testifying in court.

In order to reduce this stress as much as possible, child witnesses must be made aware beforehand of exactly what they can expect. They must know what they will have to do while testifying, such as answering questions, telling the truth, stopping until the judge tells them to start again if the prosecutor or defense attorney objects, and so forth.

When possible, children should be allowed to view the inside of a courtroom before having to appear in one. They must also be made ready for the cross-examination and for the almost certain challenge of their credibility by the defense attorney. The young victims must be made aware that they don't have to agree with the defense attorney when he or she says something, and that if the defense attorney does say or suggest something to the victims that is wrong they should say so. In addition, young victims need to know that if the defense attorney asks a question they don't understand they should say so and ask to have it explained, and that they should acknowledge to the defense attorney that they don't know the answer to a question if they don't.

Young victims must also be assured before the trial that nothing bad is going to happen to them during the trial, and that they should just simply tell their story as it happened. The children should also be assured that what they are doing is not just brave and important, but that it is also the right thing to do. Often, to lessen a child's stress, a friend or family member who isn't testifying can sit in the audience and the child, when on the witness stand, can look to him or her for reassurance if frightened.

For detectives testifying in a trial for child sexual abuse, all of the rules discussed in Chapter 2 for courtroom demeanor also apply here. In addition, sex crimes detectives can be sure that when defense attorneys ask about the interview with the young victims, they will almost certainly accuse the detectives of leading the victims into making certain statements, or at least imply that they did. This is when having a videotape, an audiotape, or accurate and detailed notes about what was said during the interview becomes very valuable.

Finally, my wife Melanie, who was a sex crimes detective specializing in child abuse for many years, gave me this sobering observation about the importance of a detective's work in a child sexual abuse trial: "There's a lot of pressure to get a conviction in a sex abuse case, because if you don't, you know the child will often go right back into the abusive home, and possibly be abused even worse. And just as bad, the child, if the jury comes back with a not guilty finding, will likely think that no one believes him or her. So, if you lose, you're letting down a little child who depended on you."[16]

Few people could argue that the crimes we have discussed in the first six chapters of this book are not serious offenses that deserve harsh punishment. However, there are also a number of other sex crimes that many readers would probably consider minor, pathetic, and even laughable, such as flashing or window peeping. But, as we will see in the next chapter, these offenses aren't minor or laughable at all, but are actually part of a web of sexual offenses that lead to and involve far more serious crimes.

PART III

Other Crimes and Beyond

CHAPTER 7

Other Sex Crimes

Recently, in a department store in a Virginia mall a mother noticed an oddly acting young man hovering close to her 18-year-old daughter. When she saw the man move even nearer to her daughter, whose back was turned to him, and then bend down and wave a shopping bag he carried under her daughter's miniskirt, the mother recalled a television program she had seen recently about the new breed of voyeurs.

"What's in the bag?" the mother demanded as she hurried over and confronted the man.

He jerked back and straightened up, startled. "N . . . n . . . nothing."[1] The man clutched the shopping bag to himself for a second, then broke and fled toward the door leading out of the store.

"Stop that man!" the mother yelled as she ran after him.[2] Most of the people in the store simply looked in surprise as the two flew by them. Near the exit, however, a customer finally grabbed the fleeing man and stopped him. Inside the shopping bag the mother found a small video camera the man had been using to film up her daughter's skirt. The man, the mother eventually learned from the police, had been arrested recently for similar acts at another mall.

Called "upskirting," the above incident demonstrates how voyeurs, who used to be restricted to peeping into windows, have moved forward with the times. While in the past voyeurs were forced to trespass onto others' property to peep into windows, today's voyeurs can use modern technology to peep into private areas while staying in public locations.

Although the results of upskirting are relatively tame when compared to much of the pornography now available on the Internet, it still has a very attractive allure to voyeurs. They're seeing intimate views of people, while at the same time their victims are usually totally unaware they are being violated.

"It's the forbidden quality of the experience," said Professor Paula Justice of Old Dominion University. "Like peering in a window."[3]

If their need-driven behavior demands more, using modern technology voyeurs can also photograph unsuspecting victims in much more intimate settings and in various stages of undress. And they can do this without the danger of having to trespass onto private property. Today's voyeurs can use visual recording devices small enough to conceal in innocuous items such as books and newspapers to view and record unsuspecting victims. They have been known to hide tiny video recorders in locations such as restrooms, dressing rooms in department stores, and other places where people believe they are disrobing in private.

Recently in New York, for example, the police arrested a worker at the Genesee Valley Skating Rink. The man had secretly photographed the members of a woman's hockey team as they changed into their uniforms in the locker room. In another case, a manager at a Hooters restaurant in California recently pled no contest to charges that he had secretly videotaped female job applicants trying on a Hooters uniform. Apparently, after interviewing the women the manager would tell them that they had to try on a Hooters uniform so that he could be sure they had the Hooters look. According to a number of women he filmed, he would instruct them exactly where to stand while changing, and then leave the office while they disrobed and tried on the uniform. After receiving complaints from several suspicious women, the police served search warrants on the manager's home and office, where the found videos of 82 female job applicants undressing. The police then spent days tracking down all of the victims. More than 40 of the women have joined in a lawsuit against Hooters.

"They were simply looking for jobs," said attorney Gloria Allred, who is representing the women in the lawsuit. "But as a result of their harrowing experience they have been embarrassed, humiliated and emotionally violated."[4]

Because of the unit I am now in charge of, Organized Crime, I often receive catalogs from companies that manufacture surveillance equipment for police and the public. Thumbing through these catalogues, I find that individuals can now purchase surveillance cameras that are hidden in such things as smoke detectors, ballpoint pens, men's ties, pagers, buttons for clothing, clocks, three-ring binders, sunglasses, hats, framed pictures, and many other seemingly innocent items. While these can of course be extremely useful for police officers conducting undercover operations, unfortunately, they can also be used by voyeurs to clandestinely observe and film unsuspecting victims. And readers should be especially aware that voyeurs who use this type of surveillance equipment are not just strangers that pick their victims at random. A number of cases have appeared recently around the country in which voyeurs have planted hidden cameras in the bathrooms and bedrooms of their friends and acquaintances, filming them in various stages of undress.

Some voyeurs, however, simply have to have the excitement of forbidden acts and will still trespass onto private property and peep in windows. But even many of these traditional voyeurs use modern technology. In April 2005, for example, the wife of a Chicago police lieutenant saw a man lurking around their house near midnight. She woke her husband, who then went outside and reportedly saw a 50-year-old psychiatric nurse, Ronald Jabczynski, filming with a digital video recorder through the window of a house nearby. While Jabczynski held the video recorder in one hand, the officer noted, he masturbated with the other. When the police lieutenant approached Jabczynski and identified himself, Jabczynski pulled up his sweat pants and fled.

After a short foot chase and scuffle, the officer placed Jabczynski under arrest and confiscated the recorder. The device, the police found, could record either video or still photographs, and it contained the images of nine women and three girls. The police also confiscated a computer filled with pornography from Jabczynski's home.

"[Jabczynski told] detectives he knows he has a problem," said Lieutenant John Lewison of the Jefferson Park Police Department.[5]

As it turned out, Jabczynski lived only a block or so from where he was caught peeping, and all of the images on his camera were of unsuspecting neighbors or friends and family of neighbors. On April 12, 2005, the Illinois Department of Financial and Professional Regulation suspended Jabczynski's nursing license.

Minor sex crimes such as voyeurism, very likely occur in numbers far beyond what the police receive reports on. This is because usually the victims are unaware the activity is going on, and, even in those cases where the voyeurism is discovered, often the police aren't called because the victims see the damage done as minimal. Most victims consider the perpetrators as simply pathetic, but basically harmless, losers. Consequently, reports of the activity never get to the police. But while some of the perpetrators are just that, pathetic losers, many are much more dangerous than they appear. Many dangerous sex offenders begin their criminal careers by committing minor sex crimes and then move on to more serious activities, while many others may commit minor sex crimes such as voyeurism at the same time they are committing much more serious sex crimes such as rape and child molesting.

A study that supports the danger of minor sex crimes compared child molesters who abducted their victims with those who seduced them. The study found that more than half of the subjects in both groups reported being involved in voyeurism and exhibitionism, as well as molesting children. Another study, this one of more than 4,000 child molesters, had this to say about serious sex criminals being involved in minor sex crimes: "Of the pedophiles who molested girls, 17 percent were *also* exhibitionists and 36 percent were *also* voyeurs. Of the pedophiles who molested boys, 20 percent were *also* exhibitionists and 33 percent were *also* voyeurs."[6]

In addition, while a window peeper might be only a voyeur, readers should keep in mind that he could also be a rapist scouting his next victim. Duncan Proctor, the serial rapist discussed in Chapter 1, was also a voyeur. Many rapists admit in their statements to the police that before they break into a home and rape a woman, they often scout their victim first. They want to know when is the best and safest time to attack her. This scouting is done partly through window peeping. For these reasons it is imperative for the victims of voyeurism to report any incidents to the police, and for police departments to aggressively investigate any such incidents.

Voyeurism, however, isn't the only minor sex crime that the police deal with. For example, they regularly receive complaints of frotteurism, which is the rubbing against or touching of the body of a nonconsenting person. In September 2004, in Springfield, Oregon, the police arrested a 48-year-old man, a registered sex offender, for touching the buttocks of a 13-year-old girl in a movie theater. The theater had previously received complaints from other teenage girls of a man inappropriately touching them. In Indianapolis in November 2004, a court convicted a former police officer of returning and fondling a woman whose house he had earlier searched with another officer for a wanted subject. In Palo Alto, California, in September 2004, a nursing home worker pled guilty to groping an elderly resident. In actuality, probably every woman who has regularly ridden on a crowded subway or bus system has experienced this crime.

Exhibitionism, or the exposing of one's private parts to unsuspecting people, also flourishes everywhere. In Rye, New Hampshire, in June 2005, the police received the report of a man wearing nothing but a mask exposing himself to women on Odiorne Beach. In Naperville, Illinois, in February 2005, the police arrested a 28-year-old man for walking naked down the halls of a high school. In Mesa, Arizona, in April 2005, the police arrested a man who had been leaving Polaroid photographs of his genitals on the windshields of women's cars. The previous three incidents, of course, involved male perpetrators. Women also commit exhibitionism, as anyone who has been to a beach during spring break or attended Mardi Gras can attest to, but the police receive few complaints because of it.

Like voyeurs, exhibitionists and frotteurists can be simply exhibitionists and frotteurists, or they can be dangerous sex criminals who are also exhibitionists and frotteurists. For example, in a 2001 case in Massachusetts, a man drugged six girls, ages 10 to 14, who had attended a slumber party given by his daughter. While the girls were unconscious, the man repeatedly raped them and filmed himself doing it. When his daughter found the video and took it to the police, the man fled the state. The police arrested him several weeks later, after they caught him exposing himself to several people on a California beach. He had also been a suspect, the police learned, in an exposing incident several years before in Mississippi. In November 2002, a judge sentenced him to a term of 25 to 30 years in prison for the rapes.

Due to the advent of Caller ID, Automatic Call Back, and other telephone services, obscene telephone calls are no longer as prevalent a minor sex crime as was once the case. However, they still do occur occasionally. Some sex criminals are controlled so intensely by their paraphilias that they simply cannot resist the impulse to commit certain actions. In a case involving the kidnapping and murder of a 27-year-old woman by a sexual predator, discussed in the book *Practical Aspects of Rape Investigation*, the suspect in the case, just months before the kidnapping and murder, had been involved in making obscene telephone calls.[7]

When most people hear about cases involving voyeurs, flashers, obscene callers, and even gropers, they usually just shake their heads. Most people don't consider these individuals dangerous, just pests. But this simply isn't so. As is clear from the incidents described above, many of the people who peep, flash, make obscene calls, and grope also kidnap, rape, molest, and kill.

Unfortunately, the public isn't alone in dismissing those who commit minor sex crimes as hardly worthy of concern. Most police departments routinely route calls of voyeurs, flashers, and so forth to their uniformed district cars to handle, which means that there will be a report made but little or no follow-up investigation. Unless the offender has shown a pattern of repeated incidents or increasing aggressiveness, a report is made, filed away, and that is that.

I have had my own experience with police departments' lack of concern with minor sex crimes. Six months ago, my 10-year-old niece was spending the night with a friend. While they were watching television, the father of my niece's friend walked into the room and exposed himself to the two 10-year-old girls. The night before he had walked naked into the room, but my niece had thought it was just a mistake. Naturally upset by the incidents, my niece told her mother about it, who called the police and made a complaint.

When, after several weeks, my sister-in-law hadn't heard anything from the police department, she called them. They brushed her off by saying they were working on it, even though they hadn't talked to my niece yet. She called me and asked if I could do something. The incident had occurred in an adjoining jurisdiction to the Indianapolis Police Department, so I called the captain in charge of that department's sex crimes branch. I knew the man casually, and I asked him if he would check on the status of the case for me. I found out that not only had no one yet interviewed my niece, no one had talked to the suspect yet either. The captain assured me that he would get his detective moving on the case.

As it turned out, nothing significant was ever done on the case. Although the detective did finally talk to the suspect and to the two victims, who both told the exact same story, the case was dropped and never sent for prosecution, even though my sister-in-law had told them she wanted to prosecute. And this was one police captain asking another police captain to do something. Readers can imagine how much response an ordinary citizen gets to his or her complaint.

The courts, too, often minimize the seriousness of these offenders. For example, in Indianapolis in February 2005, a neurologist pled guilty to six counts of criminal confinement, admitting that he inappropriately touched women in his care. He had reportedly given breast exams to women who had come to him complaining of headaches. Although the prosecutor asked the judge to sentence him to prison, and one of the women he assaulted said, "I would like to see him go to jail," the judge instead opted for home detention and probation.[8]

In September 2004, a Columbus, Ohio, attorney pled guilty to 53 charges. He had reportedly exposed himself to a large number of women and then photographed their shocked expressions. The judge, however, decided not to sentence him as a sex offender, and also modified his sentence so that he would be allowed to keep his law license.

In Richmond, Texas, in August 2004, a jury convicted a man of exposing himself to a 13-year-old girl who was visiting his home. He also faced additional charges that, in another incident, he had sexually touched another 13-year-old girl. Although he could have been sentenced to 2 to 10 years in prison, the judge sentenced him instead to simply probation.

A final sex crime that many people see as minor, and consequently don't believe is as dangerous as the crimes talked about in the first six chapters of this book, is child pornography. While most people will agree that those who bribe, coerce, or force children to take part in pornographic productions should be arrested and imprisoned, many of these same people don't believe that the possession of child pornography by private individuals should be against the law. After all, many of them argue, while the acts shown in the child pornography are illegal, so are many of the acts shown on the evening news and often dramatized in movies, such as robberies and murders, and it is not illegal for individuals to watch or possess these. Individuals who possess child pornography, they insist, are no more responsible for the acts perpetrated against the children than would be a person who owned a movie about a serial killer. In addition, many people argue that the First Amendment doesn't allow the government to control what people read or view in their own homes.

The U.S. Supreme Court disagrees, and has ruled that child pornography does not fall under the protection of the First Amendment. In their 1990 decision in *Osborne v. Ohio*, the Court agreed with government attorneys that the danger child pornography presents outweighs the rights of citizens to possess and view such material in the privacy of their own homes. In their ruling, the Court held that a state's interest in preventing the sexual abuse of children justified these states outlawing the possession and viewing of child pornography.[9] As a consequence, all 50 states and the District of Columbia have statutes outlawing the production, distribution, and/or possession of child pornography.

In *Osborne v. Ohio*, the U.S. Supreme Court said in its ruling that it made its decision based not only on the harm done to children when making pornography, but also on the harm caused when child pornography is used as a tool to help seduce and coerce children into sexual activity. Consequently, First Amendment protections do not apply.

Noted attorney and child advocate Andrew Vachss had this to say about the First Amendment rights of child pornography possessors and distributors: "In truth, when it comes to child pornography, any discussion of censorship is a sham, typical of the slight-of-hand used by organized pedophiles as a part of their ongoing attempt to raise their sexual predations to the level of civil rights."[10]

Arguments about First Amendment rights aside, child advocates, who know that making child pornography requires the sexual molestation of children, which is reason enough to outlaw it, also know that child pornography has many ominous uses other than just the viewing of it by those sexually aroused by children. "For them [pedophiles], such material has two essential purposes," said Andrew Vachss. "One, it self-refers the possessor to 'normality' (i.e. it tells pedophiles they are not alone, that others share their practices, that it is not they who are deviant—it is the oppressive laws which prohibit their 'love'); and two, it de-sensitizes children especially susceptible to peer pressure by displaying graphic proof that 'lots of kids like to do this,' thus paving the way for the victimization of their targets."[11]

According to a report on child pornography from the American Bar Association, "Offenders use child pornography for many purposes. Five of the most common ones are:

1. Create a permanent record for arousal and gratification.
2. Lower children's inhibitions.

3. Validate and confirm the child sex offender's belief systems.
4. Blackmail victims and other co-defendants.
5. Sell for profit or trade."[12]

A U.S. Department of Justice document about online dangers for children had this to say about child pornography: "Although not all molesters collect pornography and not all child pornography collectors molest children, significant consensus exists among law enforcement officers about the role pornography plays in recruiting and controlling new victims."[13] The document goes on to tell how child molesters use child pornography to make children believe that such acts between adults and children are normal, and also how molesters use the pornography they create with their victims to blackmail them if they ever threaten to tell about their victimization. As further evidence of the damaging uses of child pornography, in a study of convicted child molesters, 77 percent of those who molested boys and 87 percent of those who molested girls admitted to the habitual use of pornography in the commission of their crimes.[14]

"It has been my experience that pornography is often used in child molestation cases," Detective Kevin Hammel of the Trumbull, Connecticut, Police Department told me. "The offender will use the pornography to stimulate and groom adolescents and teens."[15]

Another study, this one by the Federal Bureau of Prisons, compared individuals imprisoned for possessing or trading child pornography with those imprisoned for contact sex offenses, and found that those incarcerated on child pornography charges had more than three times the number of undocumented and unreported contact sex crimes as did those actually incarcerated for contact sex offenses (an average of 30.5 offenses versus 9.6 offenses). The study concluded that "these offenders may be more physically active than suggested by the perceived passiveness of trading or possessing child pornography."[16]

A final study involving individuals who used the U.S. Postal System to distribute child pornography stated, "A U.S. Postal Inspectors Service anti-child pornography program reports that at least 35 percent of cases involving 595 individuals arrested since 1997 for using the mail to sexually exploit children were active abusers."[17]

While readers may believe, or want to believe, that those who possess or seek to possess child pornography are degenerates on the fringes of society, this simply isn't so. For example, in Boise, Idaho, in June 2005, an FBI agent received a year in prison for possessing child pornography. Fellow employees caught another FBI employee at the agency's Headquarters in Washington, D.C., viewing child pornography on his laptop computer. In March 2005, the former head of pediatric medicine at a hospital in Rochester, New York, pled guilty to receiving child pornography on his home computer. A retired Orleans County (New York) judge pled guilty in October 2004 to attempted possession of a sexual performance by a child. A college professor in Pennsylvania pled guilty to downloading child pornography onto a college computer. The police in Jefferson Parish, Louisiana, arrested a fifth-grade teacher after they searched his home and found 25 boxes of computer discs and videos of child pornography. A Boy Scout official who ran a national task force designed to protect children from sexual abuse pled guilty to possession and distribution of child pornography. In Colorado, a 15-year veteran of the Aurora Police Department pled guilty to the possession of child pornography.

The point to all of these examples (and there are literally thousands more) is that the sexual interest in children knows no social boundaries. Those who become sexually aroused by children pervade every corner of our society, and as a result, child pornography flourishes. In fact, security experts believe that child pornography is present somewhere in almost every large corporate, academic, or government computer network in our country.

"If you've got a big company system, I can almost guarantee that you have child pornography on it," said Kenneth Citarella, deputy chief of investigations for the Westchester County (New York) District Attorney's Office. "It's there somewhere."[18]

Edward Appel, chief operating officer of the Joint Council on Information-Age Crime, agrees, saying that there is "almost a 100 percent probability of finding child pornography on corporate networks."[19]

As with the other sex offenders discussed in this book, many of the people who are sexually aroused by children are extremely need-driven. What else could explain an employee downloading child pornography onto a company computer system, all the while knowing that these systems are routinely audited and that the downloading can easily be traced back to him?

The many individuals who apparently possess this overwhelming need to view depictions of sex acts between adults and children in effect constitute a market, and the child pornography industry has naturally responded to meet this demand. Fortunately, the government has also responded. In a 2001 investigation dubbed "Operation Avalanche," the authorities targeted an Internet company owned by a husband and wife in Fort Worth, Texas. Paying a fee to this company allowed Internet users to have access to various child pornography sites, some with some very frightening content.

"We're talking about children being raped, crying, it was disturbing, it was so disturbing," said Assistant U.S. District Attorney Terri Moore.[20]

The Internet company, surprised law enforcement officials found during their investigation, had over 250,000 customers. It grossed almost $1.5 million a month. Authorities closed it down and made a large number of arrests.

In another large-scale investigation of child pornography, dubbed "Operation Candyman," authorities served a court order on the Internet company Yahoo! and obtained the e-mail addresses of more than 7,000 individuals who belonged to an online group that exchanged child pornography. Members of this group included school bus drivers, preschool and daycare workers, members of the clergy, guidance counselors, and police officers. Again, law enforcement officials closed the operation down and made a large number of arrests.

In January 2004, the police made over 1,000 arrests worldwide during their investigation of a company called Regpay, which handled the Internet billing for more than 50 child pornography websites. Although Regpay is located in Minsk, Belarus, it had affiliate offices all over the world, including in California and Florida, where four officials of Connections USA and LB Systems have pled guilty for their roles in processing U.S. credit card transactions for Regpay.

According to a press release about Regpay from the office of U.S. Immigration and Customs Enforcement, "Some of the subscribers arrested to date include an elementary school teacher, priests, school principals, school coaches, school janitors, camp counselors, campus ministers, pediatricians, circus clowns, Boy Scout leaders, police officers, firefighters, and many others with direct access to children. Some of these individuals were also found to have been involved in the production and distribution of child pornography."[21]

Of course, the production and distribution of child pornography can also involve much smaller operations. In April 2005, a 9-year-old boy in Florida told the authorities that his mother had filmed his rape by a

27-year-old man and then sold the videotape. In San Antonio, Texas, in May 2005, a woman took nude pictures of her 13-year-old daughter and then sent them to a man she had met on the Internet who said he could sell them. In 2002, the police discovered that members of a group called STATTSAR, whose stated purpose was to search for missing children, also supplied drugs to underaged children and then photographed them engaging in sex acts.

As the anecdotes and information supplied in this chapter clearly show, minor sex crimes are not really minor. Many dangerous sexual predators who rape, molest, and kill, also have a number of other paraphilias that involve crimes such as voyeurism, exhibitionism, and so forth. Consequently, these seemingly minor sex crimes must be taken seriously, and those caught committing them must be examined carefully by the authorities for involvement in other much more serious crimes.

While so far this book has focused on the millions of sex crimes committed every year in our country, and the devastating effects they have on their victims, there is hope. In the next chapter we will talk about the many ways to stop sex crimes before they occur, and, if this is not possible, the programs available across the country that have been designed to help people recover from the destructive and debilitating effects of a sex crime.

CHAPTER 8

Prevention of and Recovery from Sex Crimes

One afternoon, when I was a police officer running a beat car on the south side of Indianapolis, I had just radioed the dispatcher to put me back into service after lunch. Less than a minute later, I heard my car number over the radio.

"Charles 9, we have a report of a rape at 1122 South Sloan. Believe the perpetrator has left the scene. No description at this time. Detectives are in route."

I okayed the run and started in that direction. As a uniformed police officer, I knew that my job would be to find the victim, assure her safety, get enough of her story to verify that a crime had actually been committed, give first aid if needed, protect the crime scene, and obtain enough of a description to put out a wanted broadcast on the suspect.

When I pulled to the curb in front of the address I noticed that the house had a For Sale sign in the front yard. A disheveled woman stood on the front porch, looking as though she wasn't sure what she should do.

"Ma'am, are you the one who called the police?" I asked as I hurried up to the porch.

She nodded and seemed to be gasping for air.

"Is the man still here?" I asked, my hand on my gun as I looked around the porch and then peeked through a window into the house.

The woman finally seemed to catch her breath and told me that she had seen him run out the back of the house and up the alley toward

Southeastern Avenue. Then she told me her story. She was a real estate agent and had received a call from a man that morning. He had told her that he was very interested in this house, and would likely want to make an offer on it. The woman said she had tried to get him to come into the office, but he insisted on meeting her at the house. She told me she usually wouldn't do that but the house had been on the market for well over a year and had no prospects.

She went on to tell me that when she got to the house the man was waiting for her on the porch and she didn't see a car. He told her his wife had dropped him off and would join them in a few minutes. The woman said that something just didn't feel right about the man, that he had made her feel creepy. But she really wanted to sell the house and he seemed very interested. Once they got into the house and looked around for a few minutes, he suddenly grabbed her, produced a knife and threatened to kill her if she screamed or resisted, then dragged her to the basement, where he raped her. When he had finished, he ran up the stairs and out through the back door. She ran up a few seconds later and locked the door, fearing he might come back.

As far as I know, the detectives, who arrived twenty minutes or so after I did, never made an arrest in this case. More relevant to this chapter, could this case have been prevented to begin with? Yes, it possibly could have, as could many rapes every year.

Police officers and others who deal with sex offenders have learned that many of them represent a lifelong danger, because, even after lengthy prison stays and intense treatment programs, they still often return to their crimes. For example, a study of sex offenders who had been released from a maximum-security psychiatric facility in California found that nearly 20 percent of those who had been convicted for rape were reconvicted of rape within five years of their release, and most of these within the first year of their release.[1] No one knows how many rapes these men committed that they got away with. According to a document about managing sex offenders in the community: "A 'cure' for sex offending is no more available than is a cure for epilepsy or high blood pressure."[2]

Since so many sex offenders will always be a danger to the community, in order to avoid the possibility of becoming a rape victim, citizens must follow the safety rules below:

1. Be aware and alert. To be truly safe, women must broadcast clear signs to those watching them that they are aware of their

surroundings, that they know exactly what's going on around them, and that they will not be easy targets. Rapists are looking for easy victims. Rapists don't want to be caught and sent to prison, and so they search for victims who will minimize this risk for them. A study of serial rapists found that a rapist's decision about whether or not to attack a victim depended mostly on his perception of her vulnerability. In other words, how easy did he think it would be to overpower, subdue, and rape her? In the study, 69 percent of the rapists said that the primary reason for their decision to attack a woman or not was based on whether they believed the victim was easy prey.[3] So consequently, don't be so preoccupied with other matters, such as talking on a cell phone or listening to music on an iPod, that you don't notice what's happening around you. Look attentive and assertive. Don't look like easy prey.

2. Don't go into potentially dangerous situations by yourself. Have someone with you. The real estate agent in the incident described above should have realized the possibility of danger and brought along another person. This is not a guarantee that nothing will happen, but two people are more difficult to control than one. This precaution includes parking lots, stores late at night, apartment lobbies, and so forth.

3. Don't let any promised outcomes cloud your sense of good judgment about a situation you may be getting yourself in. In the incident above, the woman let her belief that she could make a sale on a hard-to-sell house cloud her better judgment. Other rapists have lured women to remote locations through offers of jobs, modeling contracts, and other incentives.

4. When driving at night, keep the car doors locked, and, when stopped for traffic signals, always maintain enough space between your car and the car in front of you so that you will be able to maneuver your car away if someone should try to get into it.

5. Never admit strangers into your home, no matter what their reasons. If they claim they have an emergency, offer to call 911 for them. A woman home alone looks like an easy target.

6. Be particularly alert just before entering your home or apartment. Rapists will often hide or lurk nearby, and shove a woman inside once the door is unlocked.

7. Always trust your instincts, and don't be afraid to take action on your fears. The real estate agent in the incident above told me that the man had made her feel creepy, but she didn't do anything about it. Trust your feelings. If something doesn't feel right, or if a person makes you feel uncomfortable, get away from the situation.

8. A safety precaution all women should take is to carry a cell phone. And don't be afraid to use it to call 911 if you appear to be in danger. Although some might object to this advice based on cost, the cost of a cell phone is minimal compared to that of recovering from a rape. I also advise women to carry in their purses a small air horn, such as the ones used on boats. Don't be afraid to use the air horn if it appears you need to draw attention. From a rapist's perspective, a woman blasting an air horn is certainly not an easy target. So, if a person approaches you in a manner that makes you think an attack may be imminent, use the air horn. If the person is a rapist he knows he has not done anything illegal yet and will likely just quickly leave the area. If he's not a rapist, then the worst that can happen is that you will have to apologize.

9. As for physically or even verbally resisting a rapist, this is difficult advice to give because different types of rapists respond differently to physical or verbal resistance. Serious resistance will cause some rapists to break off the attack and flee. However, for other rapists resistance will only increase their enjoyment of the attack, and for some it may incense them to the point where they respond with serious and possibly deadly force. The decision of whether or not to resist an attack should be made by the woman based on the totality of her situation, and whatever decision she makes should always be supported and never second-guessed by family members and friends.

It is always easy to imagine what we would do if we were caught in certain situations, such as facing a rapist, but the actions we take are always different in real life. When I first became a police officer, I always imagined how fearless and heroic I would be if I ever got into a gunfight. However, when it actually happened I was anything but fearless and heroic. I dove for cover and fired back blindly. The same is true of a rape situation. No one really knows what he or she will do until confronted with the real situation. Consequently, family and friends should never question a victim's decision about offering resistance, but accept what the victim did as the best response under the circumstances.

Experienced sex crimes detectives will always take the time to meet with family members of rape victims and explain to them how important their reaction to the victim can be. The victim doesn't need people telling her "that's what happens when you go out late by yourself, date certain people, venture into certain parts of town, etc." The victim needs a sympathetic, nonjudgmental family who will listen to and comfort her without recriminations. No woman deserves to be raped, no matter how foolish her activities before the rape. Although we might all shake our heads and say that we wouldn't do whatever the victim did that made her vulnerable, we have all done stupid things in our lives that we look back on and feel thankful that nothing bad happened to us because of them.

10. If a rape cannot be prevented or successfully resisted, it is important for the victim to note and remember things, such as a description of the rapist, any tattoos, birth marks or scars, the type of car he drove, and anything else that could assist the police in identifying him. Many rapists are repeat offenders and just a little help from the victim can make identification much easier. If the victim is transported in a car or held in a strange location somewhere, she should try to leave behind as many fingerprints as possible. Leaving behind a personal item, such as an earring, can help the police tremendously in making their case against the rapist. In the FBI study of 41 serial rapists cited in Chapter 1, the researchers found that the majority of the rapists used their own cars in the commission of the crime, and, when identified and confronted by the police, almost half fully admitted their crimes.

11. To prevent drug-induced rapes, women should never accept a drink from someone they don't know, take a drink from a punch bowl, or leave their drink unattended. If a woman should suddenly feel a sensation of drunkenness that isn't in keeping with the amount of alcohol consumed, she should immediately notify friends, family, or anyone else nearby she trusts that she suspects she has been drugged.

12. Since many rapes occur in the victim's home, women should make certain their house or apartment is not an easy target for surveillance or a break-in. Many rapists like to scout their victims first through window peeping, and often they will enter a victim's home ahead of time in order to familiarize themselves with the interior. Then, when rapists decide the time is right, they know how to get into the victim's home and they know their way around inside. To discourage rapists, women should make window peeping and entry into their homes difficult and noticeable. For information on tips about how to make your home burglarproof, see my book *The Complete Guide to Personal and Home Safety* (2002).

Just how important is home security? Along with preventing a rape, it might also be the difference between life and death, as was shown on May 16, 2005, in Coeur D'Alene, Idaho.

Early in the morning of May 16, 2005, eight-year-old Shasta and nine-year-old Dylan Groene, a brother and sister who lived with their mother Brenda, her boyfriend Mark McKenzie, and their 13-year-old brother Slade, heard their mother call to them to come into the living room. When the two children walked sleepy-eyed into the living room, they saw a stranger, later identified as 42-year-old registered sex offender Joseph Edward Duncan III, standing there with a shotgun.

Although no one in the house knew it, Duncan was on the run from child molesting charges in Minnesota. Even though Duncan had been listed as a high-risk sex offender, a judge in Minnesota set his bail at only $15,000 after the police arrested him for molesting a six-year-old boy on a playground. Before this last arrest, Duncan had spent many years in prison for another sex offense against a child. Prior to his incarceration, because he had shown an aggressive sexual attraction to children, Duncan been ordered into a sex offender treatment program. However, as many sex offenders will, he refused to cooperate with the program managers, and a judge sent him to prison.

The terrified children saw that their mother, her boyfriend, and their older brother had been bound with zip ties and duct tape. Duncan quickly tied up the two children, and then took them outside and placed them on the ground next to a swing set. He then went back into the house and allegedly bludgeoned to death the three people tied up inside. Shasta would later tell the police that she and her brother Dylan could hear their mother's boyfriend yelling, and that they saw their brother Slade, covered with blood, stagger out of the house. Shasta and Dylan called to Slade to untie them, but apparently he had been too injured to comprehend what they said. Duncan later told Shasta, apparently in an attempt to frighten her and make her more compliant, that he had killed her family with a hammer, which he would then hold out and show her.

Although there was considerable speculation about the reason for the murders, including gangs and drug debts, the police now believe that Duncan was the only one involved and that he murdered the three simply so that he could have the two small children to molest. "We believe Joseph Duncan is the only one responsible for these crimes," said Captain Ben Wolfinger of the Kootenai County Sheriff's Department.[4]

After taking Shasta and Dylan from the scene, Duncan soon transferred the two children to a stolen red Jeep and headed for one of three remote campsites he would use in Montana. According to Shasta's later statement to the police, at these campsites Duncan repeatedly sexually molested both her and her brother.

In the following weeks, Duncan moved continuously with the children, who would not be recognized, even though the police had distributed and posted thousands of flyers with Dylan and Shasta's pictures on them. Some time during this period, Duncan reportedly murdered 9-year-old Dylan, and then moved on with Shasta, sexually molesting her regularly.

Finally, at around 2:00 A.M. on July 2, 2005, Amber Deahn, a waitress in a Denny's restaurant in Coeur D'Alene, Idaho, where Duncan and Shasta were having breakfast, recognized Shasta from the police posters and called the authorities. She stalled Shasta's milkshake order until the police could arrive and arrest Duncan. No one is sure why Duncan returned to the Coeur D'Alene area, where people were more likely to recognize Shasta.

When the police talked to Shasta they found out the real reason for the three murders and the kidnapping of the children. "He told her he was out driving around looking for children to kidnap," Kootenai County Sheriff's Detective Brad Maskell testified during a probable cause hearing. "He . . . saw her playing in the yard with her brother and wearing a bathing suit. At that point he chose them as possible kidnap victims."[5] Court documents filed by the police go on to say that he told Shasta he had studied the family's habits and peered into their home to learn the layout of the house.

The police eventually recovered from the stolen red Jeep a pair of dark gloves Shasta described him as wearing the night of her kidnapping, a 12-gauge shotgun, and an empty zip tie bag. According to reports in the *Pacific Northwest Inlander*, the police recovered from the Jeep a video recorder with footage of Duncan abusing and threatening Shasta and Dylan. The *Pacific Northwest Inlander* also reported that Duncan allegedly shot Dylan to death and then burned his body at a campsite in Montana.[6] On July 10, 2005, lab technicians identified human remains found by the police at a remote campsite in Montana as those of 9-year-old Dylan Groene.

During their investigation, the police also discovered that for several months prior to the murders and kidnappings in Idaho, Duncan had kept a blog, or journal, on the Internet. In it he talked about his struggles with pedophilia. "God has shown me the right choice, but my demons have tied me to a spit and the fire has already been lit," he wrote on April 24, 2005, soon after he had jumped bail in Minnesota on child molestation charges.[7] The police also learned that Duncan had complained anonymously online to the Fargo, North Dakota, police chief about the unfairness of that state's sex offender registry laws.

The police have so far charged Duncan with four counts of first-degree murder and various kidnapping charges. It is expected that charges involving the sexual abuse of Shasta and Dylan will also be filed. In addition, federal charges may possibly be sought, since Duncan took Dylan and Shasta across state lines.

After her release from the hospital, Shasta went to live with her father. "This little girl really went through more than any little girl should ever have to think about," said Captain Ben Wolfinger of the Kootenai County Sheriff's Department.[8]

Would following tip #12 above, making the Groene home harder to break into, possibly have saved four people from death and Shasta from weeks of horror she will likely never totally recover from? Yes, it possibly would have. Apparently, Duncan found a way to slip into the home and catch everyone by surprise. If instead he'd had to make a lot of noise breaking in, someone might have had time to call the police. Many victims of rape tell the police that they were awakened by a man standing over their bed, and that they hadn't heard him break into their house. This can be prevented. While it might not be possible to make a home totally burglarproof, any home can still be made secure enough that anyone breaking into it will have to make a lot of noise.

This is important because individuals like Duncan, those who target children as sexual victims, are often resistant to treatment that practitioners hope will make them safe. An encyclopedia article about pedophilia stated, "Behavioral treatment of pedophilia does not affect recidivism, nor apparently does incarceration. The condition remains chronic, and for this reason, societal interest in incarceration prevails over what is generally seen as equivocal behavioral treatment."[9] Further, not only doesn't the treatment for pedophilia usually work, but many child molesters simply refuse to even take part in it.

Pedophilia, many researchers believe, never disappears from a person's psyche. Although pedophiles may abstain, the desire is always there. And though some pedophile child molesters may be able to abstain for long periods, many others go right back to their deviant behavior the moment they get the chance. The same is true of sex offenders who target adults. Many of these individuals simply can't control the need-driven behavior that compels them to be sex offenders.

Because many experts consider both sex offenders who target adults and those who target children to be incurable, more than a dozen states, in order to decrease the threat that these criminals present, have instituted an "undetermined sentencing rule." What this means is that dangerous sex offenders in these states are not released from custody, even after the completion of their prison sentences, if the state can show that they still present a threat to society.

Washington is one of the states that has a mechanism for keeping sex offenders incarcerated even after they have served their time in prison. The state must show that the person has been convicted of a sexually violent crime, and that the person suffers from a mental abnormality or personality disorder that makes it likely that, if released, he or she will become involved in acts of predatory sexual violence. Because this can be difficult to prove, every year in the state of Washington less than 1 percent of the individuals released from prison for a sex offense charge are referred to the attorney general for a petition to declare them a danger to society. The attorney general, on average, files a petition on only a third of this 1 percent. This means that many dangerous sexual predators, such as Joseph Edward Duncan III, can slip through the system and return to society with the same intense sexual urges that landed them in prison to start off with.

A study designed to verify this danger of released sex offenders slipping through the system tracked 61 individuals in the state of Washington

who had been recommended for retention as dangerous sexual predators, but on whom, for various reasons, the attorney general did not file.
Fifty-nine percent of this group, within 70 months of their release, had
been arrested for a new crime, 28 percent for a new sex offense.[10] Keep in
mind, however, that these are just the sex offenses that were reported to
the police and for which a perpetrator was known; most sex offenses are
never reported, and a perpetrator is never identified.

Earlier we discussed the defenses against rape, and after reading all
I have said about child molestation, many people may wonder whether
there are any practical ways to stop children from becoming the victims
of sexual abuse. Yes, there are.

But first, parents and others must be aware that the sexual abuse of
children is even happening. Because it is so often well hidden, sexual
abuse of children can have been going on for months, or even years,
without the parents knowing about it. Fortunately, there are a number of
signs that can alert parents and others to the possibility that child sexual
abuse is occurring. They include:

1. A sudden fear and avoidance of someone the child shouldn't be
   afraid of or want to avoid.
2. A sudden onset of nightmares or sleep disturbances.
3. Unusual sexual curiosity or a sudden sexual knowledge beyond
   what the child should have.
4. A change in behavior, such as extreme mood swings, excessive
   crying, or a sudden desire for isolation in a formerly outgoing
   child.
5. Pain or itching in private areas.
6. Someone suddenly wanting to spend a lot of time alone with
   your child and who is always trying to get you out of the way.
7. A child suddenly receiving gifts from a source not known to
   do this.

It should be cautioned right away that any of the signs above could
be caused by something other than child sexual abuse. So if they appear,
don't immediately jump to conclusions, but instead investigate with an
open mind.

However, remember that if your child does reveal information about
sexual abuse, the reaction of the person the child reports the abuse to can
be crucial to the child's eventual psychological and emotional recovery

and to his or her determination to carry through with the complaint. If a child does tell you about sexual molestation, don't react with horror, shock, anger, disgust, or disbelief. This is just what the molester likely told the child would happen if he or she ever told. Also, don't talk badly about the person the child accuses. This may be a person that the child has confused feelings for, involving both affection and dislike, and your attitude could make the child want to protect him.

Keep in mind, it takes a lot of courage for children to tell adults about sexual abuse, and when they do it they are making themselves very vulnerable. Consequently, listen with a nonjudgmental attitude, and assure the child that what happened was not his or her fault. Another very important point to remember is never to assume that any story a child tells is too outrageous or outlandish to have happened. Molesters will often select children as their victims because they are embarrassed to ask adults to do what they want to do. Obviously, if the person the child reports as the abuser is a parent or guardian, steps must be taken to protect the child from more abuse or retaliation for telling.

If a child does go to an adult and complains of sexual abuse, or if an adult comes into information that appears to indicate reasonable suspicion of child sexual abuse, 49 of the 50 states and the District of Columbia legally require that person to report the abuse to the authorities. Not doing so can carry serious criminal sanctions. Reasonable suspicion means that a normal person coming into a set of facts would suspect child abuse.

Along with possible criminal sanctions for not reporting child sexual abuse, other penalties can also befall a person who ignores the complaint. For example, in Columbus, Ohio, school officials fired a high school principal because she failed to report accusations that a 16-year-old special education student had been raped at school. Reportedly, the principal had also tried to talk the girl's parents out of calling the police, fearing adverse publicity for the school. In another case, this one in California, a high school girl had been involved in a sexual relationship with her basketball coach. The girl's parents notified the school of the relationship, but the school did not report it to the police. The relationship affected the underaged girl so negatively that she required extensive counseling. The coach, eventually arrested after the parents complained to the police, pled guilty to child abuse and sexual molestation. The parents sued the school and the coach and received a judgment of $1.55 million.

While so far I may have painted a dismal picture of the problem of child sexual abuse in our country, something can be done. There are a number of things parents can do that will greatly reduce the chances that their children will be sexually molested. They are:

1. Most important, listen to your children. If they want to tell you about someone acting oddly, listen to them. The police find that children will often tell someone other than their parents about sexual abuse or attempted sexual abuse because they were scared or embarrassed, or because they tried and the parents apparently didn't have the time to listen to them. Only in relationships where the children feel loved and important enough to be listened to can parents expect them to tell about sexual molestation. Put simply, children who feel they can talk to their parents about absolutely anything, and who know their parents will take the time to listen to them, will be more likely to tell their parents about sexual abuse or attempts at sexual abuse.

   In this same area, parents must talk to their children, and at an early age, about sexual matters. They must talk to them before they can fall victim to sexual abuse, as the following comment by a child molester attests to: "Parents are partly to blame if they don't tell their children about [sexual matters]—I used it to my advantage by teaching the child myself." Another convicted child molester added, "Parents shouldn't be embarrassed to talk about things like this—it's harder to abuse or trick a child who knows what you're up to."[11]

   Police Sergeant Terry Hall, who runs a child molestation prevention program, related an incident to me about the importance of talking to children about sexual abuse: "I asked a child molester one time, 'What can I tell parents who do not educate their kids about people like you?' He sat back in the chair and smiled and said, 'Don't tell a child about it and I will be glad to talk to them when I get out.' It sent a chill up my spine. He had just confessed to 300 molestations, and unfortunately only got 12 years. He is out now."[12]

2. Be suspicious of any house or person all the children in the neighborhood want to hang around. While this may be just a nice person who likes children, molesters often attempt to make themselves and their homes attractive to children.

3. Teach your children that they have the right to say no to anyone who wants to touch them in a way that makes them feel uncomfortable, and that they should always tell you about any incident of this type.
4. Never assume that anyone could not be a child molester. As I hope I have shown, sexual predators come in all guises, from priests to police officers, from janitors to CEOs. There is absolutely no one in any position or any occupation who can't be a child molester. No one!
5. Know where your children are at all times and with whom. Know your children's friends and activities.
6. If you suspect someone you don't know well might be a sexual predator, check with your state's sex offender registry. All states have a sex offender registry, and most states now include photos of the sex offenders in these registries. On March 5, 2003, the U.S. Supreme Court ruled that it is legal for states to post the pictures of sex offenders on the Internet. Some critics of sex offender registries had complained that putting photos online punished sex offenders twice for the same crime. The Court didn't agree.

    "Our system does not treat dissemination of truthful information in furtherance of a legitimate government objective as punishment," wrote Supreme Court Justice Anthony Kennedy. "The purpose and the principal effect of notification are to inform the public for its own safety, not to humiliate the offender."[13]

    You can find information about the sex offender registry in your state by going to the Web site of The National Center for Missing and Exploited Children at www.ncmec.org. In 2005, Senator Charles Schumer of New York sponsored Senate Bill 1086, which would create a national sex offender database that would be searchable by the public. If this bill becomes law, it will be a powerful tool for parents wanting to protect their children.

    Parents might also want to consider checking their state's sex offender registry for the leaders of any youth group their children want to join. Cautious parents should also make unannounced visits to activities their children are involved in. They should drop by band rehearsals, sporting practices, day-care centers, and so forth.

    When considering enrolling a child in a program whose leader seems remarkable with children, keep in mind that he may well be remarkable, but at the same time be alert to the possibility that he could be a child molester. Check to find out. "If someone appears too good to be true to your kids, he very well may be too good to be true," warns police sergeant Terry Hall.[14]

7. Monitor your child's computer use. As discussed earlier, child molesters who once had to go out into the streets to find their victims can now find millions of them at the click of a computer mouse. Children are often much too trusting and may give out personal information to people they meet on the computer, not suspecting that these individuals are not the teenage boys or girls they claim to be but rather middle-aged child molesters. Child molesters exploit this blind trust of children in their selection, grooming, and seducing of victims.

Computer chat rooms are particularly hazardous for children. These are very often visited and used by child molesters who hide in the assumed identity of a teenager or even a younger child. To prevent a child from being approached and set up for grooming by a child molester, parents should consider keeping children's computers where they can see them being used and also consider installing software that can filter out sites they don't want their children to visit. For further information, the FBI has published a booklet titled *A Parent's Guide to Internet Safety*. It is available at www.fbi.gov. Click on "Reports and Publications."

But most important, since children can't be watched every second, parents need to talk to them about the hazards of computer use. Parents need to make their children aware of the dangers of giving out personal information, and of the possibility that people on computers aren't always who they claim to be. For help with this, in addition to the FBI publication mentioned above, a number of other government and private organizations have set up child-friendly Web sites that educate children about the dangers of the Internet. One such very useful site is www. netsmartz.org.

Although some frightened parents may want to do so, taking away a child's access to a computer is not the answer. Doing this will only make him or her go online in secret somewhere away from home, such as at school, the library, or a friend's house. And this is exactly what child molesters want, a way to drive a wedge between the parent and child. This is important because police officers who work sting operations by going into chat rooms and pretending to be young girls or boys can attest to the fact that within minutes of doing so they are hit with sexual overtures.

"Every time I'm representing myself on the Internet as a 12- or 13-year-old girl, within one or two sentences the conversation goes to sex. Every time," said Colorado Springs detective Joel Kern.[15]

This danger is borne out by real-life examples. A 36-year-old Wisconsin man who met a 15-year-old girl on the Internet persuaded her to meet him, have a sexual relationship with him, and then run away with him to California. He received a 20-year prison sentence. A 23-year-old New York man who posed as a teenager on the Internet lured two 14-year-old girls to a meeting, where he raped them. A 33-year-old Michigan man met an 11-year-old girl on the Internet, lured her to his house, tied her up, and raped her.

For anyone who needs further proof, recently the television program *Dateline* rented a house, wired it up for sound and video, and then had people go online in a chat room posing as under-aged children who said they were home alone and interested in sex. Within the next two and a half days, *Dateline* had 50 men knocking on the door of the house wanting to have sex with what they thought was a minor child.[16] If you believe you know a child who is being exploited online, you can report it to the authorities at www.cybertipline.com or by calling 1-800-843-5678.

While the advice I have given can significantly lessen a person's chances of becoming a sexual assault victim, and consequently should be adhered to whenever possible, the reality of life is that sometimes, no matter what precautions are taken, no matter how careful individuals are, an incident occurs and a victim is sexually assaulted. Some sex criminals are simply so obsessed that even knowing they will be caught will not stop them. The concern then, along with making certain the perpetrator is arrested, tried, convicted, and incarcerated, is to provide healing for the victims. This is crucial. In a survey of 2,000 women, 19.2 percent of the women who had been raped had also attempted suicide, compared to only 2.2 percent of those women who had not been raped.[17] Another study found that approximately 50 percent of rape victims had experienced serious depression during the first year after the attack, while 40 percent also reported serious sexual dysfunctions for up to six years following the attack.[18]

Along with these problems, many victims of rape experience a psychological malady called Rape Trauma Syndrome, which is very similar to PTSD (post-traumatic stress disorder). PTSD often strikes those who have experienced a traumatic event far outside the experience of ordinary people. For example, rescue workers responding to a large-scale disaster in which people are horribly mutilated, soldiers in combat, police officers involved in killing an offender, and others in such circumstances often suffer PTSD.

Like those with PTSD, those suffering from Rape Trauma Syndrome have experienced a traumatic event far outside of a person's ordinary experiences. And, as in cases of PTSD, individuals who suffer from Rape Trauma Syndrome often have flashbacks to the incident, report feelings of numbness or detachment from reality, and have difficulty sleeping and eating. In addition, Rape Trauma Syndrome sufferers may experience an exaggerated startle response, become emotionally upset for no apparent reason, go through long periods of depression, and have a fear of meeting new people. Rape Trauma Syndrome sufferers are also often especially alert to verbal and nonverbal signs from family members and friends. These victims are looking for signs of approval or disapproval concerning their action or inaction during the sexual assault.

It has been found over the years that every victim's recovery from sexual assault takes a different route and has its own timetable. However, as the following incident demonstrates, occasionally a victim can not only recover from a sexual assault, but find fulfillment in devoting her life to helping others whom have suffered through a similar crime.

In the spring of 1989, Debbie Smith's life seemed very normal. One afternoon she was doing housework at her home in Williamsburg, Virginia, while her husband, a police lieutenant, slept upstairs after working the night shift the evening before. Soon, however, everything would be far from normal.

A man with a gun slipped into her house, catching her unawares, grabbed her, warned her to be quiet, blindfolded her, and then dragged her to a nearby wooded area, where he raped her. Before leaving her after the attack, he warned her, "Remember, I know where you live and I will come back if you tell anyone."[19]

Debbie fled back to her house, woke her husband, and, between sobs, told him what had happened. Still in fear of her attacker, she begged her husband not to report the crime. She just wanted to clean herself and try to forget about it. "I felt dirty," she said. "I wanted to take a shower and wash it away."[20] Her husband, however, persuaded her that the man was obviously very dangerous and that they needed to do everything they could to get him off the street. He convinced her to let him report the rape and also take her to the hospital for a forensic medical examination.

Debbie later looked through the police department's mug shot books, but she couldn't find her attacker, and so the case wore on with no resolution. For various reasons, Debbie put off going to counseling for several years after the attack and found herself experiencing many of the symptoms of Rape Trauma Syndrome, including nightmares, spontaneous emotional outbursts, and thoughts of suicide.

Five years after her rape, a local reporter wanted to do a follow-up story about Debbie's case. The reporter contacted Debbie and assured her that they wouldn't use her name. After discussing it with her family, and thinking it might help her heal, Debbie decided to allow the reporter to use her name after all. She found to her surprise that after the news story named her as a sexual assault victim, she received an outpouring of response from other sexual assault victims.

Although Debbie felt inspired by the response, her own sexual assault still remained an open case. Because of a huge backlog of work, it took years for the state of Virginia to get around to trying to match the DNA the hospital had recovered from Debbie with a suspect, but they finally did. On July 26, 1995, more than six years after the attack, a laboratory technician identified Norman Jimmerson, who had already been in prison for five years for the abduction and robbery of two other women, as Debbie's attacker. The police charged Jimmerson with Debbie's attack, and a court eventually convicted and sentenced him to a prison term of two consecutive life sentences plus 25 years.

Because of the need to decrease the long turnaround time for doing DNA analysis, a spectator at Debbie's trial, the director of the Virginia Division of Forensic Science, who sat on the national Committee on the Future of DNA, asked her to speak before the committee about the necessity of expediting these cases. Although normally very shy, Debbie finally agreed to do it, and she impressed the committee members with the depth of her commitment. Debbie then began making more and more public appearances, speaking out for women who had been sexually assaulted.

"Working past my shy nature, daring to speak of such an intimate subject and learning to express my heart to perfect strangers is not an easy task but I have to do everything I can to help other victims of sexual assault," Debbie said. "It is not a choice for me, but an overwhelming urgency."[21]

Debbie and her husband eventually founded an organization to assist the victims of sexual assault. It is called H-E-A-R-T (Hope Exists After Rape Trauma). The organization's Web site can be found at www. H-E-A-R-T.info.

Because, as the case above shows, DNA can often sit for months or even years in police laboratories before being analyzed, and during this time a serial rapist can strike many times, a group in Chicago, the Women's DNA Initiative, has recently begun funding the sending of DNA samples to private laboratories, where the turnaround time is much shorter. In July 2004, the results of one of these expedited DNA tests led to the arrest of a man who admitted to 19 rapes, and likely would have committed many more if not arrested.

"We are pleased to see that the testing is getting serial rapists off the street," said Sheri Mecklenburg, chief counsel to the Chicago Police Department.[22]

However, while this expedited DNA analysis may save women from becoming future sexual assault victims, those who have already been victimized are looking for something else: they are looking for resources that will help them heal. Fortunately for the victims of sexual assault, there are numerous programs and resources around the country that can assist them in reclaiming their lives and moving forward. No program will ever be able to return things to the way they were before the sexual assault, as such an event changes a victim's life forever, but still these programs can often help victims begin functioning normally again.

Sometimes what victims need immediately after a sexual assault is just a sympathetic, nonjudgmental ear. Unfortunately, this isn't always available within the victim's circle of family and friends. These people can often be too close emotionally to the victim, are embarrassed to talk about such things, or simply don't want to hear about it. Fortunately, a number of agencies, detailed below, have counselors available to listen to and talk with victims, along with group therapy settings available for later.

Selfhelp Magazine had this to say about sexual assault victims receiving counseling and group therapy: "A hot line counselor or even an in-person rape crisis counselor can be a supportive listener when family and friends are unavailable or are too emotionally involved to be helpful." The article goes on to say: "After the initial crisis, a support group can help break down isolation, secrecy, and shame. The survivor can see that women she likes and respects have had experiences similar to her own, and that they like and respect her. Because members of the group are at different stages of healing, she can gain perspective on how far she has come and see evidence that further progress is possible."[23]

As important as it is for adults, therapy and counseling for child molestation victims is perhaps even more crucial because of the long-term detrimental effects sexual abuse can have on children's emotional and psychological development. In a study of men who had been sexually abused as children, 80 percent had a history of substance abuse, 50 percent had suicidal thoughts, 23 percent had attempted suicide, and 31 percent had violently victimized others. All of these percentages are far above the percentages for non–sexually victimized men.[24]

Practitioners have found group counseling to be one of the best and most successful treatments for the victims of child sexual abuse. Undergoing this therapy, a victim can see that the abuse he or she has suffered is not that uncommon, and that child sexual abuse victims look just like everyone else.

Where then can a victim, or the loved ones of a victim, find the organizations that can help sexual assault victims, both children and adults? Individuals should first check with their local victim assistance unit, usually housed with the police department or prosecutor's office. These units can often put sexual assault victims in contact with local organizations that can help. Those looking for help should also consider contacting the Rape, Abuse and Incest Network (RAINN) at 1–800–656-HOPE or at www.rainn.org. This organization can help with both support groups and with assistance in locating a sexual abuse crisis center near where the victim lives.

Many other organizations also assist sexual assault victims, or maintain lists of agencies that can assist sexual assault victims in their recovery. A few of these are: www.survivingtothriving.org/link, www.vachss.com/help_text/circle_of_trust.html, and www.saiwso.org.

For those victims at an advanced stage of recovery who want to reach out and help others avoid becoming victims, a detailed listing of the various agencies across the United States that are working to decrease the threat of sexual violence can be found at the National Sexual Violence Resource Center. This organization can be reached at 1-877-739-3895 or www.nsvrc.org. Ask for their 45-page booklet titled *Directory of Projects Working to Eliminate Sexual Violence*.

Some Final Thoughts

Victim assistance counselor Senobia Pervine, who has worked in the field for over 15 years, told me this when I asked her about the effects sexual assault has on a victim: "In my experience in working with sexual assault victims I find that, besides physical injury, they experience a host of emotions because of their victimization: embarrassment, anger, guilt, depression, self-blame."[1]

As Miss Pervine points out, few sexual assault victims will not be marked by the event, and some may even be scarred for life. While a sex crimes detective cannot do anything to erase this event from a victim's life, he or she can see that the perpetrator is identified, arrested, and convicted for the crime. Then, since all states now have sex offender registries and there are plans for a national registry, if the perpetrator ever gets out of prison, he or she will never again be able to hide behind the secrecy that often shrouds sex offenders.

Sex crimes detectives perform a critical job in our country, because sex offenders don't just sexually assault people. They also steal their victims' innocence and feelings of security. A sexual assault victim can never truly feel safe again anywhere.

As I hope I've shown, being a sex crimes detective is not a job that just anyone can do. These detectives must deal with extremely fragile victims who have been violated in the most personal way. They must also deal with some of society's most dangerous and degenerate criminals. Fortunately for all of us, there are thousands of officers across our country who are willing to go to work every day and face this challenge.

Notes

Chapter 1

1. U.S. Department of Justice, *Rape and Sexual Assault: Reporting to Police and Medical Attention, 1992–2000* (Washington DC: U.S. Government Printing Office, 2002), p. 1.

2. L. Risin and M. Koss, "Sexual Abuse of Boys: Prevalence, and Descriptive Characteristics of Childhood Victimizations," *Journal of Interpersonal Violence*, March 1987, pp. 309–23.

3. David G. Curtis, "Perspectives on Acquaintance Rape," The American Academy of Experts in Traumatic Stress, 1997, http://www.aaets.org/arts/art13htm.

4. D.E.H. Russell, *Rape in Marriage* (New York: Macmillan, 1990).

5. I. Johnson and R. Sigler, *Forced Sexual Intercourse in Intimate Relationships* (Brookfield, VT: Dartmouth/Ashgate, 1997), p. 22.

6. U.S. Department of Justice, *Rape and Sexual Assault*, p. 2.

7. Warren Wise, "Proctor Verdict: Guilty," *Charleston (SC) Post and Courier*, March 5, 1998, http://archives.postandcourier.com.

8. Phillip Caston, "High Court Reverses Ruling That Proctor Was Denied Fair Trial," *Charleston (SC) Post and Courier*, April 21, 2004, http://archives.postandcourier.com.

9. Warren Wise, "Proctor Gets Life Without Parole," *Charleston (SC) Post and Courier*, April 3, 1998, http://archives.postandcourier.com.

10. William Ernoehazy, "Sexual Assault," *eMedicine*, January 21, 2002, http://www.emedicine.com/EMERG/topic527.htm.

11. Michael T. Dreznick, "Heterosocial Competence of Rapists and Child Molesters: A Meta-Analysis," *Journal of Sex Research*, May 2003.

12. Robert R. Hazelwood and Ann W. Burgess, "An Introduction to the Serial Rapist: Research by the FBI," *FBI Law Enforcement Bulletin*, September 1987, pp. 16–24.

13. A. N. Groth and Ann W. Burgess, "Sexual Dysfunction During Rape," *New England Journal of Medicine*, April 1977, pp. 764–66.

14. Hazelwood and Burgess, "An Introduction to the Serial Rapist," pp. 16–24.

15. Tim Moore, "Florida Department of Law Enforcement Adds Burglary Convictions to DNA Database," *Florida Police Chief*, September 2000.

16. Hazelwood and Burgess, "An Introduction to the Serial Rapist," pp. 16–24.

17. Ibid.

18. S. K. Bardwell, "Pair Charged in Robberies, Assaults," *Houston Chronicle*, February 26, 2005, www.chron.com.

19. J. Briere and N. Malamuth, "Self-Reported Likelihood of Sexually Aggressive Behavior," *Journal of Research in Personality*, 1983, pp. 315–23.

20. Diana Russell, "Males' Propensity to Rape," Web site excerpts from Russell's books, November 7, 2004, www.dianarussell.com/menrape.html.

21. Curtis, "Perspectives on Acquaintance Rape."

22. Barbara E. Johnson, "Rape Myth Acceptance and Sociodemographic Characteristics: A Multidimensional Analysis," *Sex Roles: A Journal of Research*, June 1997.

23. D. E. Herman, "The Rape Culture," in *Women: A Feminist Perspective*, ed. Jo Freeman (Mountain View, CA: Mayfield, 1984).

24. U.S. Department of Justice, *Crime in the United States* (Washington, DC: U.S. Government Printing Office, 2004), p. 27.

25. U.S. Department of Justice, *Criminal Victimization in the United States, 2002 Statistical Tables* (Washington, DC: U.S. Government Printing Office, December 2003), p. 29.

26. U.S. Department of Justice, *Sexual Assault of Young Children as Reported to Law Enforcement: Victim, Incident, and Offender Characteristics* (Washington, DC: U.S. Government Printing Office, July 2000), p. 2.

27. U.S. Department of Health and Human Services, "Sexual Assault," research document issued by the U.S. Department of Health and Human Services, April 2001, http://www.4woman.gov/faq/sexualassault.htm.

28. U.S. Department of Justice, *Rape and Sexual Assault*, p. 1.

29. National Center for Victims of Crime, *Sexual Assault*, research document, 1998, http://www.ncvc.org/ncvc/main.aspx?dbName=DocumentViewer&DocumentID=32369.

30. Nathan W. Pino, "Gender Differences in Rape Reporting," *Sex Roles: A Journal of Research*, June 1999.

31. U.S. Department of Justice, *Rape and Sexual Assault*, p. 3.

32. Dan Dove (detective, Provo, Utah, Police Department), interview by author, August 29, 2005.

33. Sabrina Garcia and Margaret Henderson, "Blind Reporting of Sexual Violence," *FBI Law Enforcement Bulletin*, June 1999, p.13.

34. D. Nibert, "Assaults Against Residents of a Psychiatric Institution," *Journal of Interpersonal Violence*, March 1989, pp. 342–49.

35. KCRA 3 TV, "52 Registered Sex Offenders Found Living in California Nursing Homes," February 8, 2005, http://www.kcra.com/print/4178106/detail.html.

36. Margaret T. Gordon and Stephanie Riger, *The Female Fear* (Champaign, IL: University of Illinois Press, 1991).

37. National Center for Victims of Crime, *Sexual Assault*.

38. U.S. Department of Justice, *The Sexual Victimization of College Women* (Washington, DC: U.S. Government Printing Office, December 2000), p. 10.

39. *KATU 2 News*, "Excerpts from Probable Cause Statement in Ward Weaver Case," August 21, 2002, http://www.katu.com/printstory.asp?ID=49607.

40. Ibid.

41. *KATU 2 News*, "Next Step for Ward Weaver Is Evaluation," September 23, 2004, http://www.katu.com/news/story.asp?ID=71303.

Chapter 2

1. Roy Hazelwood and Stephen G. Michaud, *Dark Dreams* (New York: St. Martin's, 2001).

2. Joe Kafka, "Death Row Inmate Found Dead in Cell," *Rapid City (SD) Journal*, March 30, 2003, www.rapidcityjournal.com.

3. Lance Hamner (prosecutor, Johnson County, Indiana), interview by author, August 13, 2005.

4. Senobia Pervine (rape victim assistance counselor, Marion County, Indiana, Victim Assistance Unit), interview by author, August 23, 2005.

5. U.S. Department of Justice, *Crime Scene Investigation: A Guide for Law Enforcement* (Washington, DC: U.S. Government Printing Office, January 2000), p. 16.

6. David W. Rivers, "Crime Scene Investigation," handout from Homicide and Forensic Death Investigation Conference held at Public Agency Training Council, Indianapolis, January 2004.

7. Larry Cahill (sex crimes detective, Indianapolis Police Department), interview by author, August 1, 2005.

8. U.S. Department of Justice, *Sexual Assault Nurse Examiner (SANE) Programs: Improving the Community Response to Sexual Assault Victims* (Washington, DC: U.S. Government Printing Office, April 2001), p. 1.

9. U.S. Department of Justice, *Sexual Assault Evidence: National Assessment and Guidebook* (Washington, DC: U.S. Government Printing Office, January 2002), p. 70.

10. Kimberly A. Crawford, "Crime Scene Searches," *FBI Law Enforcement Bulletin*, January 1999, p. 27.

11. *Mincey v. Arizona*, 437 US 385 (1978).

12. *Katz v. United States*, 88 S. Ct. 507 (1967).

13. Alfred Allan Lewis and Herbert Leon MacDonell, *The Evidence Never Lies: The Case Book of a Modern Sherlock Holmes* (New York: Bantam, 1989).

14. Bill Pender (former police officer; crime scene technician, Marion County, Indiana, Crime Laboratory), interview by author, August 4, 2005.

15. Royce Taylor (consultant, Automated Fingerprint Identification Systems [AFIS],), interview by author, August 3, 2005.

16. Pender, interview by author, August 4, 2005.

17. Tom Spalding (reporter, Gannet newspapers), interview by author, August 10, 2005.

18. American Psychiatric Association, *Diagnostic and Statistical Manual of Mental Disorders* (Arlington, VA: American Psychiatric Association, 2000).

19. Brent E. Turvey, *Criminal Profiling* (New York: Academic Press, 2002), p. 34.

20. R. Prentky, "Recidivism Rates Among Child Molesters and Rapists: A Methodological Analysis," *Journal of Law and Human Behavior*, 1997, p. 642.

21. Eugene J. Kanin, "False Rape Allegations," *Archives of Sexual Behavior*, February 1994, pp. 81–84.

22. David E. Zulawski and Douglas E. Wicklander, "Special Report 1: Interrogations: Understanding the Process," *Law and Order*, July 1998, p. 87.

23. Tom Tittle (captain, Marion County, Florida, Sheriff's Department), interview by author, August 2, 2005.

24. David Vessel, "Conducting Successful Interrogations," *FBI Law Enforcement Bulletin*, October 1998, p. 6.

25. *Miranda v. Arizona*, 384 US 436 (1966).

26. *Dickerson v. United States*, 530 US 428 (2000).

27. Joe Navarro, "A Four-Domain Model for Detecting Deception," *FBI Law Enforcement Bulletin*, June 2003, p. 19.

28. Charles L. Yeschke, *The Art of Investigative Interviewing* (New York: Butterworth-Heinemann, 2003), pp. 24–26.

29. Joe Navarro and John R. Schafer, "Detecting Deception," *FBI Law Enforcement Bulletin*, July 2001, p. 12.

30. David Phillips (former head of Indianapolis Police Department Polygraph Unit; homicide lieutenant, Indianapolis Police Department), interview by author, September 9, 2005.

31. Joe Mason (former homicide lieutenant, Indianapolis Police Department), interview by author, August 19, 2005.

Chapter 3

1. *CBS 2—New York News*, "No Parole for Connecticut Rapist," March 3, 2005, http://cbsnewyork.com/topstories/topstoriesny_story_062144202.html.

2. Ibid.

3. Lance Hamner (prosecutor, Johnson County, Indiana), interview by author, August 13, 2005.

4. Kevin Hammel (detective, Trumbull, Connecticut, Police Department), interview by author, September 15, 2005.

5. Jennifer Mertens, "Lessons from the Body Farm," *Law Enforcement Technology*, June 2003, p. 37.

6. Marni Becker-Avin, "The Real Purpose of Voir Dire," *Trial Techniques Committee Newsletter—American Bar Association*, Fall 2001, p. 10.

7. Veronica Whitney, "Suspect in Bryant Case Threats Pleads Guilty," *Vail DailyNews*, March 30, 2005, www.vaildaily.com.

8. Seth Stern, "Bryant Case Tests Limits of 'Rape Shield Laws,'" *Christian Science Monitor*, October 22, 2003, www.csmonitor.com.

9. *Forensic Nurse*, "Assault on Rape Shield Law Puts Victims at Risk, Says Advocacy Group," October 2003, www.forensicnursemag.com.

10. Michelle J. Anderson, "From Chastity Requirements to Sexuality License: Sexual Consent and a New Rape Shield Law," *George Washington Law Review*, 2002, p. 51.

11. *UIC News Tips*, "UIC Researchers Study 'Second Rape' Phenomenon," December 17, 2001, http://www.uic.edu/depts/paff/opa/releases/2001/secondrape_release.htm.

12. Patricia Tjaden and Nancy Thoennes, *Extent, Nature, and Consequences of Intimate Partner Violence* (Washington, DC: U.S. Government Printing Office, 2000), p. 10.

13. Randy Wyrick, "Bellman in Bryant Case Breaks Silence," *Vail Daily News*, April 6, 2005, www.vaildaily.com.

14. *Vail Daily News*, "Kobe Bryant, Accuser Settle," March 2, 2005, www.vaildaily.com.

15. David Zeman, "The Kobe Bryant Case: Spotlight Shatters Accuser's Privacy," *Detroit Free Press*, July 26, 2003, www.freep.com.

16. Ibid.

17. Ed Timms, "DNA Alters Thinking on Swift Justice," *Dallas Morning News*, July 30, 2001.

18. Carole Moore, "Taking the Stand," *Law Enforcement Technology*, July 2005, p. 79.

19. Ibid., p. 81.

Chapter 4

1. *TCM Breaking News*, "Child Molester Gets Life under 'Three Strikes' Law," April 15, 2004, http://archives.tcm.ie/breakingnews/2004/04/15/story143075.asp.

2. Richard Nanan (detective, Manchester, New Hampshire, Police Department), interview by author, August 8, 2005.

3. Dan Dove (detective, Provo, Utah, Police Department), interview by author, August 29, 2005.

4. U.S. Department of Justice, *Sexual Assault of Young Children as Reported to Law Enforcement: Victim, Incident, and Offender Characteristics* (Washington DC: U.S. Government Printing Office, July 2000), p. 4.

5. Ibid.

6. McCay Vernon, "Issues in the Sexual Molestation of Deaf Youth," *American Annals of the Deaf*, December 2002.

7. Nancy Faulkner, "Sexual Abuse Statistics," *Pandora's Box: The Secrecy of Child Sexual Abuse*, a promotional Web site for programs that combat child sexual abuse, August 29, 2005, http://www.prevent-abuse-now.com/stats.htm.

8. Steve Twedt, "Trash Passing," *IRE Journal*, November/December 2000.

9. U.S. Department of Justice, *Sexual Assault of Young Children*, p. 10.

10. Janet Kornblum, "Meet the Child Molester Next Door," *USA Today*, January 28, 2003, www.usatoday.com.

11. Karen Thomas, "Who Are the Child Molesters Among Us?" *USA Today*, March 12, 2002, www.usatoday.com.

12. United States Conference of Catholic Bishops, *A Report on the Crisis in the Catholic Church in the United States* (Washington, DC: United States Conference of Catholic Bishops, 2004), pp. 22–23.

13. Ibid., p. 84.

14. Ibid., p. 107.

15. Ken Kusmer, "Catholic Group: Abuse Scandal Could Cost up to $3 Billion," *Indianapolis Star,* July 10, 2005.

16. Torcuil Crichton, "Jehovah's Witnesses Accused of Building 'Pedophile Paradise,'" *Sunday Herald,* July 2002.

17. Gene G. Abel and Nora Harlow, *The Stop Child Molestation Book* (Philadelphia: Xlibris, 2002).

18. Ibid.

19. Richard Nanan (detective, Manchester, New Hampshire, Police Department), interview by author, August 8, 2005.

20. Association for the Treatment of Sexual Abusers, *Reducing Sexual Abuse through Treatment and Intervention with Abusers* (Beaverton, OR: Association for the Treatment of Sexual Abusers, 1996).

21. *KFMB TV,* "Marcus Wesson Guilty in Murders of Nine of His Children," June 17, 2005, http://www.kfmb.com/story.php?id = 15527.

22. Cyndee Fontana, "The Many Portraits of Marcus Wesson," *Fresno Bee,* April 18, 2004.

23. Ibid.

24. *ABC 30,* "Marcus Wesson Asks to Fire Attorneys," June 24, 2005, http://abclocal.go.com/kfsn/news/print_062405_nw_wesson. html.

25. David Finkelhor, *Online Victimization: A Report on the Nation's Youth* (Alexandria, VA: National Center for Missing and Exploited Children, 2000), p. ix.

26. Kenneth V. Lanning, *Child Molesters: A Behavioral Analysis* (Alexandria, VA: National Center for Missing and Exploited Children, 2001), p. 55.

27. American Psychiatric Association, *Diagnostic and Statistical Manual of Mental Disorders* (Arlington, VA: American Psychiatric Association, 2000).

28. *Indianapolis Star,* "Repeat Molester Eluded System," June 19, 2005.

29. Ibid.

30. Kenneth V. Lanning and Ann W. Burgess, *Child Molesters Who Abduct: Summary of the Case in Point Series* (Alexandria, VA: National Center for Missing and Exploited Children, 1995), p. 11.

31. Wayne D. Lord, "Investigating Potential Child Abduction Cases," *FBI Law Enforcement Bulletin,* April 2001, pp. 1–10.

Chapter 5

1. *CBS 11 TV,* "Wife Says She Selected Corpse in Fake Death Scheme," May 5, 2005, http://cbs11tv.com/localstories/local_story_125102307.html.

2. Associated Press, "Couple Faked Death with Stolen Corpse," May 7, 2005, www.lineofduty.com/blotterstory.asp?storyid=75491.

3. Ibid.

4. Kenneth V. Lanning, "Investigator's Guide to Allegations of 'Ritual' Child Abuse," research paper, January 1992, http://web.mit.edu/harris/www/lanning/html.

5. Richard Nanan (detective, Manchester, New Hampshire, Police Department), interview by author, August 8, 2005.

6. Cathy Redfern, "Jury Convicts Live Oak Man of Child Abuse," *Santa Cruz Sentinel*, March 15, 2005, www.santacruzsentinel.com.

7. Kenneth V. Lanning, *Child Molesters: A Behavioral Analysis* (Alexandria, VA: National Center for Missing and Exploited Children, 2001), p. 30.

8. Ann W. Burgess, "Contemporary Issues," in *Practical Aspects of Rape Investigation*, ed. Ann W. Burgess and Robert R. Hazelwood (New York: CRC, 2001), pp. 21–22.

9. *San Jose Mercury News*, "How Child Molester Got to Thousands," June 18, 2005, http://www.lineofduty.com.

10. K. C. Faller, *Child Sexual Abuse: Intervention and Treatment Issues* (Washington DC: U.S. Government Printing Office, 1993).

11. D. Muram, "Child Sexual Abuse: Relationship Between Sexual Acts and General Findings," *Child Abuse and Neglect* (1989), pp. 211–16.

12. William P. Heck, "Basic Investigative Protocol for Child Sexual Abuse," *FBI Law Enforcement Bulletin*, October 1999, p. 22.

13. Lanning, *Child Molesters*, p. 5.

14. Tom Tittle (captain, Marion County, Florida, Sheriff's Department), interview by author, August 16, 2005.

15. Ibid.

16. Gillian Murphy, *Beyond Surviving: Toward a Movement to Prevent Child Sexual Abuse* (New York: Ms. Foundation for Women, 2002), p. 8.

17. Seth L. Goldstein and R. P. Tyler, "Frustrations of Inquiry," *FBI Law Enforcement Bulletin*, July 1998, p. 1.

18. Merrilyn McDonald, "The Myth of Epidemic False Allegations of Sexual Abuse in Divorce Cases," *Court Review*, Spring 1998, p. 15.

19. Heck, "Basic Investigative Protocol," pp. 21–22.

20. Margaret Rieser, "Recantations in Child Sexual Abuse Cases," *Child Welfare*, November/December 1991.

21. Ibid.

22. Bill Montgomery, "Girl Details Rape at Trial," *Atlanta Journal-Constitution*, June 23, 2004.

23. Donna Pence and Charles Wilson, *The Role of Law Enforcement in the Response to Child Abuse and Neglect* (Washington, DC: U.S. Government Printing Office, 1992), p. 5.

24. Michael R. Napier, "Magic Words to Obtain Confessions," *FBI Law Enforcement Bulletin,* October 1998, p. 15.

25. Kim Smith, "Child-Sex Case Draws Life Sentence," *Las Vegas Sun,* May 8, 2002, www.vachss.com/help_text/archive/george_gibbs.html.

26. Christopher Smith, "Suspected Kidnapper in Idaho Kept Blog," Associated Press, July 7, 2004, www.wireservice.wired.com.

Chapter 6

1. Leroy Sigman, "Jury Recommends Six Life Terms Plus 90 Years," *Daily Journal,* October 6, 2004, www.mydjconnection.com.

2. Ibid.

3. Kenneth V. Lanning, *Child Molesters: A Behavioral Analysis* (Alexandria, VA: National Center for Missing and Exploited Children, 2001), p. 20.

4. Jeremy Browning, "Craig Man Found Guilty of Incest," *Craig (CO)Daily Press,* August 25, 2003, www.craigdailypress.com.

5. Ibid.

6. Renee Z. Dominguez, et al., *Encyclopedia of Crime and Punishment* (Great Barrington, MA: Berkshire, 2001).

7. Suzanne O'Malley (prosecutor, Marion County, Indiana), interview by author, September 6, 2005.

8. Lynne Tuohy, "A Payback for Nightmares—Judge Describes Child Victims' Anxiety, Self-Loathing as He Sentences Giordano to 37 Years," *Hartford (CT) Courant,* June 14, 2003.

9. *Maryland v. Craig,* 497 US 836 (1990).

10. Associated Press, "Judge Must Allow Children's Taped Testimony," July 7, 2005, www.duluthsuperior.com.

11. Donna Pence and Charles Wilson, *The Role of Law Enforcement in the Response to Child Abuse and Neglect* (Washington, DC: U.S. Government Printing Office, 1992), p. 33.

12. Lanning, *Child Molesters,* p. 44.

13. Ross Cheit and Erica Goldschmidt, "Symposium: The Treatment of Sex Offenders: Child Molesters in the Criminal Justice System: A Comprehensive Case-Flow Analysis of the Rhode Island Docket," *New England Journal on Criminal and Civil Confinement,* 1997, p. 267.

14. Cary Brunswick, "Tougher Sentences for Child Sex Abusers," *Daily Star,* July 21, 2001, www.thedailystar.com.

15. Lanning, *Child Molesters,* p. 132.

16. Melanie Snow (former sex crimes detective, Indianapolis Police Department), interview by author, August 15, 2005.

Chapter 7

1. Joanne Kimberlin, "New Technology Offers Peeping Toms More," *Virginian-Pilot*, June 8, 2004, www.hamptonroads.com.

2. Ibid.

3. Ibid.

4. Lisa Sweetingham, "More Women Join Lawsuit against Hooters," *Court TV*, April 9, 2004, www.radford.edu/~maamodt/aamodt%20(4th)/hooters%20privacy.htm.

5. Robert Herguth, "Cops Arrest Man Suspected of Being Serial Peeping Tom," *Chicago Sun-Times*, April 11, 2005.

6. Gene G. Abel and Nora Harlow, *The Stop Child Molestation Book* (Philadelphia: Xlibris, 2001).

7. Robert R. Hazelwood and Kenneth V. Lanning, "Collateral Materials in Sexual Crimes," in *Practical Aspects of Rape Investigation*, ed. Robert R. Hazelwood and Ann W. Burgess (New York: CRC, 2001), p. 228.

8. Vic Ryckaert, "Doctor Sentenced to Home Detention," *Indianapolis Star*, February 26, 2005, www.indystar.com.

9. *Osborne v. Ohio*, 495 US 103 (1990).

10. Andrew Vachss, "Age of Innocence," *London Observer*, April 16, 1994, www.vachss.com/av_dispatches/disp_9404_a.html.

11. Ibid.

12. Eva J. Klain, et al., *Child Pornography: The Criminal-Justice-System Response* (Alexandria, VA: National Center for Missing and Exploited Children, 2001), pp. 6–7.

13. Michael Medaris and Cathy Girouard, *Protecting Children in Cyberspace: The ICAC Task Force Program* (Washington, DC: U.S. Government Printing Office, 2002), p. 2.

14. Enough Is Enough, *Take Action Manual* (Washington, DC: Enough Is Enough, 1996), p. 9.

15. Kevin Hammel (detective, Trumbull, Connecticut, Police Department), interview by author, September 15, 2005.

16. Medaris and Girouard, *Protecting Children in Cyberspace*, pp. 2–3.

17. Klain, *Child Pornography*, p. 4.

18. Sharon Gaudin, "Analysts: Child Porn Hidden on Corporate Networks," *Internetnews*, February 14, 2003, http://www.internetnews.com/bus-news/article.php/1584551.

19. Ibid.

20. *CBS News*, "Child Cyberporn Patrons Busted," August 8, 2001, www.cbsnews.com.

21. U.S. Immigration and Customs Enforcement, "Internet Child Pornographers," Fact Sheet, March 9, 2005, www.ice.gov/graphics/news/factsheets/cybercrime.htm.

Chapter 8

1. V. H. Sturgeon and J. Taylor, "Report of a Five-Year Follow-Up Study of Mentally Disordered Sex Offenders Released from Atascadero State Hospital in 1973," *Criminal Justice Journal*, April 1980, p. 50.

2. Kim English, *Managing Adult Sex Offenders in the Community: NIJ Research in Brief* (Washington, DC: U.S. Government Printing Office, 1997), p. 6.

3. D. J. Stevens, *Inside the Mind of a Serial Rapist* (San Francisco: Austin and Winfield, 1999), pp. 55–67.

4. *CBS News*, "Idaho Suspect's Chilling Record," July 6, 2005, www.cbsnews.com.

5. Nicholas K. Geranios, "Idaho Murder/Abduction Suspect Allegedly Staked Out Home," Associated Press, July 13, 2005, http://www.lineofduty.com.

6. Nicholas K. Geranios, "Girl's Account Could Be Key in Idaho Case," Associated Press, July 16, 2005, http://www.comcast.net.

7. Christopher Smith, "Suspected Kidnapper in Idaho Kept Blog," Associated Press, July 7, 2005, http://wireservice.wired.com.

8. *CBS News*, "Idaho Kids' Ordeal Described," July 6, 2005, www.cbsnews.com.

9. Lauri R. Harding, "Pedophilia," *Gale Encyclopedia of Psychology* (Independence, KY: Gale, 2001).

10. Donna Schram and Cheryl D. Milloy, *Sexually Violent Predators and Civil Commitment* (Olympia, WA: Washington State Institute for Public Policy, 1998), p. i.

11. Gregory M. Weber, "Grooming Children for Sexual Molestation," Web site dedicated to fighting child sexual abuse, March 20, 2005, http://www.vachss.com/guest_dispatches/grooming.html.

12. Terry Hall (sergeant and head of child molestation prevention program, Indianapolis Police Department), interview by author, August 4, 2005.

13. *CNN.com/Law Center*, "Supreme Court Upholds Sex Offender Registration Laws," March 5, 2003, http://www.cnn.com/2003/LAW/03/05/scotus.sex.offenders.ap.

14. Hall, interview by author, August 4, 2005.

15. Charlie Brennan, "Tide of Internet Sex Crimes Rising," *Rocky Mountain News*, December 18, 2004, www.rockymountainnews.com.

16. Chris Hansen, "Dangers Children Face Online," *MSNBC*, November 11, 2004, www.msnbc.msn.com.

17. Sandra L. Bloom, "Sexual Violence—The Victim," *Psychiatric Aspects of Violence: Issues in Prevention and Treatment*, 2000, pp. 63–71.

18. R. Moscarello, "Psychological Management of Victims of Sexual Assault," *Canadian Journal of Psychiatry*, 1990, pp. 25–30.

19. U.S. Department of Justice, *Case Studies: The Power of a DNA Match* (Washington, DC: U.S. Government Printing Office, 2001).

20. Bill Hewitt, "No Time to Wait," *People Magazine*, June 3, 2002, http://www.law-forensic.com/cfr_funding_backlog_10.htm.

21. *Resource*, "Changed Forever: From Homemaker to Advocate," Fall/Winter 2003, p. 11.

22. Carlos Sadovi and Hal Dardick, "Private DNA Test Leads to First Arrest," *Chicago Tribune*, July 21, 2004.

23. Clare G. Holzman, "Recovering from Rape," *Selfhelp Magazine*, March 29, 2005, www.selfhelpmagazine.com/articles/trauma/raperec.html.

24. David Lisak, "The Psychological Impact of Sexual Abuse: Content Analysis of Interviews with Male Survivors," *Journal of Traumatic Stress*, April 1994, pp. 525–48.

Some Final Thoughts

1. Senobia Pervine (victim assistance counselor, Marion County, Indiana, Victim Assistance Unit), interview by author, August 23, 2005.

Bibliography

ABC 30. "Marcus Wesson Asks to Fire Attorneys." June 24, 2005, http://abclocal. go.com/kfsn/news/print_062405_nw_wesson. html.

Abel, Gene G., and Nora Harlow. *The Stop Child Molestation Book*. Philadelphia: Xlibris, 2002.

American Psychiatric Association. *Diagnostic and Statistical Manual of Mental Disorders*. Arlington, VA: American Psychiatric Association, 2000.

Anderson, Michelle J. "From Chastity Requirements to Sexuality License: Sexual Consent and a New Rape Shield Law." *George Washington Law Review*, 2002, pp. 45–61.

Associated Press. "Couple Faked Death with Stolen Corpse." May 7, 2005, www. lineofduty.com/blotterstory.asp?storyid=75491.

———. "Judge Must Allow Children's Taped Testimony." July 7, 2005, www. duluthsuperior.com.

Association for the Treatment of Sexual Abusers. *Reducing Sexual Abuse through Treatment and Intervention with Abusers*. Beaverton, OR: Association for the Treatment of Sexual Abusers, 1996.

Bardwell, S. K. "Pair Charged in Robberies, Assaults." *Houston Chronicle*, February 26, 2005, www.chron.com.

Becker-Avin, Marni. "The Real Purpose of Voir Dire." *Trial Techniques Committee Newsletter—American Bar Association*, Fall 2001, pp. 9–11.

Bloom, Sandra L. "Sexual Violence—The Victim." *Psychiatric Aspects of Violence: Issues in Prevention and Treatment*, 2000, pp. 63–71.

Brennan, Charlie. "Tide of Internet Sex Crimes Rising." *Rocky Mountain News*, December 18, 2004, www.rockymountainnews.com.

Briere, J., and N. Malamuth. "Self-Reported Likelihood of Sexually Aggressive Behavior." *Journal of Research in Personality*, 1983, pp. 315–23.

Browning, Jeremy. "Craig Man Found Guilty of Incest." *Craig (CO) Daily Press*, August 25, 2003, www.craigdailypress.com.

Brunswick, Cary. "Tougher Sentences for Child Sex Abusers." *Daily Star*, July 21, 2001, www.thedailystar.com.

Burgess, Ann W. "Contemporary Issues." In *Practical Aspects of Rape Investigation*, ed. Ann W. Burgess and Robert R. Hazelwood. New York: CRC, 2001.

Caston, Phillip. "High Court Reverses Ruling That Proctor Was Denied Fair Trial." *Charleston (SC) Post and Courier*, April 21, 2004, http://archives. postandcourier.com.

CBS News. "Child Cyberporn Patrons Busted." August 8, 2001, www.cbsnews.com.

———. "Idaho Kids' Ordeal Described." July 6, 2005, www.cbsnews.com.

———. "Idaho Suspect's Chilling Record." July 6, 2005, www.cbsnews.com.

CBS 2—New York News. "No Parole for Connecticut Rapist." March 3, 2005, http://cbsnewyork.com/topstories/topstoriesny_story_0621442.02.html.

Cheit, Ross, and Erica Goldschmidt. "Symposium: The Treatment of Sex Offenders: Child Molesters in the Criminal Justice System: A Comprehensive Case-Flow Analysis of the Rhode Island Docket." *New England Journal on Criminal and Civil Confinement*, 1997, pp. 251–289.

CNN.com/Law Center. "Supreme Court Upholds Sex Offender Registration Laws." March 5, 2003, http://www.cnn.com/2003/LAW/03/05/scotus.sex. offenders.ap.

Crawford, Kimberly A. "Crime Scene Searches." *FBI Law Enforcement Bulletin*, January 1999, pp. 26–31.

Crichton, Torcuil. "Jehovah's Witnesses Accused of Building 'Pedophile Paradise.'" *Sunday Herald*, July 2002.

Curtis, David G. "Perspectives on Acquaintance Rape." The American Academy of Experts in Traumatic Stress, 1997, http://www.aaets.org/arts/art13htm.

Dickerson v. United States. 530 US 428 (2000).

Dominguez, Renee Z. *Encyclopedia of Crime and Punishment*. Great Barrington, MA: Berkshire, 2001.

Dreznick, Michael T. "Heterosexual Competence of Rapists and Child Molesters: A Meta-Analysis." *Journal of Sex Research*, May 2003.

English, Kim. *Managing Adult Sex Offenders in the Community: NIJ Research in Brief*. Washington, DC: U.S. Government Printing Office, 1997.

Enough Is Enough. *Take Action Manual*. Washington, DC: Enough Is Enough, 1996.

Ernoehazy, William. "Sexual Assault." *eMedicine*, January 21, 2002, http://www. emedicine.com/EMERG/topic527.htm.

Faller, K. C. *Child Sexual Abuse: Intervention and Treatment Issues*. Washington, DC: U.S. Government Printing Office, 1993.

Faulkner, Nancy. "Sexual Abuse Statistics." *Pandora's Box: The Secrecy of Child Sexual Abuse*. Web site dedicated to combating child sexual abuse, August 29, 2005, http://www.prevent-abuse-now.com/stats.htm.

Finkelhor, David. *Online Victimization: A Report on the Nation's Youth*. Alexandria, VA: National Center for Missing and Exploited Children, 2000.

Fontana, Cyndee. "The Many Portraits of Marcus Wesson." *Fresno Bee*, April 18, 2004, www.fresnobee.com.

Forensic Nurse. "Assault on Rape Shield Law Puts Victims at Risk, Says Advocacy Group." October 2003, www.forensicnursemag.com.

Garcia, Sabrina, and Margaret Henderson. "Blind Reporting of Sexual Violence." *FBI Law Enforcement Bulletin*, June 1999, pp. 12–16.

Gaudin, Sharon. "Analysts: Child Porn Hidden on Corporate Networks." *Internetnews*, February 14, 2003, http://www.internetnews.com/bus-news/article.php/1584551.

Geranios, Nicholas K. "Girl's Account Could Be Key in Idaho Case." Associated Press, July 16, 2005, http://www.comcast.net.

———. "Idaho Murder/Abduction Suspect Allegedly Staked Out Home." Associated Press, July 13, 2005, http://www.lineofduty.com.

Goldstein, Seth L., and R. P. Tyler. "Frustrations of Inquiry." *FBI Law Enforcement Bulletin*, July 1998, pp. 1–6.

Gordon, Margaret T., and Stephanie Riger. *The Female Fear*. Champaign, IL: University of Illinois Press, 1991.

Groth, A. N., and Ann W. Burgess. "Sexual Dysfunction During Rape." *New England Journal of Medicine*, April 1977, pp. 764–66.

Hansen, Chris. "Dangers Children Face Online." *MSNBC*, November 11, 2004, www.msnbc.msn.com.

Harding, Lauri R. "Pedophilia." *Gale Encyclopedia of Psychology*. Independence, KY: Gale, 2001.

Hazelwood, Robert R., and Ann W. Burgess. "An Introduction to the Serial Rapist: Research by the FBI." *FBI Law Enforcement Bulletin*, September 1987, pp. 16–24.

Hazelwood, Robert R., and Kenneth V. Lanning. "Collateral Materials in Sexual Crimes." In *Practical Aspects of Rape Investigation*, ed. Robert R. Hazelwood and Ann W. Burgess. New York: CRC, 2001.

Hazelwood, Roy, and Stephen G. Michaud. *Dark Dreams*. New York: St. Martin's, 2001.

Heck, William P. "Basic Investigative Protocol for Child Sexual Abuse." *FBI Law Enforcement Bulletin*, October 1999, pp. 19–25.

Herguth, Robert. "Cops Arrest Man Suspected of Being Serial Peeping Tom." *Chicago Sun-Times*, April 11, 2005.

Herman, D. E. "The Rape Culture." In *Women: A Feminist Perspective*, ed. Jo Freeman. Mountain View, CA: Mayfield, 1984.

Hewitt, Bill. "No Time to Wait." *People Magazine*, June 3, 2002, http://www.law-forensic.com/cfr_funding_backlog_10.htm.

Holzman, Clare G. "Recovering from Rape." *Selfhelp Magazine*, March 29, 2005, www.selfhelpmagazine.com/articles/trauma/raperec.html.

Indianapolis Star. "Repeat Molester Eluded System." June 19, 2005.

Johnson, Barbara E. "Rape Myth Acceptance and Sociodemographic Characteristics: A Multidimensional Analysis." *Sex Roles: A Journal of Research*, June 1997.

Johnson, I., and R. Sigler. *Forced Sexual Intercourse in Intimate Relationships.* Brookfield, VT: Dartmouth/Ashgate, 1997.

Kafka, Joe. "Death Row Inmate Found Dead in Cell." *Rapid City (SD) Journal*, March 30, 2003, www.rapidcityjournal.com.

Kanin, Eugene J. "False Rape Allegations." *Archives of Sexual Behavior*, February 1994, pp. 81–84.

KATU 2 News. "Excerpts from Probable Cause Statement in Ward Weaver Case." August 21, 2002, http://www.katu.com/printstory.asp?ID=49607.

———. "Next Step for Ward Weaver Is Evaluation." September 23, 2004, http://www.katu.com/news/story.asp?ID=71303.

Katz v. United States. 88 S. Ct. 507 (1967).

KCRA 3 TV. "52 Registered Sex Offenders Found Living in California Nursing Homes." February 8, 2005, http://www.kcra.com/print/4178106/detail.html.

KFMB TV. "Marcus Wesson Guilty in Murders of Nine of His Children." June 17, 2005, http://www.kfmb.com/story.php?id=15527.

Kimberlin, Joanne. "New Technology Offers Peeping Toms More." *Virginian-Pilot*, June 8, 2004, www.hamptonroads.com.

Klain, Eva J. *Child Pornography: The Criminal-Justice-System Response.* Alexandria, VA: National Center for Missing and Exploited Children, 2001.

Kornblum, Janet. "Meet the Child Molester Next Door." *USA Today*, January 28, 2003, www.usatoday.com.

Kusmer, Ken. "Catholic Group: Abuse Scandal Could Cost up to $3 Billion." *Indianapolis Star*, July 10, 2005.

Lanning, Kenneth V. *Child Molesters: A Behavioral Analysis.* Alexandria, VA: National Center for Missing and Exploited Children, 2001.

———. "Investigator's Guide to Allegations of 'Ritual' Child Abuse." Research paper, January 1992, http://web.mit.edu/harris/www/lanning/html.

Lanning, Kenneth V., and Ann W. Burgess. *Child Molesters Who Abduct: Summary of the Case in Point Series.* Alexandria, VA: National Center for Missing and Exploited Children, 1995.

Lewis, Alfred Allan, and Herbert Leon MacDonell. *The Evidence Never Lies: The Case Book of a Modern Sherlock Holmes.* New York: Bantam, 1989.

Lisak, David. "The Psychological Impact of Sexual Abuse: Content Analysis of Interviews with Male Survivors." *Journal of Traumatic Stress*, April 1994, pp. 525–48.

Lord, Wayne D. "Investigating Potential Child Abduction Cases." *FBI Law Enforcement Bulletin*, April 2001, pp. 1–10.

Maryland v. Craig. 497 US 836 (1990).

McDonald, Merrilyn. "The Myth of Epidemic False Allegations of Sexual Abuse in Divorce Cases." *Court Review*, Spring 1998, pp. 12–20.

Medaris, Michael, and Cathy Girouard. *Protecting Children in Cyberspace: The ICAC Task Force Program.* Washington, DC: U.S. Government Printing Office, 2002.

Mertens, Jennifer. "Lessons from the Body Farm." *Law Enforcement Technology*, June 2003, pp. 31–40.

Mincey v. Arizona. 437 US 385 (1978).

Miranda v. Arizona. 384 US 436 (1966).

Montgomery, Bill. "Girl Details Rape at Trial." *Atlanta Journal-Constitution*, June 23, 2004.

Moore, Carole. "Taking the Stand." *Law Enforcement Technology*, July 2005, pp. 76–84.

Moore, Tim. "Florida Department of Law Enforcement Adds Burglary Convictions to DNA Database." *Florida Police Chief*, September 2000.

Moscarello, R. "Psychological Management of Victims of Sexual Assault." *Canadian Journal of Psychiatry*, 1990, pp. 25–30.

Muram, D. "Child Sexual Abuse: Relationship Between Sexual Acts and General Findings." *Child Abuse and Neglect*, 1989, pp.211–16.

Murphy, Gillian. *Beyond Surviving: Toward a Movement to Prevent Child Sexual Abuse.* New York: Ms. Foundation for Women, 2002.

Napier, Michael R. "Magic Words to Obtain Confessions." *FBI Law Enforcement Bulletin*, October 1998, pp. 11–15.

National Center for Victims of Crime. *Sexual Assault*, research paper, 1998, http://www.ncvc.org/ncvc/main.aspx?dbName=DocumentViewer& DocumentID=32369.

Navarro, Joe. "A Four-Domain Model for Detecting Deception." *FBI Law Enforcement Bulletin*, June 2003, pp. 19–24.

Navarro, Joe, and John R. Schafer. "Detecting Deception." *FBI Law Enforcement Bulletin*, July 2001, pp. 9–13.

Nibert, D. "Assaults Against Residents of a Psychiatric Institution." *Journal of Interpersonal Violence*, March 1989, pp. 342–49.

Osborne v. Ohio. 495 US 103 (1990).

Pence, Donna, and Charles Wilson. *The Role of Law Enforcement in the Response to Child Abuse and Neglect.* Washington, DC: U.S. Government Printing Office, 1992.

Pino, Nathan W. "Gender Differences in Rape Reporting." *Sex Roles: A Journal of Research*, June 1999.

Prentky, R. "Recidivism Rates Among Child Molesters and Rapists: A Methodological Analysis." *Journal of Law and Human Behavior*, 1997, pp. 635–59.

Redfern, Cathy. "Jury Convicts Live Oak Man of Child Abuse." *Santa Cruz Sentinel*, March 15, 2005, www.santacruzsentinel.com.

Resource. "Changed Forever: From Homemaker to Advocate." Fall/Winter 2003, pp. 10–11.

Rieser, Margaret. "Recantations in Child Sexual Abuse Cases." *Child Welfare*, November/December 1991.

Risin L., and M. Koss. "Sexual Abuse of Boys: Prevalence, and Descriptive Characteristics of Childhood Victimizations." *Journal of Interpersonal Violence*, March 1987, pp. 309–23.

Rivers, David. "Crime Scene Investigation." Handout from Homicide and Forensic Death Investigation Conference, held at Public Agency Training Council, Indianapolis, IN, January 2004.

Russell, D.E.H. *Rape in America.* New York: Macmillan, 1990.

Russell, Diana. "Males' Propensity to Rape." Web site of excerpts from Russell's work, November 7, 2004, http://www.dianarussell.com/menrape.html.

Ryckaert, Vic. "Doctor Sentenced to Home Detention." *Indianapolis Star*, February 26, 2005, www.indystar.com.

Sadovi, Carlos, and Hal Dardick. "Private DNA Test Leads to First Arrest." *Chicago Tribune*, July 21, 2004.

San Jose Mercury News. "How Child Molester Got to Thousands." June 18, 2005, http://www.lineofduty.com.

Schram, Donna, and Cheryl D. Milloy. *Sexually Violent Predators and Civil Commitment.* Olympia, WA: Washington State Institute for Public Policy, 1998.

Sigman, Leroy. "Jury Recommends Six Life Terms Plus 90 Years." *Daily Journal*, October 6, 2004, www.mydjconnection.com.

Smith, Christopher. "Suspected Kidnapper in Idaho Kept Blog." Associated Press, July 7, 2004, http://wireservice.wired.com.

Smith, Kim. "Child-Sex Case Draws Life Sentence." *Las Vegas Sun*, May 8, 2002, www.vachss.com/help_text/archive/george_gibbs.html.

Snow, Robert L. *The Complete Guide to Personal and Home Safety.* Cambridge, MA: Perseus, 2002.

Stern, Seth. "Bryant Case Tests Limits of 'Rape Shield Laws.'" *Christian Science Monitor*, October 22, 2003, www.csmonitor.com.

Stevens, D. J. *Inside the Mind of a Serial Rapist.* San Francisco: Austin and Winfield, 1999.

Sturgeon, V. H. and J. Taylor. "Report of a Five-Year Follow-Up Study of Mentally Disordered Sex Offenders Released from Atascadero State Hospital in 1973." *Criminal Justice Journal*, April 1980, pp. 31–63.

Sweetingham, Lisa. "More Women Join Lawsuit against Hooters." *Court TV*, April 9, 2004, www.radford.edu/~maamodt/ammodt%20(4th)/hooters%20privacy.htm.

TCM *Breaking News*. "Child Molester Gets Life under 'Three Strikes' Law." April 15, 2004, http://archives.tcm.ie/breakingnews/2004/04/15/story143075.asp.

Thomas, Karen. "Who Are the Child Molesters among Us?" *USA Today*, March 12, 2002, www.usatoday.com.

Timms, Ed. "DNA Alters Thinking on Swift Justice." *Dallas Morning News*, July 30, 2001.

Tjaden, Patricia, and Nancy Thoennes. *Extent, Nature, and Consequences of Intimate Partner Violence*. Washington, DC: U.S. Government Printing Office, 2000.

Tuohy, Lynne. "A Payback for Nightmares—Judge Describes Child Victims' Anxiety, Self-Loathing as He Sentences Giordano to 37 Years." *Hartford (CT) Courant*, June 14, 2003.

Turvey, Brent E. *Criminal Profiling*. New York: Academic, 2002.

Twedt, Steve. "Trash Passing." *IRE Journal*, November/December 2000.

UIC *News Tips*. "UIC Researchers Study 'Second Rape' Phenomenon." December 17, 2001, http://www.uic.edu/depts/paff/opa/releases/2001/secondrape_release.htm.

United States Conference of Catholic Bishops. *A Report on the Crisis in the Catholic Church in the United States*. Washington, DC: United States Conference of Catholic Bishops, 2004.

U.S. Department of Health and Human Services. "Sexual Assault." Research document, April 2001, http://www.4woman.gov/faq/sexualassault.htm.

U.S. Department of Justice. *Case Studies: The Power of a DNA Match*. Washington, DC: U.S. Government Printing Office, 2001.

———. *Crime in the United States*. Washington, DC: U.S. Government Printing Office, 2004.

———. *Crime Scene Investigation: A Guide for Law Enforcement*. Washington, DC: U.S. Government Printing Office, January 2000.

———. *Criminal Victimization in the United States, 2002 Statistical Tables*. Washington, DC: U.S. Government Printing Office, December 2003.

———. *Rape and Sexual Assault: Reporting to the Police and Medical Attention, 1992–2000*. Washington, DC: U.S. Government Printing Office, 2002.

———. *Sexual Assault Evidence: National Assessment and Guidebook*. Washington, DC: U.S. Government Printing Office, January 2002.

———. *Sexual Assault Nurse Examiner (SANE) Programs: Improving the Community Response to Sexual Assault Victims*. Washington, DC: U.S. Government Printing Office, April 2001.

———. *Sexual Assault of Young Children as Reported to Law Enforcement: Victim, Incident, and Offender Characteristics*. Washington, DC: U.S. Government Printing Office, July 2000.

———. *The Sexual Victimization of College Women*. Washington, DC: U.S. Government Printing Office, December 2000.

U.S. Immigration and Customs Enforcement. "Internet Child Pornographers." Fact Sheet, March 9, 2005, http://www.ice.gov/graphics/news/factsheets/cybercrime.htm.

Vachss, Andrew. "Age of Innocence." *London Observer*, April 16, 1994.

Vail Daily. "Kobe Bryant, Accuser Settle." March 2, 2005, www.vaildaily.com.

Vernon, McCay. "Issues in the Sexual Molestation of Deaf Youth." *American Annals of the Deaf*, December 2002.

Vessel, David. "Conducting Successful Interrogations." *FBI Law Enforcement Bulletin*, October 1998, pp. 1–6.

Weber, Gregory M. "Grooming Children for Sexual Molestation." Web site dedicated to combating child sexual abuse, March 20, 2005, http://www.vachss.com/guest_dispatches/grooming.html.

Whitney, Veronica. "Suspect in Bryant Case Threats Pleads Guilty." *Vail Daily*, March 30, 2005, www.vaildaily.com.

CBS 11 TV. "Wife Says She Selected Corpse in Fake Death Scheme." May 5, 2005, http://cbs11tv.com/localstories/local_story_125102307.html.

Wise, Warren. "Proctor Gets Life Without Parole." *Charleston (SC) Post and Courier*, April 3, 1998, http://archives.postandcourier.com.

———. "Proctor Verdict: Guilty." *Charleston (SC) Post and Courier*, March 5, 1998, http://archives.postandcourier.com.

Wyrick, Randy. "Bellman in Bryant Case Breaks Silence." *Vail Daily*, April 6, 2005, www.vaildaily.com.

Yeschke, Charles L. *The Art of Investigative Interviewing*. New York: Butterworth-Heinemann, 2003.

Zeman, David. "The Kobe Bryant Case: Spotlight Shatters Accuser's Privacy." *Detroit Free Press*, July 26, 2003, www.freep.com.

Zulawski, David E., and Douglas E. Wicklander. "Special Report 1: Interrogations: Understanding the Process." *Law and Order*, July 1998, pp. 86–92.

Index

About the Author

ROBERT L. SNOW is Commander of the Homicide Branch in the Indianapolis Police Department, and author of *Deadly Cults: The Crimes of True Believers* and *Murder 101*, among other titles.